The Creative Ethnographer's Notebook

The Creative Ethnographer's Notebook offers emerging and trained ethnographers exercises to spark creativity and increase the impact and beauty of ethnographic study.

With contributions by emerging scholars and leading creative ethnographers working in various social science fields (e.g., anthropologists, educators, ethnomusicologists, political scientists, geographers, and others), this volume offers readers a variety of creative prompts that ethnographers have used in their own work and university classrooms to deepen their ethnographic and artistic practice. The contributions foreground different approaches in creative practice, broadening the tools of multimodal ethnography as one designs a study, works with collaborators and landscapes, and renders ethnographic findings through a variety of media. Instructors will find dozens of creative prompts to use in a wide variety of classroom settings, including early beginners to experienced ethnographers and artists. In the eBook+ version of this book, there are numerous pop-up definitions to key ethnographic terms, links to creative ethnographic examples, possibilities for extending prompts for more advanced anthropologists, and helpful tips across all phases of inquiry projects.

This resource can be used by instructors of anthropology and other social sciences to teach students how to experiment with creative approaches, as well as how to do better public and engaged anthropology. Artists and arts faculty will also benefit from using this book to inspire culturally attuned art making that engages in research, as well as research-based art. Readers will learn how creative ethnography draws on aspects of the literary, visual, sonic, and/or performing arts. Information is provided about how scholars and artists, or scholartists, document culture in ways that serve more diverse public and academic audiences.

Melisa Cahnmann-Taylor, Meigs Professor of Language and Literacy Education at the University of Georgia, has authored six books, including a book of poems, *Imperfect Tense*. She became a Fulbright Scholar Ambassador (Mexico) in 2022.

Kristina Jacobsen, Associate Professor of Songwriting and Anthropology (Sociocultural & Linguistic) at the University of New Mexico, is a touring singer-songwriter and Fulbright Scholar (US–Italy, 2019–2020).

"A diverse assemblage of well-documented, accessible tools and exercises that challenge and embolden aspiring ethnographers toward 'scholartistry': integrating artistic practices into their lives and ways of doing research, presenting that work in media and forms more resonant and congruent with the communities they study, and to broader academic and public audiences."

Mark Simos, *Professor, Songwriting Department, Berklee College of Music*

The Creative Ethnographer's Notebook

Edited by Melisa Cahnmann-Taylor and Kristina Jacobsen

NEW YORK AND LONDON

Designed cover image: Thomas Bethge / Alamy Stock Photo

First published 2025
by Routledge
605 Third Avenue, New York, NY 10158

and by Routledge
4 Park Square, Milton Park, Abingdon, Oxon, OX14 4RN

Routledge is an imprint of the Taylor & Francis Group, an informa business

Library of Congress Cataloging-in-Publication Data
Names: Cahnmann-Taylor, Melisa, editor. | Jacobsen, Kristina M., editor.
Title: The creative ethnographer's notebook /
edited by Melisa Cahnmann-Taylor and Kristina Jacobsen.
Description: New York, NY : Routledge, 2024. |
Includes bibliographical references and index.
Identifiers: LCCN 2024001621 (print) | LCCN 2024001622 (ebook) |
ISBN 9781032429922 (hardback) | ISBN 9781032429915 (paperback) |
ISBN 9781003365228 (ebook) | ISBN 9781003487487 (ebook other)
Subjects: LCSH: Ethnology–Methodology. | Qualitative research–Methodology.
Classification: LCC GN307.8 .C74 2024 (print) |
LCC GN307.8 (ebook) | DDC 305.80072/1–dc23/eng/20240402
LC record available at https://lccn.loc.gov/2024001621
LC ebook record available at https://lccn.loc.gov/2024001622

ISBN: 9781032429922 (hbk)
ISBN: 9781032429915 (pbk)
ISBN: 9781003365228 (ebk)
ISBN: 9781003487487 (eBook+)

DOI: 10.4324/9781003365228

Typeset in Times New Roman
by Newgen Publishing UK

From Melisa:

To the life, memory, and inspiration of my ancestors through kinship and kindred spirit. May we keep creating opportunities to embrace complexity and beauty.

From Kristina:

To my father, who taught me to love the sound and warmth of the singing voice. To my mother, who fostered that love in me with attention, creativity and care, and who taught me what it means to live an artful life.

Contents

List of Illustrations *xii*
List of Contributors *xiv*
Foreword by John L. Jackson, Jr. and Deborah A. Thomas *xxi*
Acknowledgements *xxvi*

1 Introduction to Creative Ethnography as a Field 1
MELISA CAHNMANN-TAYLOR AND KRISTINA JACOBSEN

PART I
Preparing for the Field 15

2 Creative Engagements with Social Theory: Writing through the Abstract to Arrive at the Concrete 19

Giving Meaning and Voice to Objects 20
MELISA CAHNMANN-TAYLOR

The Taste of Theory: Understanding Discursive, Materialist, and Phenomenological Approaches with Food 25
ALDER KELEMAN SAXENA

Comic Relief: Making a World of Difference in Anthropology 31
BERNARD C. PERLEY

3 Reading Ethnographies with Creative Attention to the Senses 38

Scoring the Ethnographic Episode 39
ANTHONY KWAME HARRISON

Making the Familiar Strange: Writing a Song from a Newspaper Article 43
KRISTINA JACOBSEN

Mine the Gap: Writing into a Poem's Expanse 48
SIENNA CRAIG

PART II
In the Field 53

4 Creative Approaches to What Matters and Paying Attention to What Makes You Curious 55

Working in Non-Western Literary and Linguistic Forms 56
MELISA CAHNMANN-TAYLOR

Slowing Down the Ethnographic Gaze through Observational Videomaking 60
PETER SUTORIS

Writing Silence through Ethnography: Intimate or Otherwise 65
FIONA MURPHY AND EVROPI CHATZIPANAGIOTIDOU

5 Designing Ways to Make Data Sing 70

Writing Someone Else's Life Story as a Song 71
KRISTINA JACOBSEN

Writing Along the Faction Spectrum 76
JESS FALCONE

Inside the Prose Poem: Using Fresh Metaphors and Similes to Open Up Fieldwork 80
ADRIE KUSSEROW

6 Entering the Field Site: Space and the Non-Human: Seeing the Field, Landscapes, and Non-Human Life in Places of Inquiry 85

Creating Empathy and Writing from a Picture 86
KRISTINA JACOBSEN

Writing Space and Place 91
PAUL STOLLER

Attending to Animal Stories: Listening for Lines 96
DAVID SYRING

7 Language: We Are What We Speak 101

Translingual Poetry and Scholarship 102
MELISA CAHNMANN-TAYLOR

Writing a Song in an Endangered Language 108
SARA SNYDER HOPKINS

Lyrical Storytelling and Finding Voice 114
STEVEN ALVAREZ

8 Our Bodies, Our Selves: Interrogating the Ethnographic Body, Kinship, and Food During Fieldwork 120

Temporality and Embodied Experience 121
NOMI STONE

Cultivating Appetite: Food, Travel, and Communing through Food 125
KRISTINA JACOBSEN

Artful Scholarship with Interview Data 130
MELISA CAHNMANN-TAYLOR

9 People, Places and Performance: Ritual, Religion, and Visualities 136

Production Values in Practice 137
WILLIAM LEMPERT

Creative Sensory Ethnography through Group Songwriting 141
NAOMI SUNDERLAND

War and Witness* 152
ATHER ZIA

PART III
After the Field 159

10 Creative Approaches to Social Science Data 161

Representing Ethnographic Insights through Mural Sketches 162
DEBRA VIDALI

Using a Three-Step Coding Process to Co-Compose Song Lyrics from Qualitative Interviews: A Lesson for Intermediate-Level Researchers 169
KAEL REID

For Those Who Would Wear the Whale Mask: Using Mask-Making to Perform and Transform the Ethnographic Monologue 178
SALLY CAMPBELL PIRIE

11 Writing it Up: Multimodality, Genre, and How to Translate Creative Activity for an Academic Audience 188

Recording an Ethnographic Soundscape 189
JAY HAMMOND

Write to Discover What You Truly Want to Say 193
NICOLETTA DEMETRIOU

Creating an Ethnographic Exhibit 198
KWAME PHILLIPS AND DEBRA VIDALI

After the Field Site: Writing About the Unexplained 203
CRISTINA MORETTI

12 Creative Ethnographic Fieldstarters 208

Digging Deep into the Essentials of Ethnographic Writing 209
RUTH BEHAR

Trauma and Turning around the Ethnographic Gaze 215
RENATO ROSALDO

13 Looking Back and Moving Forward 221

Ethnographic Songwriting, Deep Hanging Out, and Keeping Our Practice Alive: Intention, Showing Up, and Feeding Our Inner Scholartist 222
KRISTINA JACOBSEN

When Poetry Became Ethnography and Other Flying Pig Tales: An Ode to Dell Hymes, as well as Creative Ethnographic Mentors Past, Present, and Future 238
MELISA CAHNMANN-TAYLOR

Glossary *249*
Index *257*

Illustrations

Figures

2.1 Handsketch for the after dark theme in a "Going Native" series. 33
2.2 The final version of the after dark comic in the "Going Native" series. 34
5.1 Cluster writing. 72
5.2 Faction spectrum. 77
6.1 The baobab tree (photo by Paul Stoller). 92
10.1 Splash page from Hamdy et al. (2017, pp. 130–31). Used with permission of the University of Toronto Press. 164
10.2 *Minnie* by Phoebe Einzig-Roth (2020). Used with permission of the artist–ethnographer. 165
10.3 *Unheard Voices* by Jemila Mussa (2020). Used with permission of the artist–ethnographer. 166
10.4 *Nuestra Ciudad: Los Angeles* by Olivia Bautista (2020). Used with permission of the artist–ethnographer. 167
10.5 *The Economy of Progress* by Mikail Albritton (2020). Used with permission of the artist–ethnographer. 167
10.6 The three-step coding process. 170
10.7 Full-page graphic 1. 178
10.8 Full-page graphic 2. 179
10.9 Full-page graphic 3. 180
10.10 Full-page graphic 4. 181
10.11 Full-page graphic 5. 182
10.12 Full-page graphic 6. 183
11.1 An example of a hand-drawn mind map. 194
11.2 The "*Kabusha* Radio Remix" installation and a visitor in Le Cube, Paris (photo by Kwame Phillips, 2016). 199
13.1 The three concentric circles model. 230

Tables

2.1 The convergence between observational and analytical approaches. 28
10.1 Songwriting sheet template (standard pop song framework). 172
10.2 Macro code (dominant theme from the interview and theme of the song). *coming out.* 174

Contributors

Steven Alvarez is Professor of English at St. John's University. He's the author of *Brokering Tareas: Mexican Immigrant Families Translanguaging Homework Literacies*, *Community Literacies en Confianza: Learning from Bilingual After-School Programs*, and four books of poetry. His most recent work about "taco literacy" focuses on Mexican foodways in the USA and has been featured on Hulu, Netflix, and National Public Radio. He lives in New York City.

Ruth Behar is the James W. Fernandez Distinguished University Professor of Anthropology at the University of Michigan. She is a MacArthur Fellow, a Carnegie Corporation "Great Immigrant," a recipient of a Guggenheim Fellowship, and a member of the American Academy of Arts and Sciences. Her scholarly books include *The Presence of the Past in a Spanish Village*, *Translated Woman*, *The Vulnerable Observer*, *An Island Called Home*, and *Traveling Heavy*. She also writes for young people and is the author of the novels, *Lucky Broken Girl* and *Letters from Cuba*, as well as a picture book, *Tía Fortuna's New Home*.

Melisa Cahnmann-Taylor, Fulbright Scholar Ambassador, is Meigs Professor of Language and Literacy Education at the University of Georgia. She's authored five books addressing intersections between language education and the literary, visual and performing arts including one book of poems, *Imperfect Tense*, and her newest education title, *Enlivening Instruction with Drama and Improv*. Supported by grants and prizes from the National Endowment for the Arts, Fulbright, and Beckman Award for Professors Who Inspire, her work narrates the heartache and joy of teaching and learning language. She lives in Athens, GA with her husband and two children. Her website: www.melisacahnmanntaylor.com

Evropi Chatzipanagiotidou is an anthropologist at Queen's University Belfast. Her research interests lie in the study of migration and diasporas, conflict-induced displacement, and the politics of memory and loss. She has conducted fieldwork in Cyprus, Greece, the UK, and Turkey and has published on diverse topics, including the connections between memory and history in the Cypriot conflict, the transnational role of diasporas in peacebuilding, youth migration and precarity in Southern Europe, and the politics of silence and loss in refugee representations.

Sienna R. Craig is the Orvil Dryfoos Professor of Public Affairs at Dartmouth College. The author of six books that span a range of genres, from literary ethnography to poetry, children's literature, memoir, and fiction, she has also collaborated with visual artists, documentary filmmakers, and composers. Her book *The Ends of Kinship: Connecting Himalayan Lives between Nepal and New York* interweaves short fiction and ethnography. The website for this text includes writing prompts and a visual glossary. Her work has been supported by the John Simon Guggenheim Foundation, the National Science Foundation, and the Wenner-Gren Foundation for Anthropological Research, among others.

Nicoletta Demetriou, an ethnomusicologist based in Cyprus, is co-editor of *Music in Cyprus* (Routledge, 2015), editor of a three-volume corpus on Cypriot poetic dueling, and author of *The Cypriot Fiddler* (in Greek; 2022). Nicoletta was previously Research Fellow in Ethnomusicology and Life Writing at Wolfson College, University of Oxford, and Tutor in Narrative Non-Fiction on Oxford's MSt in Creative Writing (2012–2019). Her work has been supported by a British Academy/Leverhulme Trust grant (2013), a Fulbright grant (2017), a Visiting Fellowship at the Seeger Center for Hellenic Studies at Princeton University (2019), and an EU Widening Fellowship (2019–2021).

Jessica Marie Falcone is Professor of Anthropology at Kansas State University. Her first book *Battling the Buddha of Love: A Cultural Biography of the Greatest Statue Never Built,* published by Cornell University Press in 2018, won the Edward C. Dimock manuscript prize in the Indian Humanities. After winning a prize for ethnographic fiction from the Society for Humanistic Anthropology, Jessica served on the prize-organizing committee for several years and is a die-hard fan of the genre.

Jay Hammond is a musician, sound artist, and anthropologist. The Guardian has called his music "a shimmering homage to nature." His work explores the intersection between research and art, creativity, and inquiry. His current book project *Social Music: A Sounded Anthropology of Improvisation and Intimacy* is an ethnography of improvised music communities in North America. Through ethnographic research and the production of multimodal projects, the book elucidates how aesthetic values in improvised music communities can both facilitate and inhibit trust across the social boundaries of race, class, gender, and ability. He is Assistant Professor of Practice in Music at Georgetown University.

Anthony Kwame Harrison is the Edward S. Diggs Professor in Humanities at Virginia Tech. He holds a PhD in Cultural Anthropology and is the author of *Hip Hop Underground* (Temple University Press, 2009) and *Ethnography* (Oxford University Press, 2018). Kwame is the president of the International Association for the Study of Popular Music (IASPM), US Branch, and a past-president of the General Anthropology Division of the American Anthropological Association.

His ongoing research on Black travel through White spaces is featured in a 2019 special issue of the arts-based journal *Dysfunction.*

Sara Snyder Hopkins is an ethnomusicologist, linguistic anthropologist, Assistant Professor in the Department of Anthropology and Sociology at Western Carolina University, and Director of the Cherokee Language Program. Prior to working at WCU, Hopkins taught elementary music and arts education at New Kituwah Academy, which is the language immersion school of the Eastern Band of Cherokee Indians. Hopkins is currently editing a critical edition and translation of the 1846 *Cherokee Singing Book* and is Project Director for Eastern Cherokee Histories in Translation (ECHT), funded by the National Endowment for the Humanities, the Cherokee Preservation Foundation, and the John W. Heisse Fund.

John L. Jackson, Jr. is Provost and Richard Perry University Professor at the University of Pennsylvania. He has written several books, including *Harlemworld: Doing Race and Class in Contemporary Black America* and *Thin Description: Ethnography and the African Hebrew Israelites of Jerusalem.* Jackson's films include *Bad Friday: Rastafari after Coral Gardens*, which was co-directed with Deborah A. Thomas, and *Making Sweet Tea: The Lives and Loves of Southern Black Gay Men,* which was co-directed with Nora Gross. He is a founding member of CAMRA and the Center for Experimental Ethnography, two initiatives organized around creating and assessing visual and performative research projects.

Kristina Jacobsen is an ethnographer, singer–songwriter, and cultural anthropologist. An Associate Professor of Songwriting and Anthropology (Sociocultural and Linguistic) at the University of New Mexico, her research focuses on language reclamation, expressive culture, popular music, and arts-based research methodologies. Her first book *The Sound of Navajo Country: Music, Language and Diné Belonging* (UNC Press, 2017) was the winner of the 2018 IASPM-US Woody Guthrie Award for most outstanding book on popular music. Jacobsen is a touring singer–songwriter and a Fulbright scholar (US–Italy, 2019–2020), and she fronts the all-female honky tonk band The Merlettes. www.kristinajacobsenmusic.com, www.kristina-jacobsen.com

Alder Keleman Saxena is an Assistant Professor of Environmental Anthropology and Sustainable Food Systems based in the Department of Anthropology and the Program in Sustainable Communities at Northern Arizona University. Her mixed-methods research has examined the intersections of biodiversity conservation, food security, and food culture, with fieldwork in Mexico, Bolivia, and India. She also has a secondary interest in human-built infrastructure, particularly as it enrolls more-than-human agents in the forms of environmental damage collectively referred to as The Anthropocene. Across these arenas, her work examines the confluences between materiality and meaning making, as well as the feedback between these processes.

Adrie Kusserow is Professor of Anthropology at St. Michael's College in Colchester, Vermont. Her ethnographic fieldwork has been primarily with refugees in Uganda, South Sudan, India, Nepal, and the US. She helped to co-found Africa Education and Leadership Initiative: Bridging Gender Gaps Through Education (africaeli.org) with the Lost Boys of Sudan. She is the author of two books of ethnographic poetry, *Hunting Down the Monk* (BOA Editions, Ltd 2002) and *REFUGE* (BOA Editions, Ltd, 2013), as well as *The Trauma Mantras* (Duke University Press, 2024) and one ethnography *American Individualisms* (Palgrave Macmillan, 2004). www.adriekusserow.com

William Lempert is Assistant Professor of Anthropology at Bowdoin College in Brunswick, Maine. Since 2006, he has conducted over 2 years of ethnographic fieldwork in the Kimberley region of Northwestern Australia with Indigenous media organizations. Through collaboration on production teams, he aims to understand the stakes of Aboriginal self-representation, embedded within the dynamic process of filmmaking. His research engages the tensions between the production of films that vividly imagine hopeful and diverse Indigenous futures and the broader defunding of Aboriginal communities and organizations. www.williamlempert.com

Cristina Moretti, Department of Sociology and Anthropology, Simon Fraser University, Canada, is an urban anthropologist and a co-founder of the Centre for Imaginative Ethnography. Her research in Italy analyzes the politics of public space and the relationships between local visual cultures and city spaces. Her current project in Vancouver, Canada, examines temporality and redevelopment, and asks how sensory ethnography can help to attend to some of the paradoxes and debates that animate city transformations. Moretti's work in sensory anthropology also includes memory and multimodality, the materiality of bureaucracy, walking methodologies, and the sensorial dimension of water infrastructures.

Fiona Murphy is an anthropologist based in the School of Applied Language and Intercultural Studies (SALIS) at Dublin City University. As an anthropologist of displacement, she works with the Stolen Generations in Australia and people seeking asylum and refuge in Ireland, the UK, and Turkey. She has a particular passion for creative and public anthropologies and is always interested in experimenting with new forms and genres. See her TEDx talk on displacement (https://www.youtube.com/watch?v=hwFYBId9Uco).

Bernard C. Perley is Wolastokwiyik from Nequotkuk New Brunswick, Canada. He is the Director of the Institute for Critical Indigenous Studies (CIS) at the University of British Columbia. Dr. Perley has a Bachelor of Fine Arts degree, a Master of Architecture degree from the University of Texas at Austin, and a PhD in Anthropology from Harvard University. The knowledge and experience gained from these three programs have contributed significantly to his writing and advocacy for revitalizing Indigenous languages, cultures, and identities as place-based interdependencies. He has published on Indigenous language endangerment and language revitalization, anthropology, and Native American studies.

Kwame Phillips is Senior Lecturer in Media Practices at the Winchester School of Art, University of Southampton, England, specializing in sensory media production, visual anthropology, and audio culture. Phillips' work focuses on resilience, race, and social justice, using multimodal and experimental methodologies. His recent interest is in "mixtape scholarship," which encompasses the curation and reprocessing of sensory media to convey sonic narratives in a manner that is not bounded by academic tradition or traditional form. This has led to the visual mixtapes *The Imagined Things: On Solange, Repetition and Mantra* and *Lovers Rock Dub: An Experiment in Visual Reverberation.*

Sally Campbell Pirie is an award-winning cartoonist, anatomical illustrator, printmaker, toymaker, and anthropologist of childhood. She is also Professor of Child and Family Studies at the University of Massachusetts at Amherst. She received her PhD from the University of Colorado, Boulder, and is a graduate of Punahou School and Grinnell College. Dr. Pirie's areas of expertise include comics-based research methods and creative research in childhood. She served two terms as the Editor-in-Chief of *Anthropology and Education Quarterly* and is currently a member of the editorial collective of *Pedagogy, Culture and Society*. She was the 2020 Distinguished Visiting Professor of Liberal Arts at the University of Minnesota, Morris. You can learn about all of that and more at www.sallypirie.com

Kael Reid is Assistant Professor in the Faculty of Liberal Arts and Professional Studies at York University in Toronto, Canada. With a lengthy background in teaching and learning, including a PhD from the Ontario Institute for Studies in Education (University of Toronto), Kael teaches core and elective courses in Children, Childhood, and Youth Studies. Kael brings together their musical and academic backgrounds to conduct research using a range of participatory ethnographic songwriting methods that they have developed. Kael collaborates with children, youth, and adults to assist them in documenting and sharing their perspectives and stories through songwriting, singing, and recording. www.kaelreid.com

Renato Rosaldo, award-winning poet and cultural anthropologist, is Professor Emeritus of Social and Cultural Analysis at New York University. He is the author of five poetry collections, most recently *Into the World Outspread* (2022), *The Chasers* (2019), and *The Day of Shelly's Death* (2014), in which he revisits a fatal event that transformed his life in 1981: the accidental death of his wife Michelle Rosaldo while the couple were doing fieldwork in a remote village in the Philippines, accompanied by their young sons. The book includes a manifesto for "antropoesía," or "ethnographic poetry," and Rosaldo's classic essay "Grief and a Head-Hunter's Rage."

Paul Stoller is Professor of Anthropology at West Chester University and Permanent Fellow at the Center for Advanced Study at FAU/Erlangen-Nuremberg. During his time in anthropology among West African peoples, Stoller has explored spirit possession, systems of belief, the informal economy, immigration, social change, and the dynamics of health and wellbeing. The author of 15 books, his latest book is *Wisdom from the Edge: Writing Ethnography in Turbulent Times* (Spring–Summer 2023).

Nomi Stone, a poet and anthropologist, is the author of three books, most recently the poetry collection *Kill Class* (Tupelo, 2019), which was finalist for the Julie Suk Award, and the ethnography *Pinelandia: An Anthropology and Field Poetics of War and Empire* (University of California Press, 2022), which was the winner of the American Anthropological Association's Middle East Studies Prize (2023). Her poems have recently appeared in *The Atlantic, POETRY, American Poetry Review, Best American Poetry, The Nation,* and *The New Republic.* She recently became a Postdoctoral Researcher in Anthropology at Princeton and is currently Assistant Professor of Poetry at the University of Texas, Dallas.

Naomi Sunderland is a member of the School of Health Sciences and Social Work and Creative Arts Research Institute, Griffith University, Australia. Naomi is a proud descendant of the Wiradjuri First Nations People of Australia, alongside her mixed European heritage. She has an extensive research and publishing record in arts-inclusive, participatory, and rights-centered research in arts health, wellbeing, First Nations social justice, and arts-based development. She was awarded an Australian Research Council Fellowship (2021–2024) to study the effect of First Nations music on social and cultural determinants of health, as well as a Fulbright Senior Scholar Fellowship (2024) to study the effects of collective musicmaking on collective trauma.

Peter Sutoris is an environmental anthropologist, documentary filmmaker, photographer, and Assistant Professor at the Sustainability Research Institute at the University of Leeds, UK. He is the author of the documentary film *The Undiscovered Country* (2012) and the monographs *Visions of Development* (OUP, 2016) and *Educating for the Anthropocene* (The MIT Press, 2022, open access). His research interests include cultures of degrowth and activist pedagogies, and much of his work uses visual ethnographic methods to study how different people imagine the future differently. He frequently writes for non-academic audiences, including for *The Guardian, Scientific American, POLITICO, Undark, Salon*, and elsewhere.

David Syring writes about cultures of place, the arts, plants, and animals in human cultures, food systems, and sustainability. His book *Places in the World a Person Could Walk* was a Minnesota Book Award finalist. Since 2005, he has done frequent fieldwork in Ecuador, leading to the book *With the Saraguros: The Blended Life in a Transnational World.* He creates videos with Saraguro collaborators. For 5 years, he edited *Anthropology and Humanism* and he wrote an overview of humanistic anthropology for the *SAGE Handbook of Cultural Anthropology*. He is co-editor (with Lauren Griffith) of *The Routledge Companion to the Anthropology of Performance*.

Deborah A. Thomas is the R. Jean Brownlee Professor of Anthropology and the Director of the Center for Experimental Ethnography at the University of Pennsylvania. She is the author of *Political Life in the Wake of the Plantation, Exceptional Violence*, and *Modern Blackness* and a co-editor of the documentary films *Bad Friday* and *Four Days in May*. She is currently the co-chair of the American Anthropological Association's Commission on the Ethical Treatment of Human Remains. Prior to her life in academia, she was a professional dancer with the New York-based Urban Bush Women.

Debra Vidali is a sociocultural anthropologist, experimental ethnographer, theater-maker, linguist, and scholar–activist. Her work focuses on Indigenous sovereignty, allied solidarity, ways of knowing, and multimodal production. She works in a range of formats, including theater, creative non-fiction, poetry, installations, audio, K-12 curriculum, and conventional academic writing. In 2023, Vidali was awarded first place in the Society for Humanistic Anthropology Ethnographic Poetry Competition. Her recent publications include "Craftwork in Ethnographic Theater Making" (*Routledge Companion to the Anthropology of Performance*, 2023) and "Ethnographic Theater Making: Multimodal Alchemy, Knowledge, and Invention" (*American Anthropologist*, 2020). Vidali is a faculty member in Emory University's Department of Anthropology.

Ather Zia is a political anthropologist, poet, short fiction writer, and columnist. She is Associate Professor of Anthropology & Gender Studies at the University of Northern Colorado, Greeley. She has authored *Resisting Disappearances: Military Occupation and Women's Activism in Kashmir (June 2019)* and co-edited *Can You Hear Kashmiri Women Speak (Women Unlimited 2020), Resisting Occupation in Kashmir (Upenn 2018)*, and *A Desolation called Peace (Harper Collins 2019)*. She has published a poetry collection called *The Frame* and another is forthcoming. Ather is the founder–editor of Kashmir Lit, co-founder of the Critical Kashmir Studies Collective, and co-editor of *Cultural Anthropology*.

Foreword

John L. Jackson, Jr. and Deborah A. Thomas
University of Pennsylvania

We are penning this foreword on the heels of being given the honor of presenting the 12th annual Gerbrands lecture, which allowed us to be in community with colleagues at the University of Leiden and discuss issues of multimodal and multidisciplinary scholarship for a few days in fall 2023. The Adriaan Gerbrands lecture is an annual public engagement with scholars chosen for their contributions to the fields of visual and material culture, areas of study for which Adriaan Gerbrands (1917–1997) was an early and unapologetic advocate. For scholars committed to various forms of multimodality in anthropology and beyond, the fact that this lecture series exists at all couldn't be a more exciting indicator of how far we have come in terms of recognizing the scholarly value of extratextual ethnographic work. The useful text in your hand is another such critical indicator. It is a phenomenal intervention and tool for both pedagogy and theory that makes for an ideal primer for teachers, professors, and graduate students seeking to engage others in multimodal work. We couldn't be more thrilled to have been invited to write this brief foreword.

As scholars who landed in anthropology departments for graduate study after working in other (creative) fields, we had very different experiences in terms of the extent to which we were comfortable expressing and continuing with our artistic exploits. Deborah came to graduate school as a professional dancer, having performed for several years with a New York-based company called the Urban Bush Women (UBW). What drew her to graduate school was a process of working that the UBW had begun developing in the early 1990s, a process in which forms of dance and music were used as tools within collaborative, community-based social change work. These Community Engagement Projects (as they were then called) were oriented toward the development of critical thinking skills, historical consciousness, awareness of and trust in communities' own resources, and supporting the goals of the communities with which the company was working. The company worked with experts in popular education and what is now understood as artistic social practice to develop a curriculum for this kind of approach, which was transformative not only for members of the communities with which UBW worked but also for the company members themselves.

Deborah was inspired to learn more about how this kind of creative popular education work could be "scaled up," so to speak, so she started asking around about ways to study this. Eventually, she ended up applying to graduate schools and landed in an MA program in Latin American and Caribbean Studies at New York University. During the first semester, she took an anthropology course called "Transnational Processes," taught by Constance R. Sutton, who would eventually become her PhD advisor. In this course, Deborah was amazed to realize that there was a field of study that was capacious enough to include her interests (in which people did research on the arts and social change), there was a method that seemed to match what she had been doing as a dancer (i.e., **deep hanging out**, otherwise known as **participant observation**), and there were disciplinary ancestors (e.g., Zora Neale Hurston and Katherine Dunham), who had traveled the road before her and could provide models for what a career incorporating scholarship and the arts could look like.

At the same time, and although Deborah's senior thesis project for the Semiotics Department at Brown University was a dance–theatre production that investigated issues of race and national belonging in Cuba, Brazil, and the US, Deborah kept her life as a dancer relatively separate from her life as a researcher. She was aware that the department thought that her background as a dancer was a plus, as it meant she was disciplined. And, of course, Faye Ginsburg had already established the Center for Culture, Media, and History, through which students could get an MA in Ethnographic Film and be exposed to a range of artists engaging in research. However, her interest in dance was mostly attuned to the ways it provided a portal to broader political questions and the ways in which it reflected (and produced!) social and political transformations within communities. At the same time, she did not know how to (or want to) merge her own scholarly and artistic practices, even though one of her central methodologies for her PhD research involved dancing with the companies whose work she was studying. It wasn't until much later that she picked up a camera at the behest of a community of Rastafari, with whom she and collaborator Junior "Gabu" Wedderburn were working to document stories of police violence, that she began to reintegrate her creative and scholarly practices.

John attended Howard University in Washington, D.C., with the goal of heading out to Hollywood after completing his undergraduate degree from their School of Communication. Coming of age in Brooklyn, New York, just as Spike Lee's first few "joints" were being released to critical acclaim, John was easily persuaded about the power of telling stories through images and sound. However, he had started his attempt at charting his professional career in media even earlier with the goal of becoming a stand-up comedian. They are storytellers as well, of course, and even as a teenager, he appreciated the ways in which comics used humor to ask audiences to see their everyday worlds with new eyes.

As a high schooler, John would sneak out of the house, take a bus and two trains from southern Brooklyn to mid-Manhattan, and sign-up for open mic sessions in Manhattan comedy clubs. He'd keep a Sony cassette recorder positioned on the stage or a table up front so that he could listen to his sets, make adjustments to his jokes when he got back home, and take a revised set to the club next time. John also decided, on a lark, to stuff a couple of tapes in cushioned mailers and send them off to local radio stations in the city. His pitch: give this 10th grader his own radio program so that he can bring his comedic stylings to the airwaves. Someone took him up on that request, and he spent his final 2 years of high school hosting "The Jackson Attraction Radio" on FM radio in the largest radio market in the US.

Within a year of launching his radio show, on which John did innovative things like dragging a television into the studio and making jokes about local television shows on air, he was producing and engineering the show himself and interviewing local and national hip hop artists and celebrities. It was after graduating from Brooklyn Tech that he made the switch from radio to film, and even spent several years performing monologues and giving impromptu competitive speeches as a member of Howard University's Dr. Martin Luther King Jr. Forensics Society. This gallop through John's journey from stand-up comic to radio disc jockey to filmmaker and stage performer is simply meant to signal his long-standing interest in and attention to the diversity of modes we use to communicate and craft stories and arguments. Indeed, this interest is what drew John to the work of communication scholar E. Patrick Johnson and his fieldwork-to-performance plays, which culminated in John's work on the 2021 production of *Making Sweet Tea,* showcasing E. Patrick's research on the lives of black gay men in the south and chronicling both his long-term relationships with some of those men and a bit of the process he has used over the years to turn his in-depth interviews and interactions with research subjects (i.e., his ethnographic scholarship) into a variety of differently staged theatrical performances.

Making Sweet Tea was birthed through the intensive work that we've been doing at Penn since about 2008 or so, which is when the first cohort of about 25 graduate students, mostly PhD students, from several of the University of Pennsylvania's 12 schools committed to three semesters in a row of courses that included a mixture of film history, film/visual theory, and intensive film production. Those students began without any formal training in film, but the first semester was meant to raise their level of comfort with film and filmmaking and routinize their relationship with the technology. This first cohort of students went to documentary film festivals together, worked on each other's film projects, and eventually formed CAMRA, the Collective for Advancing Multimodal Research Arts. Several of these students also incorporated some filmic work into their dissertations. Quite a few of them landed academic jobs for which they incorporated filmmaking into their teaching and research. And just about all of them built networks that included multimodal scholars across several institutions, both around the country and around the world.

At the same time, faculty across Penn's schools who were working on extratextual projects came together in a working group designed to support and bring greater awareness to the range of multimodal work that was happening in each of our spaces. We held conferences and other events, bringing in experts in multimodal scholarship to talk about their work. We gathered policies oriented toward the evaluation of multimodal work as research practice and publication, and we learned from scholars/artists in other locations about how they were able to create space for this work within their own universities. When the opportunity came to institutionalize, we took it, thereby founding the Center for Experimental Ethnography (CEE) at Penn in fall 2018, which has become a hub for faculty and students who have creative practice at the heart of their research process. CAMRA is also now formally connected to and embedded in CEE.

At CEE, we believe that multimodal research practices transform how we conduct research, generate and disseminate knowledge, train students, and remain accountable to the communities in which we interact and through which our research circulates. We join others in understanding creative practice as intellectual work that vitally historicizes the inequalities that pervade our society and develops interventions through collaborative and participatory work. A basic premise that underlies our efforts is the contention that an expanded, multimodal definition of what counts as scholarship will help to lead to a more diverse university community; a community in which artistic practice is a cornerstone not only for engaged and participatory social justice work but also the reimagining and transformation of the university as a whole.

To these ends, CEE facilitates and supports creative research practices among undergraduates, graduate students, faculty, and our partners within the city of Philadelphia and beyond. We coordinate scholarship, research, and public partnerships related to multimodal work practices, consolidate the activities in which we (and our students) are already engaged, and grow generative connections by hosting Visiting Scholars, coordinating workshops and conferences, supporting multimodal project-based courses, facilitating visual, sonic, and performative undergraduate and graduate research projects, producing rigorous criteria for assessing those projects, engaging with arts and community-based institutions throughout Philadelphia, and forging connections with other like-minded institutions worldwide. During our first year, we were honored to host Louis Massiah (founder of Scribe Video Center) and Aimee Cox (dancer and anthropologist) as CEE fellows. They each taught a studio seminar, conducted workshops with CAMRA, and presented some of their own works-in-progress at the end of the semester. Since that year, we have welcomed two fellows each semester, all of whom have honed our students' skills in film, podcasting, performance, sound, writing, photography, and beyond! We have a graduate certificate, which is available to all terminal degree students across the university. We have also pushed the university to accept non- or extratextual dissertations and we have been able to become involved with arts initiatives in the broader university community and across the city of Philadelphia.

Things have, indeed, changed at Penn since Melisa (Cahnmann-Taylor) was a graduate student and Dell Hymes told her that artistic products could not be legitimate "products" for anthropological scholarship (as discussed by Cahnmann-Taylor in Chapter 13, this volume). And we are not alone. We have had the inspiring opportunity to collaborate with and learn from similar centers throughout the US, Canada, Europe, South Africa, and beyond, and we are heartened that as more and more of our graduate students continue on to academic positions elsewhere, they go on to build similar institutional spaces, thus proliferating these commitments and convictions. Therefore, it stands to reason that this volume would emerge in this moment!

The Creative Ethnographer's Notebook is such a gift! It offers concrete tools for thinking through creative modes of generating and analyzing ethnographic material and developing extratextual research processes and "products." The book is offered as a series of **études** and here, we use the term étude in its classical sense. When Deborah was training in classical piano, Chopin was her favorite composer, and he regularly wrote études to introduce players to novel techniques. By calling the offerings in this book études, we mean to reference these short pieces, pieces that were written to provide practice material to help players (broadly conceived) hone a skill. The études presented in this book, however, are gifts not only for the player but also for the teacher. As a pedagogical intervention, this book is a critical resource for both high school and university teachers, opening up new avenues for exploration, play, and critical thinking.

Embedded within each of these études is also the important matter of evaluation. If we are willing to accept multimodal work as scholarship, then we must also be willing to provide tools for members of reappointment and promotion committees, especially those unfamiliar with extratextual research processes, who may need help to think through what constitutes "peer review" across the various genres in which scholartists (to borrow a term from this text) work.

Before the field, in the field, and after the field, multimodality remains an incredibly vibrant and energizing way of breathing new life into our conceptualizations and concretizations of ethnographic practice. And for the next generation of ethnographic fieldworkers, *The Creative Ethnographer's Notebook* will help to provide the know-how, courage, and inspiration they need to continue pushing the limits of what counts as legitimate and valued intellectual knowledge production, offering even more opportunities for scholartists to transform academia (and beyond!) in powerful and productive ways.

Acknowledgements

During the time we spent generating this book from idea to publication, many wonderful individuals and organizations influenced and inspired us. At the risk of omitting someone, we acknowledge some for their paramount contributions to this project.

First, we would like to acknowledge the support and love of our beloved partners, family members and friends, who have given us encouragement, sustenance, and time during these years to work together in hotel rooms at the American Anthropological Association meetings, over long hours on Zoom, and during a special in-person book writing retreat along an acéquia in Albuquerque's South Valley. Thank you to the Athens Cyclists for wearing a version of this beautiful book cover on their cycling Jerseys across Georgia.

We are especially grateful to our Routledge editor, Meagan Simpson, who instantly saw the vision and value of this project from the moment we pitched it to her. Ever since, she has been at the ready with feedback, input, and support that has improved this book immeasurably and made creating a book about creative processes not only pleasurable but an artistic journey in its own right.

We also extend appreciation to our home departments and institutions, which support the hybrid spaces between the arts and the social sciences. At the University of New Mexico, the Music Department provided a semester's research leave and the Office of the Vice President for Research (OVPR), in collaboration with Academic Affairs and ADVANCE at UNM, provided a UNM WeR1 Research Development Grant, which helped to birth and support the finishing of the book. Students in Jacobsen's Creative Ethnography class also offered insights and feedback on the book prompts at a crucial stage. At the University of Georgia, we would like to thank the departments of Language and Literacy Education and College of Education that provided a semester's research leave to complete this project, as well as Theatre and Film Studies, Art Education, the UGA Arts Council, and the Willson Center for their supportive colleagueship, awards, grant funding, and other opportunities to teach and learn across interdisciplinary boundaries.

At the American Anthropological Association (AAA), support at the intersection of the arts and anthropology has been offered by the Society for Humanistic Anthropology, the Council on Anthropology and Education, the Music and Sound

Interest Group, and the Society for Cultural Anthropology. In 2021, we also received an AAA Community Engagement Grant to support a community-based performance event in Baltimore, called "Where Songwriting and Poetry Meet," which was the first public event celebrating the core themes that *The Creative Ethnographer's Notebook* would cover.

Thank you to our colleagues who support us on our creative ethnographic journeys, specifically UGA department heads Anne Marcotte, Allison Nealy, and Joel Taxel, UGA colleagues in Language and Literacy Education and on the Arts Council, Lynn Sanders-Bustle and colleagues in Art Education, David Saltz, Emily Sahankian, and colleagues in Theatre and Film Studies, and the UGA Faculty Learning Improv Group. Melisa's community of poetry–scholar friends, including Alys Wilman, Melissa Hotchkiss, Adrie Kusserow, Kuo Zhang, Dana Walrath, Elline Lipkin, the Hambidge Center, and Resplandor Scholar–Artist residency programs. At UNM, former UNM Dean of the College of Fine Arts, Kymberly Pinder, Music Department Chairs Steven Block and Michael Hix, and many Music, Anthropology, Theatre, and Dance colleagues have supported this project. Jacobsen's cowriters and creative collaborators Meredith Wilder, Christy Cook, Enrico Spanu, and Gianfranco Cossu, along with Merlettes bandmates Dair Obenshain, Sharon Eldridge, Laura Leach-Devlin, and Jackie Chacón, have been especially important in sustaining her artistic practice role throughout the writing of the book.

There have been numerous creative ethnographic scholars who have been a part of this journey, many of whom are included in this book. Our gratitude goes to these contributors for their creative ideas, as well as others, including our many colleagues in Humanistic Anthropology, those who have attended our community events and creative ethnographic salons at the annual American Anthropological Association meetings, and others who have hosted us as speakers on campuses to help us to develop and legitimize these ideas into this work. Specifically, we would like to thank those who are not in this volume but are here in spirit: Richard Siegesmund, Kakali Bhattachayra, Fred Erickson, Nancy Hornberger, Lucinda Pease-Alvarez, Margaret Gibson, Alicia Ostriker, Kent Maynard (may his memory be a blessing), Richard Bauman, Steven Feld, and a group of "singing anthropologists" who performed their songs at the Third Floor Performance Space in Washington, D.C., as part of the 2017 AAA meetings, including Aaron Fox, Alexander Dent, Alex Chávez, Clifford Murphy, and Chris Wilson.

Many opportunities, awards, mentors, and friends have helped to sustain our creative lives and articulate the scholar–artist connections. Thank you also to the following entities for allowing us to republish portions of original publications and artwork, including the University of Toronto Press and *Anthropology and Humanism.*

Finally, and most importantly, many students have contributed indirectly to this book, helping us to articulate ideas in creative ethnographic courses and mentorship through creative ethnographic scholarship. We would like to thank four students in particular whose time, talent, insights, and collaboration helped us to complete this book: Surya Blasiole, Laura Olson, Maira Serik, and Joel Sisson. Our deepest gratitude goes to our students and the students of our students, who can continue to define creative ethnographic power by the examples they will provide into the future.

1 Introduction to Creative Ethnography as a Field

Melisa Cahnmann-Taylor and Kristina Jacobsen

Whether painting *alebrije* figurines alongside Oaxacan artists, performing music with Navajo Nation country bands, narrating vibrant dialogue with a Songhai medicine man, scholars exploring ethnographic methods often engage in artistic practice during **fieldwork**. Anthropologists include the arts as part of ethnographic approaches to data collection, data analysis, and the representation of findings for many reasons; for example, they may have previous or ongoing training in the literary, visual, or performing arts, they may be compelled by arguments that the arts provide invaluable inquiry tools (e.g., Cahnmann-Taylor and Siegesmund 2008; 2018), or they may be working on studies that include artists as participants or **interlocutors**. Not only do **ethnographers** observe and interview artists for studies, they also at times engage themselves as artists for inspiration during analysis and/or to share their findings and fieldwork experience in evocative and impactful ways. The best of this creative ethnographic work is accessible to and valuable for a wide and diverse set of audiences, thereby increasing meaningful impact and engagement with study collaborators, as well as communities within and beyond academia.

How and when do anthropologists, educators, sociologists, and other social scientists innovate using the arts and **ethnography**? How do they start to think, write, draw, sing, photograph, or perform with the collected data? What is the result of these innovations? Ethnographers are often trained to understand **theory**, document keen observations, and make sense of human patterns, yet they are not often trained in the art of representation. Creative practices are usually left up to each individual social scientist, some of whom may be lucky enough to have an artistic practice that they keep silent or on the side of their more "official" work. Yet these practices can expose differences in the impact, depth, and reception between pieces of research or in the dissemination of important political messages regarding social justice or human rights issues within the given field. We believe that if more **creative ethnographers** shared their tips, prompts, and artistic exercises, social science work could have more meaning for individual scholars, the fields of inquiry, and the broader public. We also believe that, for artists, deeper engagement with ethnographic specificity and cultural inquiry leads to deeper, more nuanced, and more impactful art.

DOI: 10.4324/9781003365228-1

This is what *The Creative Ethnographer's Notebook* is all about. This resource can be used by instructors to teach students (and the instructors themselves) how to engage with creative approaches to ethnography, as well as how to conduct better *public* anthropology.

With contributions from emerging scholars and leading creative ethnographers working in various social science fields (e.g., anthropologists, educators, ethnomusicologists, political scientists, geographers, social workers, etc.), this volume offers readers a variety of creative exercises that ethnographers have used in their own work and classrooms to deepen their ethnographic practice. The contributions foreground different approaches in creative practice, broadening the tools of multimodal and multisensory ethnography as readers design studies, work with interlocutors and landscapes, and render ethnographic findings.

This book recognizes the complex relationships between innovation, fact, and fiction in creative artmaking and aims to document many kinds of truths in social science work. Facts and cultural specificity matter deeply in ethnography and ethnographic practice; however, rather than seeing the complex relationship between art and facts as a divide, we see it as an invitation. How and when the arts matter in sustaining meaningful social science and when social science can and should matter to the arts are central concerns for the editors and contributors of this volume. Ethnographic inquiry and practice in the arts have greater impact when the craft and practice of creating, thinking, doing, making, and **deep listening** are taken seriously.

Why don't we see more ethnographies being shared and read by neighbors and friends or discussed in public discourse? In her book to help ethnographers improve the ways in which they write culture, Ghodesee (2016) writes: "How ironic that scholars who research the intimate experiences of ordinary people cannot write for them." In other words, so much of what we write is rarely read by the communities about whom we write, nor is it very often read by friends, family members, or others in our communities. This is not because the themes or topics don't matter or aren't interesting or relevant; rather, the impact of ethnographic work can also be about the **genre** or style in which we write that can feel at best exclusive to other trained anthropologists and at worst alienating or boring due, in part, to the lack of artistry in the prose representations of our studies. Several texts, including Ghodesee's, have been written to energize "Writing Culture," beginning with Clifford and Marcus' (1986) famous book by that title, as well as more recent books by accomplished ethnographers who are striving to make ethnographic writing more engaging, vulnerable, and beautiful (Behar 1996; Gottlieb 2014;VanMannen 2011; Narayan 2012; Rosaldo 2013). Increasingly, scholars now incorporate more varied artistic innovations to enhance the quality of their perceptions during fieldwork and analysis, as well as to help communicate the impact of their work to broader audiences. Many scholars have begun to work artistically and in multimodalities, including and going beyond the written word. The line between "art" and "science" has become blurred and there are now new and complex possibilities for collaboration, energizing research methods and approaches for the staple anthropological method known as ethnography.

As with any artform, to do this well takes practice, intention, attention, and time. This book offers a starting point for various modes of entry into the practice of creating more accessible, socially relevant anthropologies and encourages the use of instructional time to teach creative engagement in social science classrooms.

What is Ethnography? What Does Creative Ethnography Mean?

Ethnography, defined as the in-depth study of a culture (either our own or another) at a given moment in time, is premised on intercultural inquiry and the ability to create empathy for communities, places, and persons that we may not otherwise come to know. Taking apart the Greek root words of "ethnos" (culture) and "graph" (writing), ethnography is a qualitative research method that literally "writes culture," helping us to understand the meaning of daily life among humans around the world through their interactions with human communities and non-human environments. Ethnographies can offer insights into specific (and sometimes controversial) cultural communities of practice, such as men's boxing (Wacquant 2021), urban high schools (Olsen 1997), artisanal cheesemaking (Paxson 2012), New Age communities in Venice Beach (Orey 2016), urban "skinhead" communities (Blazak 1995), or BDSM communities in San Francisco (Weiss 2006). These insights can, in turn, render more universal understanding about what it means to be located along the human–non-human continuum. The more precise, lyrical, and evocative the representation, the greater impact that these works (including books, photographs, poems, songs, films, and soundscapes) can have within varied academic fields (e.g., anthropology, education, sociology, geography, political science, business, etc.), as well as with public audiences.

In the pursuit of documentation that evokes greater feeling, lyricism, and emotional impact, ethnographers have increasingly turned to expanded understandings of "graph" not only as text but inclusive of multi-genre and multimodal documentations which may or may not include the written word, or may represent it, differently. Creative ethnography draws on aspects of the literary, visual, sonic, and/or performing arts to inform how scholars and artists document culture in ways that serve more diverse public and academic audiences. **Ethnographic poetry** (e.g., Cahnmann-Taylor 2016; Kusserow 2002; 2013; Rosaldo 2013; Stone 2008; Zia 2019), **ethnographic songwriting** (Jacobsen 2017; 2019; 2024; Hauge & Reid 2019; Reid, Jacobsen, and Hopkins, current volume), ethnographic artmaking (Perley, current volume), ethnographic memoirs (e.g., Behar 1996; Bessire 2021; Narayan 2012; Stoller 1989), and **ethnographic fiction** (Isbell 2009; Subrahamian 2018) are just a few of the many creative exploits pursued by those working across artistic practices and social science documentation. Many creative ethnographers have contributed to this book with their innovative guidance on ethnographic practice and artmaking. For both emerging and experienced practitioners alike, *The Creative Ethnographer's Notebook* offers exercises that have proved useful for faculty and students around the world who aim to experiment with the arts as a means to increase the impact and beauty of ethnographic study, insights, and products and present research findings in engaging, accessible, multimodal, and multigenre ways.

How and Why Do Ethnographers Apprentice in the Arts?

While artists can receive specialized training in arts departments, this kind of training is more difficult to come by within the social sciences and humanities. Moreover, in university settings where different disciplines are often siloed in separate colleges that are located on different parts of large campuses, interactions between artists and researchers across the arts and social sciences are rare. However, there are increasing numbers of ethnographers and "**scholartists**" (scholars who are artists or use the arts as integral parts of their study, as discussed in Cahnmann-Taylor and Siegesmund 2008; 2018) integrating art and the social sciences in research findings who are also looking for training in their artistic crafts. Cahnmann-Taylor recalls attending a poetry writers' conference as a graduate student and her shock at seeing famous anthropologist "Renato Rosaldo's" name on the name card table. An emerging and an experienced social scientist both studying poetry far away from their home universities and official institutional roles! This was an exciting discovery but also illuminated just how rare it was, and often still is, to find other social science creatives engaged in creative writing pursuits. In this book, we hope to build a greater sense of community and possibility, giving explicit permission and encouragement for current and future generations of scholars to pursue artistic training within their programs of study rather than only finding this on the outskirts of the academy on one's own time, resources, and initiative.

The approaches offered in this book can guide ethnographic practice that includes the arts as part of fieldwork, from how we conceptualize data and interactions with participants in studies to approaches to notetaking, interviews, and documentation. We focus on methods that help both teachers and learners of ethnography to embrace what is joyful, rigorous, creative, and surprising from the beginning of a project (e.g., Part I: Preparing for the Field), throughout the project (e.g., Part II: In the Field), and to the end (e.g., Part III: After the Field).

Throughout this book, we refer to both teachers and learners as "creative ethnographers." While some pursue excellence in their artistic crafts to the levels of publishing poems in both literary and academic journals, exhibiting artwork in galleries and museums, and performing songs and plays in public venues, we recognize these as only a small part of the creative ethnographer's process. Instead, qualitative researchers who engage in the "craft, practice, and possibility" (Cahnmann-Taylor 2003; 2009) of creative practice may find their way to more scintillating and accessible writing styles in academic prose, more creative ways to collaborate with study participants, and new perspectives on how to visualize, voice, taste, touch, feel, smell, and hear what is resonant in the field. Additionally, scholar–artists may find new and surprisingly personal connections to their research by approaching it in this way. In other words, this book focuses on creative processes just as much as creative products, providing exercises and prompts to awaken sensory and aesthetic awareness in our work.

We ask the primary questions: how can ethnographers take art seriously and what can the arts offer to ethnography and all of the social science fields that employ this form of inquiry?

Ethics, Moral Compass, and Researcher Responsibility in Creative Ethnography

There have always been ethical concerns about ethnographic fieldwork practices that take information for scholarly gain without giving anything directly back to the communities under study. Critics argue that ethnographic methods are too often extractive and exploitative of the cultures, persons, and landscapes under study to the exclusive benefit of the scholar's reputation, position, and royalties from publication (Denzin 2008; Smith 2021). In addition, much anthropological research has taken place, and continues to take place, in spaces of colonial occupation (past and present), where there can be vast differences in power between the ethnographer and research collaborator(s) or interlocutors. For example, performance artist Guillermo Gómez-Peña (2000) incites dialogue concerning traditional anthropology and the juxtaposition of Chicanx experience and scholarship in his provocative piece "Mexterminator," a sharp critique of the way in which American media "engineers" Mexican communities through often unflattering images, as told through the genre of science fiction (Gómez-Peña 2013). This process of cultural othering is what Gómez-Peña refers to as "a stylized anthropomorphization of Chicano postcolonial demons" (2000: 132).

To address ethical, anti-racist, and postcolonial concerns, ethnographers have sought to develop practices that are collaborative, representative of multiple voices beyond the singular voice of the scholar, and reciprocal in terms of care and responsibility. For example, the concept of conducting research "with, by, and for" the communities under study has become a fundamental tenet of critical Indigenous studies (see Hokowhitu et al. 2020) and beyond (Robinson 2020; Smith 2021). At the same time, ethnographic work has often provided vital data regarding community advocacy, language documentation and reclamation, and drawing public attention and scrutiny to structures of colonization, racialization, state surveillance, and social and political oppression that need concrete and assertive responses. Authors in this book (e.g., Cahnmann-Taylor in Chapter 8) also advocate for artful approaches to ethnographic practice, such as interviews, that expand rather than simplify divergent perspectives on any given topic.

When ethnographers innovate using artistic methods, what new ethical considerations arise? Following Murphy and Dingwall (2001), this book addresses not only aesthetics but also questions of ethics when engaging creatively with, by, and for research collaborators, including ourselves, in our studies. This also includes engaging with our own experiences as scholartists in what is often referred to as ***auto-ethnography***, or ethnography about the self. We consider how to write about communities as insiders and outsiders, through arts-based approaches to ethnography, with dignity, care, and creativity, including collaborative, co-created, and co-authored works. This includes directly addressing the "messiness" involved in doing anthropological fieldwork and the complexities involved in making art. Finally, we examine the American Anthropological Association's mandate to "Do No Harm" and how to graciously work through, and repair, unintended harm. As time passes, scholars are increasingly reflecting on unintended biases in earlier points of inquiry (either their own or those of others frequently cited in their field) with the goal of naming and transforming biases (e.g., sexism, racism, ethnocentrism, homophobia, ableism, etc.) that were previously invisible to them. For example, in Wolcott's (2010) chapter *Ethics and Intimacy in Fieldwork*, he reflects on earlier concerns regarding physical intimacy with a collaborator in his study on unsheltered youth: "The criterion of intimacy in my list of customary attributes of ethnography has become more problematic for me over the years and seems to warrant special attention" (p. 112).

Arumugam (2023) describes the fraught personal–professional dilemma of doing fieldwork on reproductive fertility while herself experiencing infertility and undergoing assisted reproductive treatment. For these and many other anthropologists, self-reflexivity includes paying attention to the subjects of our studies, as well as our own **positionality** in relation to our subjects. Rigorous and ethical disciplinary fields require the space to expose and interrogate ethical dilemmas as they arise. The arts can offer the perfect place to present the complicated, affective, and nuanced aspects of power with which anthropologists are implicated, as are all of society. This is also addressed in Rego's (2018) award-winning poem, which appeared in an anthropology journal, reflecting on her research in Cape Verde when a mother offered up her own child to Rego as she passed by.

Unadvisable
(Rego, 2018)

Try not to feel too guilty
for having just stopped at the ice cream shop
and bought yourself a delicious scoop of pure mango on a sugar cone.

And try not to feel self-conscious
As you walk along the main fair, licking it quickly before it melts.

Try not to feel like a spoiled child
who's had too many ice creams,
too many opportunities,
and more than your share of love.

Try not to feel ashamed
when a small mob of children come up from behind you
to ask for a lick of your ice cream,
and the first thing that crosses your mind is communicable diseases.

And try not to lose sleep that night,
when a woman sitting under a tree tries to give you her baby
and you say no, you can't, sorry,
as if you were saying no to a warm loaf of bread.

As the poetry editor of *Humanistic Anthropology*, Cahnmann-Taylor notes that ethnographic poems provide an important container for this complexity, discussing the ways in which ethnographic poems appearing in the journal can address moral issues precisely because they "avoid heavy-handed moral certainty" (Cahnmann-Taylor 2018: 129). Cahnmann-Taylor also writes:

> While ethnographers may all hold political and moral conviction, ethnographic poetry falls short of its goals when verse lines are used primarily to deliver political messages. Climate change, excessive class privilege, poverty, racism, colonialism, political oppression, public health—these are just some of the moral issues addressed in these winning poems. But what makes these poems successful is the grounding of these big ideas in unique and specific moments, rich with precise detail and layered with complexity… .these poems work not because they tell readers how to feel, but because their images and language help us feel for ourselves (Ibid. 2018: 129).

Crafting art and artful ethnography allows creative scholars to reconnect with ourselves, and, in turn, to more meaningfully connect with participants and with one another in our academic and artistic communities. Artful ethnography and artwork that emerges from ethnography can restitch, or reconfigure, our (undone) social worlds. However, scholars must also be responsible for making art that is rigorous and attends to craft with practiced attention. After all, lackluster art created by scientists can also pose troubling dilemmas and ethical considerations. Who has the "right" to make art and who does not? And when? Is there a threshold of training that must be defined and passed? Additionally, artists may benefit from being aware of the types of ethical considerations in which anthropology is deeply engaged, e.g., whose stories are considered worth emphasizing and whose are not? When inviting new scholars into creative ethnography, we must all attend to how the experience of trauma (whether intergenerational or recent) interacts with creative work. The idea of marrying the increased and very necessary attention to the politics of positionality and identity within academia to the increased sense of vulnerability that comes with attempting to learn a new artform can, for some students, be paralyzing. A major tenet of using **trauma-informed** pedagogies involves always offering choices and different entry and exit points (Sunderland et al. 2022; Chapter 9, this volume). For this reason, many contributors offer multiple entry and exit points into single assignments, depending on skill and experience levels, as well as lived experience and desire to engage with the prompts, which allows each prompt to be approached differently. We hope that readers will learn from the diverse range of authors in this book who teach from a variety of vantage points and identities, including those born in the US and those born elsewhere, those with new graduate degrees and those with tenure, those writing from positionalities of relative privilege (e.g., job security, race, gender, age, etc.), those who identify first and foremost as artists, scholars, or both, and those with more vulnerability within or at the fringes of academia.

Remembering that it wasn't that long ago that the renowned anthropologist, Ruth Benedict, had to create a pen name in order to give herself permission to write and publish poetry under the pseudonym, Anne Singleton (Singleton 1928), we begin to understand the enormity of the perceived chasm between anthropology and art (see also Cahnmann-Taylor and Siegesmund 2017). While Benedict's poetry has not been without its critics (see, for example, Ruth Behar in Cahnmann-Taylor and Siegesmund 2008: 63), anthropologists, and perhaps female-identified anthropologists in particular, have needed to create alter-egos in order to be artists and not jeopardize their careers as "serious" anthropologists. Indeed, as scholartists, we (the editors) have both been deeply influenced and inspired by the work of poet–anthropologist, or ***antropoeta***, Renato Rosaldo (Chapter 12, this volume), who has, in different ways, given us both "permission" to joyously join our art with our lives and "day jobs" as anthropologists. In this sense, reconnecting art to anthropology (and being our fullest selves, whatever that may look like) within academia happens one person, and one artist, at a time.

A Brief Note on Ethnographic and Creative Focus

Many of the prompts in this book cross multiple artistic genres, including ethnographic poetry, songwriting, creative non-fiction, artmaking, memoir, and filmmaking. Many of the contributors have also already collaborated with each another, in multiple cross-genre projects outside the scope of this book. Part of the intention of this book is to invite creative ethnographers to think about genre more expansively, more creatively, and with greater license to experiment with multimodal and multigenre forms of **knowledge production**. At the same time, and despite the complexity of genre identification, we have attempted to identify for those facilitating and teaching these prompts the different forms of artmaking that they primarily focus on. This is so that those engaging with these prompts have a roadmap and a general gist of where each prompt is leading. However, these lists are not exhaustive and we welcome you to play and experiment between and across prompts.

We have also chosen to use the term "creative ethnographic toolkit" as a conceptual basket encompassing *both* the artistic genre being learned and the ethnographic skillset being developed. Thus, a prompt focusing on poetry reads simply as "poetry" rather than "ethnographic poetry" but may be followed by a skillset such as "fieldnotes." This is for several reasons. First, all of the prompts in this book are intended to enrich, augment, and push our ethnographic practice as anthropologists. Second, we want the art created by the prompt to stand on its own as art. Too often, adding the qualifier "ethnographic" before an artform can suggest that the work is not able to circulate in broader art fields or, worse yet, that the creator may not be qualified to work with that specific artform. In other words, "ethnographic poetry (fiction, filmmaking)" is also just "poetry (fiction, filmmaking)." Our hope is that the work that is produced as a result of these prompts can stand on its own two feet, whether in a room full of anthropologists, a room full of artists, or ideally, someday, a room full of "antropoetas" (Rosaldo, Chapter 12, this volume).

We hope that each reader will find a place in this book and be able to see their full potential in creative ethnography, take anthropology to new places, and make it more inclusive and alive than it has ever been. Our hope is that, in and through this book, we can practice falling down and getting back up together, both as artists and anthropologists. Practicing this kind of growth mindset at any stage in our careers has the potential to change "what is" to "what might be" (to use Maxine Greene's (2007) phrasing), where we move from the actual present to an imagined future.

When engaging in creative ethnographic work, instructors and students may consider discussing these and other questions related to ethical and responsible practice:

- What brought us to the subjects of our study?
- What are the considerations of power and status (both our own and those of our collaborators) that we should reflect upon?
- How does our creative inquiry "give back" to our collaborators, scholarship, and the public at large and what are the limitations of our inquiry?
- Where are the "hard parts" of our study (i.e., the struggles, questions, tensions, and uncertainties)?

Ethical approaches to creative ethnography do not hide these tensions and questions but serve to reveal and yield more and better questions. *The Creative Ethnographer's Notebook* aims to respond to these and other questions for creative ethnographic practice, such as:

- How do we begin to creatively engage with ethnographic inquiry?
- What does it mean to personalize or creatively consider **social theory**?
- How can we awaken our senses and sensibilities to detailed evocations that are grounded in lived experience?
- What lessons can we learn from fiction writers, poets, film makers, musicians, and painters to stimulate new thoughts and diverse representations in social science?
- How do we remain conscious of ethical concerns and allow the arts to help us to become more adept at nuanced understanding?

The exercises in *The Creative Ethnographer's Notebook* are presented as "prompts" to guide readers to try new, arts-based methods of inquiry that strive to complexify and generate ever more provocative and complicated social science. This book draws on the instructional creativity of scholars and artists representing a wide variety of artistic genres, academic fields, heritage languages, and identities across the lines of race, gender, ability, and nationality. For example, contributors hail from Australia, Latin America, the UK, Southern Europe, Eastern Europe, and various regions (including Native Nations) in the US and Canada. Importantly, the contributors carried out their graduate training in anthropology, education, the visual arts, music, political science, and writing and now work in a broad range of departments and disciplinary fields. Many of them work across disciplines and across nations, including Europe, the US, Australia, and Canada.

This volume presents creative ethnographic practice from the perspectives of a diverse range of scholars who have authored creative ethnographic work around the world. Trained in ethnography and the arts, the 28 contributors are also affiliated with related disciplines, including education, music, political science, language revitalization, creative writing, history, theatre, graphic arts, and more. As the recipients of prestigious awards, honors, fellowships, and grants acknowledging their skills as anthropologists, artists, and educators, those who have contributed prompts each have extensive experience in both creative ethnographic practice and arts-based instruction. We hope that readers are inspired by the great range of practices and perspectives that are represented in this volume.

Who Will Use This Book?

The Creative Ethnographer's Notebook is designed to be used by a wide range of advanced high school, college, and university instructors of qualitative inquiry across the social sciences and humanities in the US, Canada, Europe, and around the world. We hope that even experienced instructors of ethnographic methods can learn alongside their students, using the guided exercises for creative work and to cultivate a "beginners' mind" and a sense of curiosity and play.

The primary audience for this book is students of qualitative research methods in anthropology and other similar fields within the social sciences and humanities, such as education, sociology, musicology, geography, communication studies, writing and rhetoric, and cultural studies. Instructors can use this as a primary textbook to introduce qualitative and ethnographic research methods in a way that is engaging, creative, and generative and as a tool for reflecting on qualitative inquiry more broadly. As it follows the flow of content presented in many introductory anthropology books (i.e., preparing for the field, in the field, and after the field), *The Creative Ethnographer's Notebook* offers a creative approach to the introduction of anthropology and the writing of ethnographic prose, as well as being a companion title for graduate or undergraduate courses in the field. This book can also be used as a secondary text to accompany large introductory courses in cultural and linguistic anthropology and sociology.

This book works well with introductory and upper level undergraduate and graduate courses in cultural anthropology, linguistic anthropology, language and communication, and introductory field courses in anthropology. Other courses for which the book is of use include those in **ethnomusicology**, performance studies, sound studies, American studies, critical Indigenous studies, and folklore studies. We hope that this book is also of value in the proliferation of **arts-based research** courses offered by colleges of education and fine art, and even those offered in nursing, social work and arts in medicine programs within schools of medicine.

The secondary audience for this book is teachers and scholars in arts-based education research (ABER) (e.g., Cahnmann-Taylor and Siegesmund 2008; 2018) and established social scientists who would like to recharge their approaches to research and teaching and begin training in more creative approaches. Finally, we hope that the book is of interest to artists working both within and outside of academia who want to add depth, intensity, and rigor to their cultural framing, as well as their approaches to cross-cultural storytelling, intercultural exchange, and the challenges that come with representing others through artistic mediums. Increasingly, members of arts faculties have to contend with tenure track processes that require connecting artistic practice to academic research endeavors. We hope that this book is helpful for artists who are interested in articulating the foundations of inquiry and the products of artistic practice.

The book is addressed to both emerging and experienced creative social scientists, as well as members of social science faculties who are unfamiliar with artistic practices. The prompts include ideas for classroom procedures, assignments, and alternate modes of teaching.

In sum, the creative sector in the social sciences is growing ever more robust across the globe. We have personally contributed to international conversations and growing interest among other nations, including in Hong Kong, Finland, Israel, Canada, Mexico, Singapore, Spain, Scandinavia, Ireland, England, South Africa, the Republic of Cyprus, the United Arab Emirates, Italy, and India. We hope that this volume continues to nourish the global trends in merging artistic and social science practices and products, thereby expanding maker profiles and audiences for this work.

How to Use This Book

The book is divided into three main parts that each contain prompts written by a broad range of scholar–artists and creative ethnographers. These three parts are called "Preparing for the Field," "In the Field," and "After the Field." Readers can follow the parts in order or may skip around the book and choose prompts at random. Each prompt is designed to be self-standing and function on its own. The prompts are crafted to engage students who are new to anthropology and/or artistic practices in the social sciences, as well as those who are more experienced in the arts and those who have already accumulated pages and pages of data. All of the prompts aim to engage a beginner's mind; thus, they are written in a way that engages creative ethnographers at the level that they are at. In the rare cases in which a higher experience level is required, we flag this for both teachers and students. Optional "extensions" are also included for more advanced students who wish to push themselves. Throughout the text, words and concepts that appear in bold are defined in the glossary or appear as pop-up definitions for E-book+ readers. Additionally, E-book only readers will see some underlined words and concepts that are hyperlinks with additional information.

In our own artistic practice as scholartists, we have found that entering into a creative space through "**art-adjacent**" spaces, i.e., artforms that are different from our primary artform, can be extremely generative and liberating. When the onus of being "good" or skillful in a particular artform can be left at the doorway, this creates more space for authentic exploration, artistic play, and openness to spontaneous artmaking in whatever form it may take. This ability to let go of the expectations we have for ourselves, both as artists and scholars, can be immensely generative for our primary artmaking practices. For example, for Jacobsen, creative writing, mindful listening, and drawing are very generative for songwriting, which is her primary artform; meanwhile, for Cahnmann-Taylor, improv theatre performance nourishes "leaping consciousness" (Bly 1975) in her poetry and vice versa. We hope that the prompts included in *The Creative Ethnographer's Notebook* encourage readers to bring a sense of play to their studies, whether these are ultimately expressed as "research," "art," or any of the beautiful boundaries and interstices that lie in between.

References

Arumugam, Indira. 2023. "Heartbreaking anthropology hurts: Studying fertility rituals while struggling with infertility." *Anthropology and Humanism*, 48(1): 40–52.

Behar, Ruth. 1996. *The Vulnerable Observer: Anthropology that Breaks Your Heart.* Boston: Beacon.

Bessire, Lucas. 2021. *Running out: In search of Water on the High Plains.* Princeton: Princeton University Press.

Blazak, Randall Evan. 1995. "The suburbanization of hate: An ethnographic study of the Skinheads subculture." PhD Dissertation, Emory University, Department of Sociology.

Bly, Robert. 1975. *Leaping Poetry: An Idea with Poems and Translations.* Boston: Beacon.

Cahnmann, Melisa. 2003. "The craft, practice, and possibility of poetry in educational research." *Educational Researcher*, 32(3): 29–36.

Cahnmann-Taylor, Melisa. 2009. "The craft, practice, and possibility of poetry in educational research." In *Poetic Inquiry: Vibrant Voices in the Social Sciences*, edited by Monica Prendergast, Carl Leggo, and Paulina Sameshima, 13–30. Rotterdam: Sense Publications.

Cahnmann-Taylor, Melisa. 2016. *Imperfect Tense.* San Pedro CA: Whitepoint Press.

Cahnmann-Taylor, Melisa. 2018. "Introducing the 2017 poetry prizes: A good year for 'good' ethnographic poetry." *Anthropology and Humanism*, 43(1): 126–134. https://doi.org/10.1111/anhu.12199

Cahnmann-Taylor, Melisa and Siegesmund Richard. 2008. *Arts-Based Research in Education: Foundations for Practice.* London: Routledge.

Cahnmann-Taylor, Melisa and Siegesmund Richard. 2018. *Arts-Based Research in Education: Foundations for Practice (2nd edition).* London: Routledge.

Clifford, James and George. E. Marcus. 1986. *Writing Culture: The Poetics and Politics of Ethnography.* Berkeley: University of California Press.

Denzin, Norman. K. 2008. "Evolution of qualitative research." In *SAGE Handbook of Qualitative Research*, edited by Lisa. M. Given, 3rd ed., 1–10. Thousand Oaks, CA: Sage.

Ghodesee, Kristen. 2016. *From Notes to Narrative: Writing Ethnographies That Everyone Can Read.* Chicago: University of Chicago Press.

Gómez-Peña, Guillermo. 2013. *Ethno-Techno: Writings on Performance, Activism and Pedagogy.* New York: Routledge.

Gottlieb, Alma. 2014. "The restless anthropologist: Crossing borders to new fieldsites." *Anthropology and Humanism*, 39(1): 1–2. https://doi.org/10.1111/anhu.12030

Greene, Maxine. 2007. Imagination and the healing arts. Retrieved from https://maxinegreene.org/uploads/library/imagination_ha.pdf

Hauge, Chelsey and Kate Reid. 2019. "A production of survival: Cancer politics and Feminist media literacies." *Studies in Social Justice*, 13(1).

Hokowhitu, Brendan, Aileen Moreton-Robinson, Linda Tuhiwai-Smith, Chris Andersen, and Steve Larkin, eds. 2020. *Routledge Handbook of Critical Indigenous Studies.* New York: Routledge.

Isbell, Bille Jean. 2009. *Finding Cholita.* Urbana-Champaign: University of Illinois Press.

Jacobsen, Kristina. 2017. *The Sound of Navajo Country: Music, Language and Diné Belonging.* Chapel Hill: University of North Carolina Press.

Jacobsen, Kristina. 2022. "Creative Ethnography: Ethnography and the Arts." Course syllabus. Published at the following website: https://www.academia.edu/120355039/_Creative_Ethnography_Ethnography_and_the_Arts_Syllabus_Fall_2022?source=swp_share

Kusserow, Adrie. 2002. *Hunting Down the Monk.* Rochester, NY: Boa Editions.

Kusserow, Adrie. 2013. *Refuge.* Rochester, NY: Boa Editions

Murphy, Elizabeth and Dingwall Robert. 2001. "The ethics of ethnography." In *The Handbook of Ethnography*, edited by Paul Atkinson, Amanda Coffey, Sara Delamont, John Lofland and Lyn Lofland. London: Sage, 2002.

Narayan, Kirin. 2012. *Alive in the Writing: Crafting Ethnography in the Company of Chekov.* Chicago: University of Chicago Press.

Olsen, Laurie. 1997. *Made in America: Immigrant Students in Our Public Schools.* New York: The New Press.

Orey, Spencer Dwight. 2016. "The dream refinery: Psychics, spirituality and Hollywood in Los Angeles." PhD dissertation, Duke University.

Paxson, Heather. 2012. *The Life of Cheese: Crafting Food and Value in America.* Oakland, CA: University of California Press.

Peña, Guillermo Gomez. 2000. *Dangerous Border Crossers: The Artist Talks Back.* New York: Routledge.

Rego, Marcia. 2018. "Unadvisable." (ethno-poetry) *Anthropology and Humanism*, 43(1): 156.

Robinson, Dylan. 2020. *Hungry Listening: Resonant Theory for Indigenous Sound Studies.* Minneapolis: University of Minnesota Press.

Rosaldo, Renato. 2013. *The Day of Shelly's Death: The Poetry and Ethnography of Grief.* Durham, NC: Duke University Press.

Smith, Linda Tuhiwai. 1999 [2021]. *Decolonizing Methodologies: Research and Indigenous Peoples.* 1999: London: Zed Books; Dunedin, N.Z.: University of Otago Press. 2012: London: Zed Books. 2021: London: Zed Books, 3rd edition.

Stoller, Paul. 1989. *The Taste of Ethnographic Things: The Senses in Anthropology.* Philadelphia: University of Pennsylvania Press.

Stone, Nomi. 2008. *Strangers Notebook.* Evanston, IL: Triquarterly Press.

Subrahamian, Mathu. 2018. "Ethnographic activist middle grades fiction: Reflections on researching and writing *Dear Mrs. Naidu.*" In *Arts-Based Research in Education: Foundations for Practice (2nd edition),* edited by Melisa Cahnmann-Taylor and Richard Siegesmund, 91–98. London: Routledge.

Sunderland, Naomi, Fiona Stevens, Kate Knudsen, Rae Cooper, and Marianne Wobcke. 2022. "Trauma aware and anti-oppressive arts-health and community arts practice: Guiding principles for facilitating healing, health and wellbeing." *Trauma, Violence, & Abuse*: 1–19. https://doi.org/10.1177/15248380221097442

Wacquant, Loic. 2021. *Body & Soul: Notebooks of an Apprentice Boxer, Expanded Anniversary Edition.* Oxford: Oxford University Press.

Weiss, Margot D. 2006. "Working at play: BDSM sexuality in the San Francisco Bay area." *Anthropologica*: 229–245.

Wolcott, Harry. F. 2010. *Ethnography Lessons: A Primer*. Walnut Creek, CA: Left Coast Press.

Zia, Ather. 2019. *Resisting Disappearance: Military Occupation and Women's Activism in Kashmir*. Seattle: University of Washington Press.

Part I

Preparing for the Field

There was a time when conducting ethnographic fieldwork implied that anthropologists were traveling far away from their homes to observe and analyze differences in human practices and cultures around the world. Horace Miner's (1956) paper in the *American Anthropologist* entitled "Body Ritual Among the Nacirema" (*Nacirema* is "American" spelled backwards) is a famous satire of fieldwork and representation in the early to mid-1900s. At that time, the field was heavily biased toward the orientations of scholars who were often White, male, cisgendered, able-bodied, heteronormative, and from Western countries (mostly Europe and the US), who often portrayed the cultural communities under observation as misguided, ignorant, or "primitive," reflecting biases that were often unconscious. Miner describes the savage "body rituals" of the "Nacirema," including the numbers of "shrine rooms" (bathrooms) in a home in which "mouth rites" (teeth brushing) occur over "charmboxes" (sinks) (1956, 503–4). These and other biases are sometimes also referred to as "androcentric bias" in anthropology (Scheper-Hughes 1983). As a work of fiction, Miner's essay held an important mirror to the discipline of anthropology to encourage it to recognize, through satire and humor, the problems of judgment and Western bias in anthropology, which helped to educate and change the field. Similar to how we discuss this in the book's introduction, art-adjacent genres such as "The Nacirema," can often provide broader, and more spacious, places for reflection and self-critique, including some overt apologies for harm caused, knowingly, in the past.

Preparing for the field means that anthropologists have already read foundational research articles, book length ethnographies, and essays such as Miner's (1956). Or, for younger students newer to the field, it can mean going to a place, having it pique your interest, and doing as much research as you can about that place, using both formal and informal sources. For many anthropologists, field sites become places we want to return to, again and again; they become a second (and sometimes a first) "home." Anthropologists and other qualitative researchers also read a great deal of theory, which helps scholars to draw on general principles or guidelines for how they see the world; for example, moving from the outdated "deficit theory," which saw non-Western practices as inferior, toward "asset" theories, where

DOI: 10.4324/9781003365228-2

observations are guided to be more neutral or positive and appraised for their value within their context. Finally, preparing for fieldwork requires us to read ethnographies from the past in order to plan for studies in the future, whether studying the kitchen table conversational habits among Italian Americans (Erickson 1981), gendered educational practices in Papua New Guinea (Johnson 1993), or corporate masculinity in Japanese hostess clubs (Allison 1994). Oftentimes, our incursion into the field is premised on making a distinction between our current work and work that has come before. Before we begin the fieldwork and research process, it is easy for social linguistic theory, or other theories generated by anthropological research, to feel abstract, far away, and as if they don't relate to our everyday, "real" lives. Oftentimes, as Jacobsen frames it in the classroom, this can lead to a sort of extreme academic perfectionism, or "analysis paralysis"[1] (this volume, Chapter 13; see also Jacobsen, "creative ethnography" course syllabus). Depending on attention to writing style and reader engagement, ethnographies can be difficult for those who are new to anthropology to read. Part I of this book aims to guide creative approaches to reading theory and various genres of creative ethnographic prose. The prompts in Part I can also act as guides later on (in Parts II and III) for the ways in which we can allow our "data" (i.e., what we observe in the field) to guide our theory rather than the other way around.

"Part I: Preparing for the Field" contains three chapters that aim to inspire creative approaches to theory and reading to help scholars to prepare for fieldwork with an artist's sense of attention. Chapter 2 engages social theory through the senses, offering prompts that help to literally taste different understandings of theory (Keleman Saxena) and understand ethnographic concepts and theoretical frameworks through persona poems from the non-human perspective (Cahnmann-Taylor) and through comic book form (Bernard Perley). By employing these different approaches, the abstraction of theory grounds itself in our bodies, our lived experiences, and our senses, allowing it to feel more approachable, more relevant and more meaningful for emerging ethnographers. The senses play key roles in both ethnographic writing and artistic creation; they also play a central role in effectively reaching audiences, whether readers, listeners, or viewers. Chapter 3 focuses on writing by preparing the senses. Paying close attention to music, songwriting, and poetry refines our appreciation of what happens when sound (music, voice, reading words on a page, etc.) is made audible. The prompts in this chapter aim to guide readers to engage with how ethnographic writing *feels* with music (Anthony Kwame Harrison), attend to silences and the unsayable (Sienna Craig), and include reading the news in local communities (Kristina Jacobsen).

Note

1 I define this as arriving at a point where we are frozen in both our creative and academic work. I am not referring to physiological paralysis; rather, it is the feeling of, after spending so much time *thinking* about anthropology, that *doing* something in the field, such as fieldwork, feels impossible to get right, i.e., the feeling of "damned if you do and damned if you don't."

References

Allison, Anne. 1994. *Nightwork: Sexuality, Pleasure, and Corporate Masculinity in a Tokyo Hostess Club.* University of Chicago Press.

Erickson, Frederick. 1981. "Money Tree, Lasagna Bush, Salt and Pepper: Social Construction of Topical Cohesion in a Conversation among Italian Americans." In *Analyzing Discourse: Text and Talk*, edited by Deborah Tannen, 43–68. Washington, D.C: Georgetown University Press.

Johnson, Peggy A. 1993. "Education and the 'New' Inequality in Papua New Guinea." *Anthropology & Education Quarterly* 24 (3): 183–204. https://doi.org/10.1525/aeq.1993.24.3.05x0967e

Miner, Horace. 1956. "Body Ritual among the Nacirema." *American Anthropologist* 58 (3): 503–507. https://doi.org/10.1525/aa.1956.58.3.02a00080

2 Creative Engagements with Social Theory

Writing through the Abstract to Arrive at the Concrete

Giving Meaning and Voice to Objects

Melisa Cahnmann-Taylor

Creative Ethnographic Toolkit: Poetry, poetic inquiry, dramatic monologue, theory.

Across many subfields of anthropology, ethnographic writing relies on participant observation as a central research method during fieldwork. This often involves observations of human life and interviews with human actors, which focus on the human participants in our studies. However, non-human objects at field sites have become increasingly important in more recent and collaborative ethnographic studies. For example, the Matsutake Worlds Research Group (2012) has "one of the world's most expensive mushrooms" (p. 411), the matsutake, as its primary object of study, where "the findings of research reports are just the fruiting body of a larger underground life process" (113). Theories of **new materialism** (Barad 2007; 2010; 2011; Coole and Frost 2010) point to the urgent consideration of natural and man-made objects in cultural worlds. New materialists focus on what Barad (2007) called agential realism: "the idea that it makes sense to understand agency as a pervasive feature of the things of this world" (Rosiek 2018). The following prompt asks writers to give meaning and voice to objects and enliven those objects with agency, opinions, histories, and stories. What would the matsutake mushroom say if it could speak from underground, from inside the harvester's bag, at the market stall, or from the frying pan? Inspired by the above research, as well as the **poetic** tradition of **dramatic monologue,** I invite ethnographers to consider animating a non-human object with voice, agency, and character.

Prompt

Make a list of non-human objects that represent some aspect of what you consider to be "your own" cultural community. Or choose an object from a cultural community where you have studied or spent time. Freewrite this list for at least 1–3 minutes without censoring yourself.

Next, review the list and choose the non-human object that resonates the most with layered meaning or significance for you. You do not need to know what or why yet!

DOI: 10.4324/9781003365228-4

Now, try writing a dramatic monologue from that object's point of view. Animate the object. How does it think? What is its history? Does the object consider itself to be part of a family? What losses or near-death experiences has the object encountered? Try doing some research about the object to help to create a voice that is more honest and convincing. For vocabulary, use terms that you find on pages that discuss the object's manufacturing or materials. What idioms and vernacular does your object use? What is the object's age and how is that reflected in the diction and syntax that you use to convey the object's voice?

Why This Assignment

When we think of "portraits," we often think of paintings, like da Vinci's *Mona Lisa* or Picasso's *Blue Man with Guitar*. Sara Lawrence-Lightfoot (1983) applies the visual arts term "**portraiture**" to articulate the kinds of careful detail and artistry that are involved in rendering ethnographic descriptions of participants in studies. Many poets and scholars spend creative time meditating on the lives of others (both human and non-human) as they have become symbolic of complicated interrelated lives. Writing in the voice of the "other," or the "not me," is a way to voice how we perceive others (humans and cultural objects) who are different from us. The poet John Keats' (1795–1821) term "negative capability" refers to a poet's ability, much like an anthropologist, to suspend their ego and imagine others from the inside out.

The prompt in this chapter allows creative ethnographers both to practice the personification of objects by giving them voice and appreciate the importance of displacing the human persona to understand human impacts on the non-human world, as well as the unique lives and perspectives of non-living materials. In Rosiek's (2018) words, new materialism "walk[s] us back from a humanist hubris that attributes all meaning to human interpretive activity." The individual exercise invites scholars to further research their object and imagine speaking from its perspective to explore and validate the quality of non-human experience. Consider this exercise as a way to engage with the affordances, risks, and ethics of cultivating the "not me" ethnographic voice when rendering both human and non-human interlocutors in our work.

What to Read and How to Extend

Read the whole poem "Casa" by Rigoberto González (2013), which is written in the voice of the house itself as witness (only the third stanza is shared here).

> when you tell me you have lost your job
> or that your wife has found another love
> or that your children took their laughter
> to another town. You feel alone and empty?
> Color me surprised! I didn't notice they were gone.

One final invitation is for the creative ethnographer to imagine, as González does, that your house can speak. What has it seen that you haven't seen or can't see? Who walked the floors before you? If your house or a house you have visited often during research could gossip about you, what would it say? In other words… what would the walls say if they could talk? Pablo Neruda's (1961/1994) "Odes to Common Things" may be the most famous poems dedicated to giving the voice and perspective of common objects such as socks or the artichoke. Notice how poems like "Siblings" in Smith's (2008) *Blood Dazzler* speak in the voices of Hurricanes themselves as well as in the voices of those who experienced Hurricane Katrina (see "Ethel's Sestina").

In my own poetic inquiry (Cahnmann-Taylor 2016), I interviewed American adults studying Spanish in Oaxaca, Mexico. I rendered these interviews as dramatic monologues (ibid, pp. 25–32) in the book *Imperfect Tense*, as well as the voices of historic figures (ibid, pp. 60–62). I also wrote a poem in the poet's voice as a meditation on an object related to my field of inquiry: bilingual education. The poem includes **anthropomorphism**, which is a form of personification in which human qualities are attributed to non-human objects. In this poem, the object is a colonial Spanish chair that is exhibited at the Georgia Museum of Art (p. 26), which reminded me of how segregated English monolingual speakers in the US can feel from Spanish–English bilingualism considering that Spanish is also, ironically, all around us, much like this common object.

Iberian Chair 1840s, Decorative Arts Collection
(Cahnmann-Taylor, 2016, p. 26)

Say *chair* and feel abstraction's weight,
        not classic mission, fabric,
        or rattan cane, not head or director,
but this decorative art unmoored

from its coupling: rocking__, electric ___.
        Hear its strained, *cherry*
        purpose, scuffed loosening
from rooms, as if *ch* might fall, leaving *air*

stacked in broken corners. Tilt
        it to *cheer* and clink glasses
        while the meat *chars,* left too long
by the sitter, the soldier, the rocker,

the curator, the one who certifies
        preservation and forbids
        touch. Survivor of the War
of Jenkin's Ear, this wooden Spaniard

is severed, too, from use, a stretched
    rawhide reminder, shrunk to sit out
    dispute. *See ya*, one might say
in its native tongue and we do

not sit on *la silla,* we don't recline
    in others' tongues because we won
    an ordinary household article,
our museums tell us so.

To read more examples of persona poems, go to www.poetryfoundation.org or poetry.org and search for "persona poem" or "dramatic monologue." Whether you are studying a community far from home such as the Songhay sorcery practices (Stoller and Olkes 1987) or craft cheese in the United States (Paxson 2012), the object of your cultural and creative attentions may expand beyond human worlds to include the material realities that inform and are informed by human existence.

References

Barad, Karen. 2007. *Meeting the Universe Halfway: Quantum Physics and the Entanglement of Matter and Meaning*. Durham, NC: Duke University Press.

Barad, Karen. 2010. "Quantum Entanglements and Hauntological Relations of Inheritance: Dis/continuities, Spacetime Enfoldings, and Justice-to-come." *Derrida Today* 3 (2): 240–268.

Barad Karen. 2011. "Nature's Queer Performativity." *Qui parle: Critical humanities and Social Sciences* 19 (2): 121–158.

Cahnmann-Taylor, Melisa. 2016. *Imperfect Tense.* San Pedro, CA: Whitepoint Press.

Cahnmann-Taylor, Melisa and McGovern, Kathleen. 2021. *Enliving Instruction with Drama and Improv: A Guide for Second and Foreign Language Teachers.* New York: Routledge.

Coole, Diana. H. and Samantha Frost. 2010. *New Materialisms: Ontology, Agency, and Politics.* Durham, NC: Duke University Press.

González, Rigoberto. 2013. *Unpeople Eden.* Four Way Books.

Grazer, Brian and Charles Fishman. 2015. *A Curious Mind: The Secret to a Bigger Life.* New York: Simon & Schuster.

Lawrence-Lightfoot, Sara. 1983. *The Good High School: Portraits of Character and Culture.* New York: Basic Books.

Matsutake Worlds Research Group. 2012. "A New Form of Collaboration in Cultural Anthropology: Matsutake Worlds." In *Ethnographic Fieldwork: An Anthropological Reader*, edited by Antonius Cornelis Gerardus Maria Robben and Jefffrey A. Sluka, 409–440. Malden, MA: Wiley-Blackwell.

Neruda, Pablo. 1994. *Odes to Common Things.* New York: Bulfinch Editions.

Paxson, Heather. 2012. *The Life of Cheese: Crafting Food and Value in America.* Berkeley: University of California Press.

Rosiek, Jerry. 2018. "Art, Agency, and Inquiry: Making Connections Between New Materialism and Contemporary Pragmatism in Arts-Based Research." In *Arts-Based*

Research in Education: Foundations for Practice, Melisa Cahnmann-Taylor and Richard Siegesmund. New York: Routledge.
Smith, Patricia. 2008. *Blood Dazzler*. New York: Coffee House Press.
Smith, Zadie. 2016. *Swing Time*. New York: Penguin Press.
Stoller, Paul and Cheryl Olkes. 1987. *In Sorcery's Shadow: A Memoir of Apprenticeship among the Songhay of Niger*. Chicago: University of Chicago Press.

The Taste of Theory

Understanding Discursive, Materialist, and Phenomenological Approaches with Food

Alder Keleman Saxena

Creative Ethnographic Toolkit: Embodied theory, sensorial anthropology.

Understanding the differences between bodies of theory (and why these differences matter) can feel overwhelming. This poses particular challenges when theory moves from the abstract space of classroom discussion to more practical applications, like developing theory-informed methods for gathering data or fitting a mess of unwieldy ethnography into a particular theoretical framing.

The following exercise is designed to help you to foster a better understanding of some of the methodological implications (and affordances) of discursive, materialist, and phenomenological theoretical framings. It aims to help you to understand the differences in the ways that each of these frameworks treat the same material objects and also, ideally, some continuities between them. To this end, the exercise aims to guide you to explore how the adoption of a given theoretical framework can direct your attention toward particular characteristics of your object of study and also demonstrates how generating data through "**thick**" **descriptions** can blur the lines between theoretical frameworks.

Why This Assignment

The exercise in this chapter draws on three common approaches in the social sciences. The first of these is the "discursive" approach; that is, an approach to method and theory that emphasizes language, symbolism, and meaning making. This approach is foundational to contemporary social science research and emerged largely from the poststructuralist **turn** in the early 1980s. This "turn" entailed a shift from social theories that assume an a priori underlying social "structure" toward theoretical frames that recognize that the ideas, meanings, and practices that guide social interactions are "socially constructed." Much of this construction happens as ideas change over time, shaping language and action. The writings of Michel Foucault (Foucault 1989; 1990; 1992; 1995), whose work emphasizes that patterns of social meaning both inscribe and enact power relationships, are key starting points for this area of theory.

The second approach used here is what, for simplicity, I termed the "classical materialist" approach. (In contrast, the "new materialist" approach is discussed at

DOI: 10.4324/9781003365228-5

the end of the prompt.) A core emphasis of the classical materialist approach is the understanding that people and objects are embedded within the larger relationships between labor and capital. These are relationships that exert "material" power (e.g., through monetized labor relations) and lend themselves to analyses that understand society in terms of larger social and economic structures. The writings of Karl Marx, particularly *Capital* (Marx 1992 [1867]), are core theories for this area of work.

Finally, the last major body of theory that this exercise draws on is what is sometimes called "**new phenomenology**." This term denotes an approach that centers on first-person, embodied, and sensory experiences of the world and uses these as the basis for understanding larger sets of relations. In many formulations, the relations under study are not limited to human–human relations but also include those that link humans and non-human or more-than-human entities. Touchstone thinkers in this arena include Donna Haraway on "situated" knowledge (cf. Haraway 1988), Annemarie Mol on embodiment (Mol and Law 2007), and Bruno Latour on actor–network theory (Latour 2007).

The exercise below has three objectives. First, it aims to demonstrate how theoretical lenses can influence observational practices (and the data that they generate). It is designed to show, in a simplified setting, to what kinds of details each of the three theoretical framings can direct your attention. Second, it aims to give you experience in analyzing the data generated by each kind of observation, with directions that correspond to each of the three theoretical lenses. Finally, it asks you to compare and contrast what you learn from each observation–lens cluster and also critically consider where the gathered data blur the boundaries between these simplified ideals.

Prompt

To start, choose a food. Just one food object (an apple, for example) is fine. Alternatively, you can choose a set of foods. Consider one homemade food (e.g., a baked good), one purchased ready-to-eat packaged food (e.g., a bag of chips, candy, or sliced bread), and one fruit or vegetable. These should be foods that can be eaten on the spot with no additional preparation… But don't start eating yet.

Part 1: Three Approaches to "Thick" Description

This exercise is broken up into three sets of tasks. For the first set of tasks, grab a pen and paper or whatever you're comfortable taking notes on. You will use these to write a "thick description" of the foods in front of you, using three steps. As you write these notes, please separate them from each other. For example, if you are using a notebook, keep your notes from the first step on one page and leave space at the bottom. Then put your notes from the second step on the second page and so on. You will use these spaces for the analytical work in the second part of the prompt.

First, examine the food objects visually but *do not touch them*. (That is, don't touch them beyond positioning them where you can see them.) With your writing tools, jot down some words describing the characteristics of these objects.

Be detailed! Use lots of adjectives. Try to keep your description close to the characteristics of the foods and not what they symbolize or evoke.

When you have completed the first part of the exercise, the second step is to handle the foods and examine them up close. You can touch them but *do not eat them*. Again, write detailed descriptions in your notes, this time on a new page or section of the page. How do they feel? Smell? Sound?

Finally, the third step of this set of tasks is to eat the foods. Eat them slowly and enjoy. Take notes! (Again, in a new place.) What is their texture? Or flavor? How do the foods feel in your mouth and your throat?

It is alright if the words that you write (or the characteristics that you note) overlap between the different steps. What is most important is that you describe what you observe in each step separately.

Part 2: Three Approaches to Analysis

After completing the first three steps, it is time to start on the second set of tasks. These can be done immediately after the previous part, but it would also be fine to take a break and come back to your notes with a fresh mind.

Now, review your notes carefully. For this part of the exercise, it is important to stay close to what you have written. If it helps, treat these notes as if you had collected them not in rapid succession about the same set of objects, but rather on different days of field work and about different foods. Then, do the following:

- Examining the first set of notes (those made without touching or tasting the food), use the words that you wrote to reflect on how the meanings (or concepts) associated with the objects relate to larger social meanings. What do they symbolize? What imaginaries, or narrative grooves, do they fit into? Which of the social meanings of these foods bear positive connotations and which bear negative ones? How do they fit into larger social processes and settings?
- Then, use the second set of notes to consider what you can discern about where the objects might have originated from, what kind of labor might have been necessary to bring them from their origin to where you are, and how they could fit into relationships of exchange. Where did the food come from, how did they get here, how were they made, and who made them? Who was involved in the production, transport, and preparation of the food? Who will be involved in its eventual disposal? What are the power relations linking (or dividing) these groups?
- Finally, using the third set of notes (those emphasizing taste), consider how these objects fit into larger spheres of relations. What kinds of relationships do these objects enable? How do they evoke social (human–human) relations? How do they enable relations with the more-than-human world, including living organisms, and non-living entities? How do these relationships unfold over time (i.e., over longer time periods than what you have observed)? How are *you* as the situated observer part of these relationships?

As in much creative and humanistic work, it's important to remember that there is no single "right" answer here. And, for that matter, the way your answers pan out may be quite different, depending on what kinds of foods you have chosen to analyze and what social contexts you imagine them to be embedded in.

Part 3: Compare, Contrast, and Question

To summarize what you have done so far: in the first set of steps, you completed a set of descriptive exercises with your food object(s). These align with the columns in Table 2.1. That is, you observed these objects and recorded data about them in ways that range across a spectrum from purely discursive to materially oriented to embodied experience. Then, in the second set of exercises, you analyzed these three sets of data about your food objects using the theoretical lenses that are commonly associated with each of the three observational approaches. These theoretical lenses are arranged in the rows in the table. You can think of these analyses as falling within the numbered squares in Table 2.1. That is, they sit at the convergence between theory and observational method.

Now, it's time to think about why any of this *matters*. Having completed these steps, the third set of tasks is to compare and contrast the descriptions and analyses that emerged from the previous exercises. How are the three sets of descriptions/analyses similar to each other? How are they different? How many of the analytical questions from each set in Part 2 were you able to answer with the descriptions that you derived *only* from the corresponding observation method? When and where may data from one of the other observational approaches be helpful?

In other words, if we think of the approaches that you just applied as they are outlined in Table 2.1, first ask yourself what belongs in boxes 1, 2, and 3, which indicate the convergences between method and theory that this exercise aims to highlight. Then, ask yourself what belongs in the boxes that have *no* numbers. Or, put another way, to which theoretical perspectives do these methods lend themselves that are different from those they are clustered with in this exercise?

For example, to someone whose family regularly made apple pie at home during childhood, the taste and smell of apple pie may evoke a particular set of personal social relations or relations with seasonally available food. However, to someone raised in the US, regardless of their family habits or region of origin, the embodied

Table 2.1 The convergence between observational and analytical approaches.

		Observational Approaches (first set of tasks)		
		Look, but don't touch	Touch, but don't taste	Taste, touch, smell
Analytical Approaches (second set of tasks)	Discursive	1		
	Classic Materialist		2	
	Phenomenological			3

experience of eating apple pie may evoke and symbolize particular ideal-type family relations or national identity (e.g., "American as apple pie"). This could be the case even if making apple pie was not a practice in their own home while they were growing up. This kind of analysis can easily draw on both phenomenological *and* discursive perspectives.

On the other hand, if someone's primary experience of apple pie was *only* of store-bought versions, the sensory experience of consuming apple pie may bring to mind a classic materialist analysis. For example, the sensory experience of the taste of food preservatives may lead an observer in the analysis direction of considering how the material characteristics of shelf-stable food make it fit into 21st-century food supply chains. Theoretically, these kinds of observations take their cue from situated knowledge but they, in turn, combine that knowledge with an analysis of the lively characteristics of the object. This kind of analysis is often carried out in a field called "new materialism."

How to Extend

If you loved doing this exercise, apply it to different kinds of objects, situations, and data! Or brainstorm the types of topics or forms of data that would be well suited to the three broad approaches discussed in the exercise. In a group of graduate students, you could do a write–pair–share exercise, with participants writing down a) the topic of their thesis, b) the key human relationships that they anticipate being pertinent to their topic, c) the kind of data they intend to work with (e.g., archival, interview, participant observation, etc.), and d) which of the theoretical framings they anticipate drawing on to analyze their data once they have collected it. Discussing how these theoretical framings aid in analyzing different types of data that are gathered from different social contexts can help to show the utility of these framings across different settings. The objective here is to demonstrate that choosing a theoretical framing is not necessarily a declaration that this framing provides the "best" interpretation of the world, but rather that different theory–method combinations may be appropriate for ethnographic writing about different contexts.

What to Listen To and Read

While re-emergent, the approaches denoted here as "new phenomenology" are perhaps the least likely to be taught in basic theory courses. For further reading in this area, I would recommend the following:

- Mol's (2005) article "I Eat an Apple: On Theorizing Subjectivities;"
- Ingold's (2021) essay "Globes and Spheres: The Topology of Environmentalism;"
- My own essay "A View from a Patch: Toward a Material Phenomenology of Climate Change" (Keleman Saxena 2021), which can be viewed in the context of the Feral Atlas project, https://feralatlas.supdigital.org/ and showcases

how more-than-human lives are intertwined and beyond human control, with destructive as well as productive effects.

References

Foucault, Michel. 1989. *Les Mots et les Choses: Une Archéologie des Sciences Humaines*. Bibliothèque des Sciences Humaines. Paris: Gallimard.

Foucault, Michel. 1990. *The History of Sexuality, Volume 1: An Introduction*. New York, NY: Vintage Books.

Foucault, Michel. 1992. *L'archéologie du Savoir*. Bibliothèque des Sciences Humaines. Paris: Gallimard.

Foucault, Michel. 1995. *Discipline and Punish: The Birth of the Prison*. New York, NY: Vintage Books.

Haraway, Donna. 1988. "Situated Knowledges: The Science Question in Feminism and the Privilege of Partial Perspective." *Feminist Studies* 14 (3): 575–599. https://doi.org/10.2307/3178066

Ingold, Tim. 2021. "Globes and Spheres: The Topology of Environmentalism." In *The Perception of the Environment*. Routledge: New York.

Keleman Saxena, Alder. 2021. "A View from a Patch: Toward a Material Phenomenology of Climate Change." In *Feral Atlas: The More-than-Human Anthropocene* edited by Anna Tsing, Jennifer Deger, Alder Keleman Saxena, and Feifei Zhou. Stanford University Press (Digital Projects): Redwood City, CA. DOI 10.21627/2020fa. https://feralatlas.supdigital.org/index?text=alder-keleman-saxena-patchy-climate-change&ttype=essay&cd=true

Latour, Bruno. 2007. *Reassembling the Social: An Introduction to Actor-Network-Theory*. Clarendon Lectures in Management Studies. Oxford: Oxford University Press.

Marx, Karl. 1992. *Capital, Volume 1: A Critique of Political Economy*. Edited by Friedrich Engels. London: Penguin Classics.

Mol, Annemarie. 2008. "I Eat an Apple. On Theorizing Subjectivities." *Subjectivity* 22 (1): 28–37. https://doi.org/10.1057/sub.2008.2

Mol, Annemarie and John Law. 2007. "Embodied Action, Enacted Bodies: The Example of Hypoglycaemia." In *Biomedicine as Culture: Instrumental Practices, Technoscientific Knowledge, and New Modes of Life*, edited by Regula Valerie Burra and Joseph Dumit. New York: Routledge. doi.org/10.4324/9780203941584

Comic Relief

Making a World of Difference in Anthropology

Bernard C. Perley

Creative Ethnographic Toolkit: Comics, graphic ethnography, Native anthropology.

Comics seem to be everywhere these days. This proliferation suggests their acceptance as a form of communication. The power of using graphics for communication and the amplification of messages through text requires some reflection. That being said, how seriously do we take comics? How seriously should we take them? In a world of heightened uncertainties about security (food, water, personal, etc.), our futures (individual, as well as collective), and the Earth (i.e., stability or catastrophic changes), the burden of anxiety often needs some relief. This is where comics can offer some measure of relief while serving as a catalyst for possible changes. In short, comic relief can make a world of difference in solving our collective crises.

I love creating the "Going Native" comics for *Anthropology News*. The editor Natalie Konopinski gives me a theme for each issue, such as **magic**, multispecies ethnography, or many worlds ethnography. Then, I think about how to create a three- or four-panel comic strip that provides reflections on or insights into that theme. The comics are collaborative projects with the editor and also, broadly speaking, my anthropology colleagues. Even though some themes are difficult and potentially controversial, the comics that I create bring me, and I hope other anthropologists, joy.

For me, there is nothing quite like the joy of hearing the sound of a pen or pencil scratching across the surface of a piece of paper. The friction between the ink or graphite and the paper adds to this delight as my hand guides the pen or pencil across a blank page. I begin to see contours of shapes in tension with one another as my ideas begin to emerge from the surface of the page. Slowly, what I had *in mind* materializes on paper. As a quick sketch is completed, I evaluate the results and begin a second quick sketch. I scribble the dialog between characters in text. Hand–eye–mind coordination, when put into words, surely surpasses words.

The old adage "a picture is worth a thousand words" is also true for comics. These sketches can take just a matter of seconds to create but can capture ethnographic conversations and experiences as a Native anthropologist that a thousand words could not convey in the same amount of time. These sketches are source

DOI: 10.4324/9781003365228-6

material for the final printed versions of the comics. Each tone and texture, every text and speech bubble, and every detail and graphic representation are carefully chosen to work together to deliver the message that the comic was intended to convey to appropriate audiences.

The *Going Native* comics are a direct development from my personal series of (mostly) unpublished comics titled *Having Reservations*. These comics have been an important part of my critical reflection on the many absurdities of the history between the Indigenous and settler peoples of Native North America. For example, when I was in grade school, I remember a history lesson in which the teacher lectured about explorers discovering a wilderness. As a Native American youngster, I knew something was wrong with that narrative. My education in American English-only schools reinforced this discomfort well into my academic career. There were many ideas, concepts, and beliefs that my teachers shared in class that provoked my critical impulse.

I had to figure out how to channel the energy of my critical impulse into something that could contribute to change. Drawing comics became my method of quickly capturing the ironies and absurdities of colonial-Indigenous relations in a format that invites all readers to laugh at those absurdities. It is comic relief from the tensions that have derived from over 5oo years of colonization across the Americas. If the comics are successful and provoke a smile or chuckle in recognition of an irony or absurdity, then my goal of bringing us together through laughter can allow us to take that critical next step: working together to remediate the harms of **colonialism**. This is how comics make a world of difference.

When comics are introduced into intense and dramatic moments, the "relief" they bring can affect the wellbeing of the participants in the drama. Ethnographic work is an experience that immerses ethnographers in varieties of drama, both local and global, over the long term. An excellent example of graphic ethnography that tackles these aspects is *Lissa* (Hamdy and Nye 2017; see the associated website for a deeper dive into the process and context). See also *Light in Dark Times* as an example of theoretical and practical engagement (Waterston 2020). These examples affirmed my own practice of graphic notetaking while doing fieldwork, as well as throughout my academic career. As a Native anthropologist, I had to deal with ironies and contradictions for both anthropologists and Native peoples. Comics became a shorthand way for me to capture complex encounters in quick semiotic notes. Those notes became source material for many of my subsequent "Having Reservations" comics.

For the *Going Native* comic series, some of my favorite themes have been care, magic, and after dark. Once the editor shares the theme, I imagine possible interpretations for illustrating the theme that would invite *Anthropology News* readers to think about the theme in new ways. Take the "after dark" theme, for example. I wanted to take advantage of the popularity of the many worlds perspective, which is often articulated as "pluriverses" (De la Cadena and Blaser 2018; Escobar 2018; 2020), and tie that in with communication technologies. I sketched out the idea in quick lines with possible text scribbled in the panels

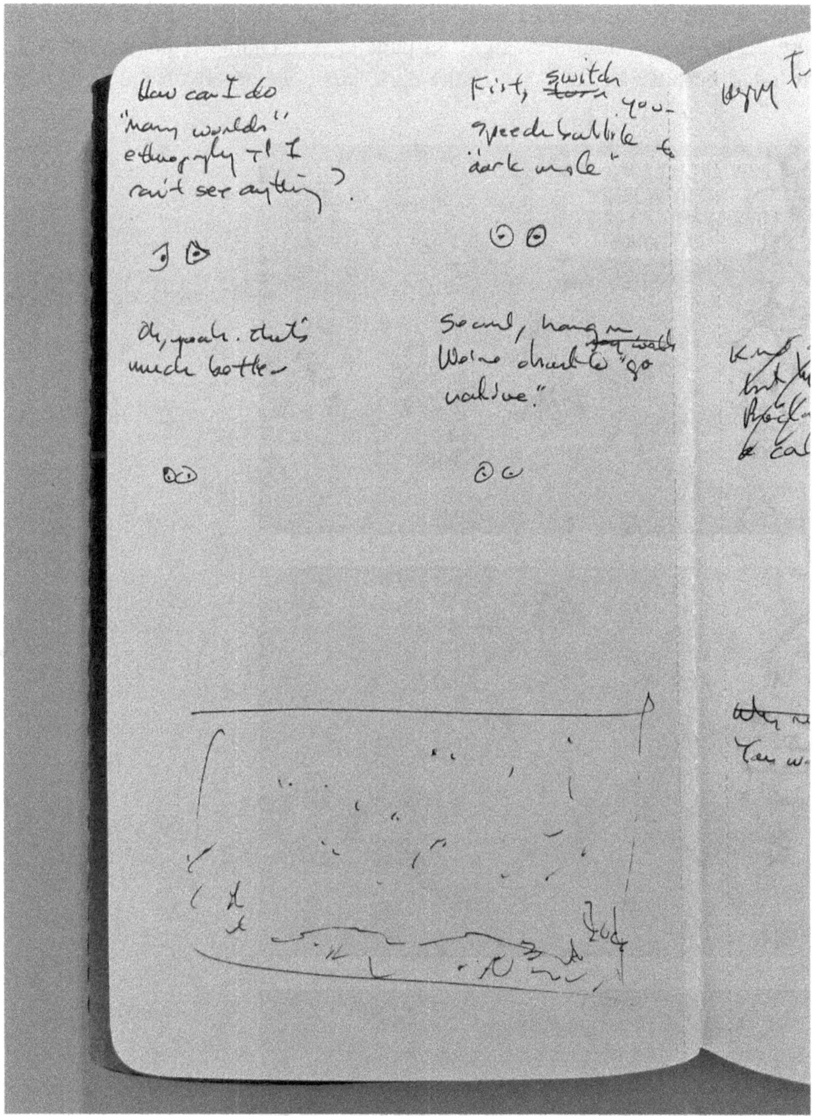

Figure 2.1 Handsketch for the after dark theme in a "Going Native" series.

(Figure 2.1). Note the sparseness of the drawing. The sketch served as the first impression of the idea.

For the final drawing, I used a template that I created, which provides the frames and text boxes in a Microsoft Word document. Once the text had been typed into the template, I converted the file into a PDF and imported it into Photoshop to be cropped to the proper size. Finally, I converted it into a JPEG file and imported that file into Procreate, where I used an iPad Pro to complete the final drawing (Figure 2.2). Ah, the final drawing… In panel 1, the character on the left (CL) is frustrated because he can't see in the dark. His counterpart on the right (CR)

Figure 2.2 The final version of the after dark comic in the "Going Native" series.

suggests a technological strategy to “see” in the dark. In the second panel CL can see but is expressing frustration while CR offers an insight that is essential for all ethnographic encounters: listening and observing. The third panel is where I switch perspectives, so I invite the reader to join the two characters in “going native” in a many worlds experience. The third image is a representation of a real place: the Salish Sea off the coast of Point Grey in Vancouver, Canada. But the night sky is for everyone. If we stop to immerse ourselves in the vastness of the universe while remaining grounded on this increasingly precarious world, perhaps we can find ways to be better relatives on this planet earth. It is our only home.

Prompt

For this exercise, you only need to create a sketch.

Choose a theme for your comic. When selecting the theme, take a moment to think about an issue or topic that has captured your attention recently. Choose a theme that can benefit from comic relief. The most important aspect of comic relief is that it does not take sides. The tensions between good and bad, right or wrong, and true or false are where both sides can come together and laugh at the absurdity of the situation or conflict. I use humor to heal wounds and traumas, not as a tool for ridicule or denigration. Also, think about a strategy to generate conversations that move toward a solution. See the third panel in Figure 2.2 for an example.

Part 1

1. Identify key words that describe the theme.
2. Identify key thinkers or activists who use those words.
3. Think about the positionality of those individuals.
4. Identify the symbols associated with those themes and people.
5. What are the ironies or contradictions in those themes?
6. What is your position within the theme?

Part 2

Begin drawing, sketching, scribbling, and reflecting on the work. Ask for two different responses to your finished draft and evaluate the effectiveness of your comic intervention.

7. Scribble a rough outline of your comic on a sheet of paper.
8. Select the structure of your comic (1 panel, 3 panels, etc.).
9. Sketch the characters and speech bubbles in the panels.
10. Scribble the dialog outside the panels.
11. Evaluate the turn-by-turn action in the panels. Does it work?
12. Start drawing details that support the theme and actions.
13. Present your comic to your class or a group of friends.

How to Extend and What to Read

Work with others to create a comic essay on your collected comics. Does your theme align with those chosen by your peers? If so, can your multiple perspectives allow readers the opportunity to see an issue from multiple perspectives? How would you work together to create a thoughtful and provocative graphic and textual exploration of a theme or issue that captures your collective imagination? See the *Cultural Anthropology* collection "Graphic Ethnography on the Rise" for a good example of how such collections can work. As you work together, ask yourselves "how sequential art can enhance the communicative capacity of multiple authors." For example, some recent collections highlighting Indigenous cultures and history have tackled the one-sided colonial history of Native North America. See, for example, collections of graphic essays such as the *Sovereign Traces* series (Henry Jr. and LaPensée 2018 and 2019; see volume two *Relational Constellations* for my contribution to the collection), *Moonshot* (Nicholson 2015; 2017; 2019), and "This Place: 150 Years Retold" (Highwater Press 2019).

Comics seem to be everywhere now. Graphic novels have started to blur into other genres. The intertextual turn of going from one genre to another presents opportunities for engagement and literacy. The popularity of movies based on Marvel and DC comics has transformed the cinematic industry. The visual vocabulary and organization of sequential art served as inspirations for the dystopian movie *The Matrix* (Wachowskis 1999). We are seeing more classic novels being retold in graphic form, such as *The Iliad* (Hinds 2019) and *The Odyssey* (Hinds 2010), *Fahrenheit 451* (Hamilton 2009, with Ray Bradbury's blessing), and *Game of Thrones* (2012–2015, with George R. R. Martin's blessing). The recent adaptation of Herbert's iconic sci-fi novel *Dune* went through the intertextual transformation from text to movie to graphic novel (Herbert and Anderson 2020). My personal favorite is the graphic novel adaptation of Philip K. Dick's *Do Androids Dream of Electric Sheep?* (2009–2011). The entire text of the novella was illustrated and it took six graphic volumes to produce the whole graphic novel. Comic relief is serious business!

Why This Assignment

We all live in a world that is full of contradictions, confusion, and challenges. Sometimes the best way to deal with particularly tense or anxiety-inducing moments is to look for humor in the event or circumstance. Recent findings in neuroscience and psychology have suggested that narrative is an effective strategy for mitigating the harms of posttraumatic stress injury (PTSI) (Gottschall 2012, Hass-Cohen and Findlay 2015, Costandi 2016). My comics are a narrative form of retelling old stories in such a way that we can collectively create narratives of healing and mutual worldmaking. Comics act as invitations to share worlds in order to create new ones. Let's start the conversation and make a world of difference.

References

Akiwensie-Damm, Kateri et al. 2019. *This Place: 150 Years Retold.* Winnipeg: Highwater Press.

Costandi, Moheb. 2016. *Neuroplasticity*. Cambridge: MIT Press.

De la Cadena, Marisol and Mario Blaser eds. 2018. *A World of Many Worlds*. Durham: Duke University Press.

Dick, Philip K. 2009–2011. *Do Androids Dream of Electric Sheep.* Los Angeles: Boom! Studios.

Escobar, Arturo. 2018. *Designs for the Pluriverse: Radical Interdependence, Autonomy, and the Making of Worlds.* Durham: Duke University Press.

Escobar, Arturo. 2020. *Pluriversal Politics: The Real and the Possible*. Durham: Duke University Press.

Gottschall, Jonathan. 2012. *The Storytelling Animal: How Stories Make Us Human.* Boston: Houghton Mifflin Harcourt.

Hamdy, Sherine and Coleman Nye. 2017. *Lissa: A Story about Medical Promise, Friendship, and Revolution.* Toronto: University of Toronto Press.

Hamilton, Tim. 2009. *Ray Bradbury's Fahrenheit 451: The Authorized Adaptation.* New York: Hill and Wang.

Hass-Cohen, Noah and Joanna Clyde Findlay. 2015. *Art Therapy & the Neuroscience of Relationships, Creativity, & Resiliency: Skills and Practices*. New York: W.W. Norton & Company.

Henry Jr., Gorden and Elizabeth LaPensée eds. 2018. *Sovereign Traces vol. 1: Not (Just) (An)Other.* East Lansing: Makwa Enewed [Michigan State University Press].

Herbert, Frank. 2020. *Dune: The Graphic Novel, Book 1.* Adapted by Brian Herbert and Kevin J. Anderson. New York: Abrams.

Hinds, Gareth. 2010. *The Odyssey: A Graphic Novel*. Somerville: Candlewick Press.

Hinds, Gareth. 2019. *The Iliad: A Graphic Novel Adaptation*. Somerville: Candlewick Press.

Lamm, Spencer ed. 2000. *The Art of The Matrix*. New York: Newmarket Press.

LaPensée, Elizabeth and Michael Sheyahshe eds. 2020. *Moonshot: The Indigenous Comics Collection vol. 3.* Inqaluit: Avanti.

LaPensée, Elizabeth ed. 2019. *Sovereign Traces vol. 2: Relational Constellations*. East Lansing: Makwa Enewed [Michigan State University Press].

Martin, George R. R. 2012, 2013, 2014, 2015. *Game of Thrones: The Graphic Novel.* New York: Bantam Books.

Nicholson, Hope ed. 2015. *Moonshot: The Indigenous Comics Collection vol. 1. Alternate History Comics: www.ahcomics.com*

Nicholson, Hope ed. 2017. *Moonshot: The Indigenous Comics Collection vol. 2. Alternate History Comics:* www.ahcomics.com

Wachowski siblings. 1999. *The Matrix*. Burbank and Los Angeles: Warner Brothers and Village Roadshow Entertainment.

Waterston, Alisse. 2020. *Light in Dark Times: The Human Search for Meaning*. Toronto: University of Toronto Press.

3 Reading Ethnographies with Creative Attention to the Senses

Scoring the Ethnographic Episode

Anthony Kwame Harrison

Creative Ethnographic Toolkit: Scoring, sonic ethnography, soundscapes, music composition.

Good ethnographic writing should convey both information and feeling. Indeed, the affective qualities of ethnography—its ability to move people—are at times as important as specific facts and details. This exercise is aimed at facilitating discussions around the feelings conveyed through ethnographic texts or **ethnographic vignettes**. It involves selecting a particular passage from an assigned ethnographic reading and focusing on how you, the reader, envision, imagine, and audialize the scene presented on the pages.

Prompt

The exercise consists of four basic steps: Selecting, Scoring, Presenting, and Discussing.

Step 1: Selecting

Choose a specific passage (i.e. an account, episode, or ethnographic vignette) from an assigned ethnographic reading. The passage should be somewhere in the range of 200 to 300 words (roughly one page). The passage should be primarily narrative, although it can involve some explanation or reflection. The most important quality is that it should place you, as the reader, in a situation and/or setting a scene that you can visualize.

Step 2: Scoring

This assignment is based on film music principles. When using music in a film, directors make a distinction between music that people in the scene would actually hear (i.e. the **soundtrack**) and music that is not part of the setting but is overlaid to enhance the atmosphere and dramatic effect (i.e. the **score**). For example, a scene

DOI: 10.4324/9781003365228-8

taking place in a country western bar might include a Hank Williams song playing on the jukebox. Yet when the female lead realizes that her lover is not there and has likely been killed, the descending drone of a clarinet or French horn might effectively accentuate the heartbreak she feels. *In other words, the score underscores the feelings, emotions, and overall mood of a cinematic moment.* It is useful to keep this difference between soundtrack and score in mind. However, in scoring the ethnographic episode the distinction need not be hard-and-fast. A certain degree of ambiguity corresponds with the complex nature of ethnographic writing, where sometimes multiple and conflicting meanings are presented at once. Such musical selections can also facilitate insightful class discussions.

The process of scoring involves pairing the selected written passage with music—preferably instrumental music. Generally, students select music they are already familiar with and that matches what they feel in the written piece. However, a non-conventional approach would be to "politicize the score" by introducing music that aesthetically conflicts with or, in some other way, disrupts the feeling of the piece. Yet another approach might involve selecting music/sounds that are rooted in the particular ethnographic setting. Although many familiar songs that might immediately come to mind contain lyrics, with a bit of effort we can often find instrumental versions. This may be as simple as doing an online search with the song title and terms such as "instrumental" or "mood music." Another option is to search through existing Karaoke websites, which feature the music of popular songs without words.

If none of the songs you know seem to fit the scene you have selected, you might also consult an open-access music resource—for example:

- www.free-stock-music.com/
- https://freemusicarchive.org/

Finally, if you are musically inclined, you may choose to compose and record your own score.

Keep in mind that the music you selected should convey sentiments that are, in your view, compatible with (or that intentionally alter) what you feel while reading the text. It is useful to think of the passage as a scene in a movie: what music would be playing in the background? Or you might want to think of the written words as song lyrics and select an instrumental piece that pairs well with the written words.

Step 3: Presenting

The presentation component of the assignment involves reading your selected passage while the musical score is playing in the background. In order to do this, you will need to play your music selection in the classroom and possibly sound-check its volume against the loudness of your speaking voice. It is important to keep your voice audible, however, some of the tension between speaking and music can be mitigated if other students in the class read along with you.

Many classrooms are equipped with sufficient audio-technologies. Bluetooth speakers, which provide good audio quality and allow students to pull up music on their phones, work well. Ultimately, decisions about audio technology should be made in collaboration with your instructor. Agreeing on one standard way to share music will simplify the transitions between different student presenters.

Finally, I recommend practicing reading your text over the music a few times prior to the in class presentation. *The presentation is essentially a performance.* Familiarity with how musical changes in the score align with the timing of your reading will allow you to read with maximum effect.

Step 4: Discussing

At the end of each presentation, you should share a few words about how you selected both the written passage and the music that accompanies it. Did you immediately know what music would work? Or did you have to look around and find something that felt right? What effect/affect were you aiming for? Ultimately, are you satisfied with the music you selected?

Following this brief overview of your process, you should engage with your classmates in a discussion about how the music fits (or does not fit) with the passage that was read. Key questions to ask include:

- What did you hear?
- What did you visualize?
- How did the musical selection enhance your feelings about, understandings of, or anticipation regarding what was being read aloud? And what do the written/spoken words add to the music?
- Does the music (alone) call to mind particular experiences for you? How are they similar and how are they different from the ethnographic passage that was read?

If you are new to ethnography, this exercise offers an effective entry point into discussing the power of ethnographic writing. Yet it can also be useful to those who are very familiar with ethnography.

Why This Assignment

We are all music listeners and most of us like sharing our music selections with friends and classmates. This exercise allows you to enjoy sharing music you like or find particularly meaningful, while also discussing the impact of a selected passage from the assigned readings. It allows you to be an active creator in meaning-making by sharing how and why a text feels a certain way for you. As such, there is no specialized knowledge needed for this assignment. Only the ability to read out loud and a willingness to share your music.

How to Extend and What to Read

This exercise can be expanded in multiple ways. One way involves working in a group (of about five) to score the same ethnographic passage. Each of you should score the passage individually, then the group should collectively decide which score to present to the class. Such an exercise forces you to discuss and deliberate on how a given piece of ethnographic writing feels similar or different to others in the group. Following the class presentation, but before asking discussion questions, your group can also share some of the deliberations surrounding your decision-making process.

A few ethnographic passages that have worked well in my classes are:

- Miles, Corey. 2019. "The Metaphysical Difficulty of Traveling While Black to the Field." *Dysfunction* 6: 12.
- Gustafsson, Mai Lan 2009. *War and shadows: The haunting of Vietnam* ("Fresh hells," pp. 66–69). New York: Cornell University Press.
- Harrison, Anthony Kwame 2009. *Hip hop underground: The integrity and ethics of racial identification* ("(Re)mixed messages," pp. 155–158). Philadelphia: Temple University Press.

The second way of expanding this exercise is to "score" your own ethnographic writing. As an introductory level students, you might write fieldnotes about the food line in the dining hall, getting on and off the bus, or a sporting event on campus. As an advanced graduate student, you might choose to score the opening vignette of a piece you are preparing to submit for publication. Such writings need not be finalized. By forcing you to be more mindful about the affective qualities of your writing, scoring the ethnographic episode can serve as an important part of the revision/reflection process. If you are an emerging scholar, this exercise can also encourage you to think about how using musical pieces might enhance such things as conference presentations, podcasts, and other multimodal presentations of your work.

Yet another way of expanding the exercise (briefly mentioned above) is to compose the music that will accompany your passage. This can be electronic, acoustic, recorded in a **Digital Audio Workstation (DAW)**, or performed live in class, in which case you will likely need to ask someone else to read the vignette while you perform. Remember, the score underscores the feelings, emotions, and overall mood of a cinematic moment.

Finally, rather than scoring a written passage, you may want to pair music with another mode of ethnographic communication, for example an ethnographic film or animation.

Making the Familiar Strange

Writing a Song from a Newspaper Article

Kristina Jacobsen

Creative Ethnographic Toolkit: Songwriting, placewriting, entering into a new fieldsite, gathering community stories, OpEds.

How do we lean into the everyday, as ethnographers, and how can we write about it with emotional acuity? How do we learn to make the familiar strange through our recognition of the cultural specificity contained in the everyday, both in our own communities and in those where we are outsiders? This prompt uses a newspaper article or **OpEd** of your choosing as an entry point into writing the first verse of a song. Like the extraterrestrial from Mars who drops down to Earth for the first time and sees everything with fresh eyes, this prompt asks you to use your keenest senses of perception to discern the context, background and social history behind the newspaper article or OpEd. Then, you will expand upon the story you found, inventing some of the details and doing research for others. Thus, the prompt focuses on the seemingly mundane events reported on by local papers to make the familiar (the everyday) strange by drawing attention to it in a song lyric. Since it is lyric-focused, it does not require knowledge of a musical instrument to complete.

Prompt

Find an article from a local newspaper where you live and/or where you are conducting research. Ideally, this should be a small, local paper and not a nationally syndicated one. The more detailed the story, the better. The smaller the town, the better. Read through it, and select a line from the story that interests you. Now, write this line down on a piece of paper. Newspaper OpEds (Opinion Editorials) can be especially rich. For example, I love to spend time with the OpEds from two newspapers close to where I live in northern New Mexico, "The Navajo Times" and "After the Thunder."

Steps

1) Begin to craft your own story from the line(s) you selected. Your story will be loosely based on these facts, but should build on your own imagination and

DOI: 10.4324/9781003365228-9

sense and memory vaults, rather than narrowly adhering to the facts from the newspaper article. If you need to, feel free to do more background research on the person, place or incident referenced. But don't let that get in the way of writing the story. This story will eventually become your song. As you write, try to use your senses as much as possible—taste, touch, sound, sight, smell, but also in your body (proprioceptive) and movement (kinesthetic).

2) Now, take the story you wrote and circle the words and phrases that you like best. From the terms you selected, begin to write a single, 4-line verse for a song. For your **rhyme scheme**, you should use ABAB, ABxBxA, or ABCB, and try to avoid rhymes that may sound cliché or are predictable. Websites like www.rhymezone.com can be very helpful in searching for more interesting and less predictable rhymes.

   We can see an example of an XAABBACCDD rhyme scheme, in which lines 2, 3 and 6 (A) rhyme with one another, lines 4 and 5 rhyme with one another (B), and lines 7 and 8 (C) and 9 and 10 (D) rhyme with one another, in the John Prine song critiquing the Vietnam War, "Sam Stone" (Prine 1971).

   1. Sam Stone came home X
   2. To his wife and family A
   3. After serving in the conflict overseas A
   4. And the time that he served B
   5. Had shattered all his nerves B
   6. And left a little shrapnel in his knees A
   7. But the morphine eased the pain C
   8. And the grass grew round his brain C
   9. And gave him all the confidence he lacked D
   10. With a purple heart and a monkey on his back D

3) For full credit, your verse should invoke/identify at least two different senses, identify a who/what/where/when, and should specify (either by name or through description) a specific geographic location. Remember, you want to show, not tell! Your songs should also have a title that relates directly to the central theme. You may choose to read/share the initial newspaper excerpt, alongside your final verse, with your peers.

Why This Assignment

Local, place-based stories can be embedded in a variety of overlooked formats. OpEds, obituaries and community interest stories in particular can offer us a raw and unfiltered view of community members' daily lives, issues of cultural and political import to local citizens, and the lived experience of what it means to be from that place/town/community. They can also be a wonderful way to enter as a guest into a new community and begin to know its intricacies and complexities. If we are from the place we are writing about, newspaper stories can also allow us to denaturalize, or make "strange," the everyday things we might otherwise take for granted, sinking into its textures, its specificities and the human stories we find through writing a song lyric.

For example, the late singer–songwriter Nanci Griffith wrote her famous song "The Loving Kind" (2009) inspired by reading an obituary about the court case, Loving vs. Virginia, a successful case challenging **anti-miscegenation** laws in Virginia in 1967. In the song, Griffith uses the last name of the plaintiff, Mildred Loving, to become the final line of the chorus, "the loving kind." It begins:

They were the loving kind
She was black and he was white
In Virginia nineteen fifty-eight
They found love amongst the hate

Well the law said they could not wed
They married anyway
The sheriff put them both in jail
Separated 'till they made their bail

Chorus:
They changed the heart of a nation
with their wedding vows
From the highest court in the land
Their union would lawfully stand
Simply Mildred and Richard
That's how they'll be remembered
They proved that love is truly blind
They were the loving kind.

What to Listen To

This prompt was first shared with me by a New Mexico singer-songwriter, Meredith Wilder, who wrote her own exquisite song inspired by a piece in the Albuquerque Journal titled "Two Men Die in Ditch Trying to Save Dog" for her song, "Along The Ditchbank (Lang's Last Goodbye):"

Clock says 6am, I'm ready to get up
Stretch my legs, take a walk with Lang and his pup
The coffee can wait 'cause I want to see the sunrise
Along the ditch bank, I'll say goodbye to the night

(....)

Spent the rest of the day dreaming and drifting
At midnight we were found, northside of 550
Lang and his pup and I jumped into the sunrise
Along the ditch bank, we howled goodbye to the night

Since then, I have also gone on to write many place-based songs inspired by newspaper excerpts while in Norway, in Sardinia, in Denmark, the United Arab Emirates, and the Navajo Nation. One song of mine that is directly inspired by an article in *The Navajo Times* "Dogs and Children," written after reading an OpEd about the abuse of stray dogs on the Navajo Nation. As a dog lover and dog owner living as a non-Native guest on the Navajo Nation at the time, I wanted to write about this topic without sounding preachy or moralistic. While journalism and songwriting are different—journalism focuses on factual truth, and songs focus on emotional truth—songs can also shed important light on place-based cultural values and ways of being in the world.

How to Extend: Putting Melody and Chords to a Song

a) For those who do sing or play an instrument: what melody would fit the mood of the story? What chord changes might you put underneath? Now, try adding these chords and melody to your verse.
b) If you are already comfortable with the basic tools of songwriting (melody, harmony, lyrics and rhythm), you may try writing a second verse and then adding a chorus (the part that repeats) after your first two verses, i.e., write a song with two contrasting parts (e.g., "verse + chorus," "verse + middle eight"). This does not have to be a completed song.
c) Additionally, if you already have some experience with songwriting and playing/performing music, you may choose to a) write an entire song, alternating verse and chorus structure and b) perform your verse and chorus for the class.
d) Finally, you may choose to memorize the portion of the song and perform it for the class. You may then hand in a copy of the song with the lyrics, chords (chords can be written in whatever way will help you remember them, later), and initial newspaper clipping.

References

Free Stock Music. 2023. Royalty Free Music for All. https://freemusicarchive.org

Griffith, Nancy. 2009. "The Loving Kind." *The Loving Kind.* Rounder Records.

Gustafsson, Mai Lan. 2009. *War and Shadows: The Haunting of Vietnam* ("Fresh hells," pp. 66–69). New York: Cornell University Press.

Harrison, Anthony Kwame. 2009. *Hip Hop Underground: The Integrity and Ethics of Racial Identification* ("(Re)mixed messages," pp. 155–158). Philadelphia: Temple University Press

Jacobsen, Kristina. 2015. "Dogs and Children." *Three Roses.* Three Roses Publishing.

Miles, Corey. 2019. "The Metaphysical Difficulty of Traveling While Black to the Field." *Dysfunction* 6: 12.

Perez, Nicole. 2017. "Two Men Die in Ditch Trying to Save Dog." March 7. www.abqjournal.com/964200/two-men-die-in-ditch-trying-to-save-dog.html

Prine, John. 1971. "Sam Stone." *John Prine.* Atlantic Records.

Wilder, Meredith. 2017. "Along the Ditchbank (Lang's Last Goodbye)." https://on.soundcloud.com/WJfRW

Yurth, Cindy. 2013. "Reporter's Notebook: Dogs and Glonnies, Strays of the Rez." *The Navajo Times.* February 14. https://navajotimes.com/opinions/2013/0213/021413notebook.php

Mine the Gap

Writing into a Poem's Expanse

Sienna Craig

Creative Ethnographic Toolkit: Poetry, free writing, affective ethnography.

Creative approaches to ethnography invite scholars to pay close attention, to think expansively about, and to experiment with form. This prompt is built around poetry and the catalytic process of reading and listening aloud. It is meant to encourage multiple forms of creative writing that can emerge from the writer's own life experience, from careful engagement with an ethnographic text, or as it relates to your own project of anthropological and/or artistic inquiry. It asks you to engage first by listening to the words of others, and then writing forward from a broad, conceptual free-write prompt—what I call an "invitation."

Poems afford us the opportunity to pose questions that often contrast with, but can also complement, what an anthropologist might ask of a moment, a scene, a feeling. They allow for different forms of vulnerability and noticing. For the purposes of this exercise, we'll be working with one poem that helps dig into some core questions asked by ethnographic practice:

- What does it mean to know?
- What are the limits of that knowing?
- How does language shape what we know?
- How do we depart from the ethnographic imperative to record what was said toward a space where we explore what might *not* have been said but that is still real, still present?
- How might we **mine these gaps** to create ethnographic writing that is attentive, vulnerable, and attuned to complexity?

The poem I've chosen is "Gimaazinibii'amoon (A Message to You)"[1] by the **Anishinaabe** poet Margaret Noodin (2020). She wrote this poem first in Anishinaabemowin, her Indigenous language, and then translated it into English. I found this poem through Pádraig Ó Tuama's podcast, "Poetry Unbound."[2] I often listen to this show to inspire my own writing and teaching. In the recording Noodin first sings this poem in Anishinaabemowin, and then reads it in English.

DOI: 10.4324/9781003365228-10

Take a moment to listen to Noodin sing and read her poem–song. Then, listen to it a second time. As you listen, feel free to take notes or just jot down feelings, words or lines that really stick with you.

Here is the beginning of the poem, as read in English:

I know there are different worlds
because our ancestors sent them messages
because lost lovers now live in them
because you just said that right now.

After you've listened to the poem twice and made a few brief notes, set a timer and free write for 7 minutes using one of the following invitations:

1. Write about a gap: in knowledge, in understanding, in comprehension.
2. Write about a moment when someone didn't say what they meant.

Pick whichever invitation most speaks to you. Although the first invitation asks this explicitly, both encourage **mining the gap**. You can write in any genre: poetry, prose, lyrics, fragments, dialogue, or ethnographic description, etc. See where this exercise leads.

To me, Noodin's (2020) poem describes the gap between different social worlds and different ways of knowing our world. As the poem goes on, it speaks about places where meaning breaks down a relationship between shoreline, sea, and "shifting wind." Both through the words in English and as the poem is sung in Anishinaabemowin, it provides a lesson in the limits, but also the power, of translation. It shows the blessings and burdens of cross-cultural communication. It touches on how people's actions and reactions can take you somewhere you didn't expect. These are all crucial elements of ethnographic practice. The poem—first sung, then spoken—is also a useful example of how form and content relate to each other, and how an ethnographer might play with form to render meaning.

When I used the first invitation myself in a free-write, I turned to something personal—my relationship with my teenage daughter. Here is some of what I wrote in those 7 minutes:

> It is impossible to know the heart of my child, even though I know her heart so well. Chasms across streaks of green-gold eye shadow, a pout, the ways she strokes our cat's head with such tenderness. All I cannot know. These architectures of understanding that live in synapses and generational structures. How is mothering like the task of writing in another language? We script care beyond what each can know. We move with and through each other like fingers intertwined. What will it mean to not have her with me? I resist the **metaphor** of the empty nest. We are not birds. Our homing instincts are different. Still, to comprehend the transition in front of us is to know that I know nothing of the world, despite the creature I've made, and who, in turn, has made me. To know

> only that I love her, with all my heart. To know only that it is sometimes the not knowing, but the holding anyway, that matters most.

I ended up using this bit of personal writing as a way into other ethnographic prose about migration and social change between Nepal and New York City. Eventually, this invitation helped me to write about a beautiful but fraught relationship between a Tibetan-speaking grandmother and her English-speaking grandchildren as they tried to appreciate each other's realities, despite not being able to understand each other well.

When I free-wrote using the second invitation, about someone who didn't say what they meant, my mind went straight to a scene from Mustang, Nepal. A tense conversation was unfolding between a village leader, a senior monk, and one outspoken woman about the future of a rural monastery: who was going to care for it; what this institution was for, now that so many young people had left the village. The *actual* conversation remained guarded and polite. Nobody yelled. Nobody accused. But so much was happening under the surface, in the gaps between words. This prompt helped me to name that, ethnographically, and to begin the work of describing why it mattered. I wrote:

> You could taste the bitterness, even in the crisp Himalayan air. It lived between words, between three languages, between social rank and gender. The words focused on material things – orders for chairs, cement, the need to build a new throne for the lama – but all of this was secondary. Nobody was saying what they meant as they talked about beams and rammed earth bricks. What they were *really* talking about was money and power: who owns the past and who might control the future.

Both poets and ethnographers must pay attention to what is unspoken or unseen, but still important. This poem by Margaret Noodin and these accompanying invitations allowed me to mine these gaps and to write into the space that they opened. Where might this prompt take you?

How to Extend

This prompt can stand on its own as an occasional exercise or a ritual with which to begin each class, meeting, or writing workshop. The writing that this prompt produces can be the first draft of a journal-based essay or expanded fieldnote "memo" that finds a place in a larger work; as the basis for class discussion that encourages close reading of a particular text; as a vehicle for producing a prose-poem of precisely 100 words (Berlant and Stewart 2019); as a starting point for a flash ethnography essay of no more than 800 words (McGranahan and Stone 2020); and more. The hope is to write something that is built from the attunement we recruit when hearing words aloud—an act that also approximates other forms of orality we might encounter through fieldwork. This, in turn, helps us to cultivate ethnographic sensibility (McGranahan 2018) that is attentive to voice, character, vernacular, and the senses (Narayan 2012). No matter what form our writing takes, a poem primes us to notice details, fragments, echoes. Writing from this place can help us to hold complexity without foreclosing meaning (Stewart 2007; Pine 2019). Some of the work to emerge from this type of prompt include meditations on loss and wonder (Ogden 2021) and locating joy in dark times through the art(s) of ethnography (Stainova and Craig 2021).

Notes

1 This whole poem can be read and listened to here: https://onbeing.org/poetry/gimaazinibiiamoon-a-message-to-you/
2 https://onbeing.org/series/poetry-unbound/

References

Berlant, Lauren and Kathleen Stewart. 2019. *The Hundreds.* Durham, NC: Duke University Press.

McGranahan, Carole. 2018. "The Importance of an Ethnographic Sensibility." *Sites: A Journal of Social Anthropology and Cultural Studies* 15(1): 1–10. https://doi.org/10.11157/sites-id373

McGranahan, Carole and Sienna Craig, eds. 2023. Un-disciplined: An Invitation to Flash Ethnography. *Anthropology and Humanism* 48(2): 353–354. https://anthrosource.onlinelibrary.wiley.com/doi/toc/10.1111/(ISSN)1548-1409.flash

McGranahan, Carole and Nomi Stone, eds. 2020. "Flash Ethnography Collection – American Ethnological Society." Accessed in February 6, 2023. https://americanethnologist.org/online-content/collections/flash-ethnography/

Narayan, Kirin. 2012. *Alive in the Writing: Crafting Ethnography in the Company of Chekov.* Chicago: University of Chicago Press.

Noodin, Margaret. 2020. "Gimaazinibii"amoon (A Message to You)." In *What the Chickadee Knows.* Michigan: Wayne State University Press.

Ogden, Laura. 2021. *Loss and Wonder at the World's End.* Durham, NC: Duke University Press.

Pine, Jason. 2019. *The Alchemy of Meth: A Decomposition.* Minneapolis: University of Minnesota Press.

Stainova, Yana and Sienna Craig, eds. 2021. "Art and Ethnographic Form in Dark Times." *Cultural Anthropology – Theorizing the Contemporary.* Accessed February 6, 2023. https://culanth.org/fieldsights/series/art-and-ethnographic-forms-in-dark-times

Stewart, Kathleen. 2007. *Ordinary Affects.* Durham, NC: Duke University Press.

Part II

In the Field

The Greek root words "ethnos" (culture) and "graph" (writing) help us to understand that ethnography refers to the written description of a people group or community, their interactions with each other, their expressive cultures, and their environments, all of which shape their way of life. There are five fields within anthropology (archaeological, biological, linguistic, sociocultural, and applied) that can help us to understand the similarities and differences in the ways people have lived and continue to live, as well as the intragroup differences between individuals within any given community. The "field" of study can be as close as our own kitchen table or as far as another neighborhood, city, or community across the world. So, in fact, the "field" is more of a conceptual framework than a geographic location, and it is certainly not a literal field with grass growing in it, as is sometimes perceived! How do we come to know about our topics of study in the field, wherever our ethnographic work may be taking place? And how do we come to know our interlocutors and build authentic and sustained relationships with them when doing fieldwork? How do we make the familiar seem strange and the strange seem familiar (as discussed by Jacobsen in Chapter 3, this volume)?

The five chapters in Part II of this book all guide creative ethnographers in aesthetic and empathetic ways of knowing and relating to ourselves and others. Curiosity can be a powerful ally in selecting a research project or in deciding upon a new fieldsite. What makes us curious, and why? What questions do we have, and how might we answer them from multiple vantage points? Chapter 4 foregrounds mindful approaches to ethnography that lead with what makes us curious, include writing poetry in formal verse forms from around the world (Cahnmann-Taylor), making videos (Sutoris), and writing silences into ethnographic narrative/creative nonfiction (Murphy and Chatzipanagiotidou). Building relationships and **rapport** in the field can often be one of the most intimidating parts of entering the ethnographic experience. Chapter 5 focuses on translating "data" into various art forms, while in the field, that can reach scholarly and public audiences, creating empathy for a diversity of lived experiences. Exploring the line between "fact" and "fiction" to tell an effective story as alternate methods to writing fieldnotes, prompts in this chapter guide creative ethnographers to make data "sing" through the genres of fairytale and songwriting (Jacobsen), through metaphor (Kusserow), and across

DOI: 10.4324/9781003365228-11

the fact-fiction spectrum (Falcone). The focus in Chapter 6 is to help readers write from perspectives that are not their own, understanding what it means to write from a photograph (Jacobsen); to be in different physical places (Stoller); and to write with perspectives of non-human and animal life (Syring). In Chapter 7, we see how language forms an essential part of our cultural identities and is embedded in many expressive cultural forms, including songs, poetry, and storytelling. In this chapter, contributors focus on second language acquisition through songwriting (Hopkins), coming of age stories-turned-poems as a method to reflect on identity, place, conflict, and growth in our own life stories (Alvarez), and **translingualism**: moving across and through languages through poetry and poetic inquiry (Cahnmann-Taylor). Chapter 8 explores the different ways we travel geographically and politically as artists and ethnographers, and our embodied experiences of time and temporality (Stone), the anthropology of food (Jacobsen) and the artful interview to grasp complexity (Cahnmann-Taylor). Lastly, Chapter 9 examines how creative ethnographers use our sight, sound and our own bodies as tools for making films (Lempert), **cowriting** songs as a group (Sunderland), and addressing trauma—our own and that of participants in our studies through writing poetry about war zones that are physical and/or psychological (Zia).

4 Creative Approaches to What Matters and Paying Attention to What Makes You Curious

Working in Non-Western Literary and Linguistic Forms

Melisa Cahnmann-Taylor

Creative Ethnographic Toolkit: Ethnopoetics, ghazal, poetry, fieldwork.

As students of culture, ethnographers eat different foods, speak different languages, and sleep in different ways in different types of accommodations. Some anthropologists study or even practice working in different aesthetic forms, including different literary structures. Coined by poet–ethnographer Jerome Rothenberg in 1968, **ethnopoetics** focuses on the aesthetic principles of Indigenous oral poetry and how these differ from those in Western literary traditions. Ethnopoetics also includes the translation of oral poetries (cf. Hymes 1981; 2003; Rothenberg 1985; Tedlock 1985). Not surprisingly, many anthropologists who have studied ethnopoetics (as well as others too) have also written poetry themselves, with verses often being written by researchers in non-Western forms based on their field of study at the time. Working within non-Western literary forms can give new meaning and possibility not only to what is said but the aesthetic choices for how something is said, as well as to whom, by whom, and to what end.

There is a long-standing tradition of English-speaking poets working in non-English forms. For example, Donald Justice (2004) famously authored "Pantoum of The Great Depression" using a Malaysian form called the **pantoum**, which consists of interlocking 4-line stanzas. A.E. Stallings (2013) pondered the ubiquity of the word "like" in the English language using a French form from the 13th century called the **sestina**. Typically, the sestina is composed of six 6-line stanzas that use a total of six different end words that are repeated six times, and are then repeated again in a final 3-line stanza. To reinforce the overuse of the word, Stallings (2013) chose to repeat "like" (and its companions "alike" and "dislike") in all 39 lines of the poem! Writing in non-English as well as non-Western forms can offer greater gifts of thought and substance.

Originally an Arabic verse form dealing with loss and romantic love, the Persian **ghazal** (pronounced "guzzle") consists of syntactically and grammatically complete **couplets**. The form also employs an intricate use of repetition and rhyme. Each couplet ends on the same word or phrase (the *radif*) and is (often) preceded by the couplet's rhyming word (the *qafia,* which appears twice with the *radif* in the first couplet and subsequently appears in the second line of the next five or

DOI: 10.4324/9781003365228-13

more stanzas). The last couplet includes a proper name, which is often the poet's. In the Persian tradition, each couplet is of the same meter and length, and the subject matters include both erotic longing and religious belief or mysticism. English-language poets who have composed in this form include Adrienne Rich, John Hollander, and Agha Shahid Ali. See Ali's (2003) "Tonight" and Patricia Smith's (2007) "Hip-Hop Ghazal." Admire the ways in which Natasha Trethewey, born in Mississippi to mixed-race parents at a time when there were anti-miscegenation laws in place, uses the ghazal form in her poem "Miscegenation." Trethewey (2006) repeats the name of the state where she was born ("Mississippi") as the end word for each couplet, using her own "Russian" name to end the poem.

Prompt

Search the internet or visit a poetry resource, such as www.poetryfoundation.org, and type "ghazal" into the search engine. Read as many ghazals as you can, such as those referenced at the end of this chapter. Then, make a list of words that you would be interested in using as the "radif" in your own poem. Like Trethewey, you could pick the state that you are from. Or like Stallings, you could choose a word from current vernacular or slang that you hear often in the present or have heard used in the past. If you are conducting research, you could choose a word that is spoken by your participants or a word that has significance within the community in which you are interested. One student in my class wrote a formal "villanelle" poem, which also uses repeated words and phrases. The repeated words that she selected were about her homestay family experience in Mexico and how difficult it was to respond to her host mother's frequent question "*¿Cómo les fue*?" [How did it go?], in her emerging Spanish fluency (Cahnmann 2019).

Following the formal structure described below, write your own ghazal. You can write two couplets or ten. Write without stopping for 10 minutes, then revise what you have written. After 20 minutes of work, share your writing with a peer or classmate. Keep the following qualities of the ghazal in mind but feel free to experiment by using all or only some of the criteria:

- The ghazal is a poem of two or more couplets.
- Each couplet is a semantically independent 2-line mini-poem. The unity to the whole poem is the repeated word.
- A rhyme–refrain (*qafia–radif*) combination occurs at the ends of both lines in the first couplet and then at the end of the second line in every couplet that follows. While the rhyme word that precedes the end word can change, the rhyme remains the same throughout the ghazal. See, for example, how Trethewey often has the long "e" and/or "n" consonant sounds preceding the final radif of Mississippi (e.g., leaving, even, green, even). Many poets dispense with the qafia.
- The last stanza includes the writer's own name and is addressed to the self.

What to Read and How to Extend

Check out a list of slang words, either in English[1] or another language, that young people use today and consider writing a ghazal with one of those words, such as *bruh, gotchoo, savage,* or *basic*. Notice how Antrobus (2020) uses the vernacular phrase "and that" to end every couplet in his poem reflecting on the usage of Jamaican English in the UK. See how McDonough (2012) integrates US cell phone slang into new languages for queer love. Additional ghazals worth reading include "Good Hair" by Sherman Alexie (1966), "Red Ghazal" by Nezhukumatathil, and Smith's (2018) "Ghazal."

In my own work with translingual youths in US schools, I have often heard teachers use derogatory terms to describe their students' translingual practices. The word "Spanglish" has often appeared in my fieldnotes. Which taboo or derogatory word from your fieldwork or life would you like to call into question? The ghazal is a wonderful form to honor words that are forbidden or judged and better understand their value and utility.

Símon Ghazal
(Cahnmann-Taylor, 2020)

A language we'll never learn in classrooms: Spanglish.
First or second language: both/and borders Spanglish.

Standard English, a blazer-dressed, distant uncle;
Tía Castellana, a black laced corset to Spanglish.

Puro amor tattooed on a gangster's knuckles.
¿What recourse *nos queda*? Implored in Spanglish.

El Paso, Las Cruces, La Brea, indelible
stains tarring place names in original Spanglish.

Implicated in languages born in exile:
Yidd-,Chingl-, Hingl-, and Kongl- ish, abhorred like Spanglish.

When certain consonants appear between vowels,
--*mojado/mojao*--they're ignored in Spanglish.

El poeta writes *culocracy*, governing *culos*,
a neologism tour de force in Spanglish.

Tranquila, Melisa, conjugating struggle's
easy. Hang out *o janguear mejor* in Spanglish.

Note

1 URL link: www.fluentu.com/blog/english/teen-slang/

References

Alexie, Sherman. 1966. "Good Hair." Accessed January 18, 2023. https://poets.org/poem/good-hair

Ali, Shahid Agha. 2003. "Tonight." Accessed January 18, 2023. www.poetryfoundation.org/poems/51652/tonight-56d22f898fcd7

Antrobus, Ray. 2020. And that. Accessed January 18, 2023. www.poetryfoundation.org/poetrymagazine/poems/153197/and-that

Cahnmann-Taylor, Melisa. 2019. "Teachers as Poets." *Teachers as Writers Magazine*. Accessed August 3, 2023. https://teachersandwritersmagazine.org/teachers-as-poets-helping-educators-develop-personal-literary-practices/

Cahnmann-Taylor, Melisa. 2020. "*Simón* Ghazal." *Journal of Latina Critical Feminism*. Accessed January 18, 2022. www.facebook.com/journallcf/

Hymes, Dell. 1981. *In Vain I Tried to Tell You: Essays in Native American Ethnopoetics*. Philadelphia: University of Pennsylvania Press.

Hymes, Dell. 2003. *Now I Know Only So Far: Essays in Ethnopoetics*. Lincoln: University of Nebraska Press.

Justice, Donald. 2004. "Pantoum of the Great Depression." In *Collected Poems*, edited by Donald Justice. New York: Alfred A. Knopf, Inc.

McDonough, Jill. 2012. "Husky Boys' Dickies." *Where you live*. NY: Salt Publishing. Accessed February 8, 2023. www.poetryfoundation.org/poems/57190/husky-boys-dickies

Nezhukumatathil, Aimee. 2003. "Red Ghazal." Accessed January 18, 2023. www.poetryfoundation.org/poems/56133/red-ghazal

Rothenberg, Jerome. 1968. *Technicians of the Sacred: A Range of Poetries from African, America, Asia & Oceania*. Doubleday: New York.

Rothenberg, Jerome ed. 1985. *Technicians of the Sacred: A Range of Poetries from Africa, America, Europe and Oceania*. 2nd revised and expanded edition. Berkeley: University of California Press.

Smith, K. Tracy. 2018. "Ghazal." Accessed January 18, 2023. https://poets.org/poem/ghazal-1

Smith, Patricia. 2007. "Hip hop ghazal." Accessed January 18, 2023. www.poetryfoundation.org/poetrymagazine/poems/49642/hip-hop-ghazal

Stallings, Alicia Elsbeth. 2013. Sestina: Like. Accessed January 18, 2023. www.poetryfoundation.org/poetrymagazine/poems/56250/sestina-like

Tedlock, Dennis. 1985. *Popol Vuh: The Definitive Edition of the Mayan Book of the Dan of Life and the Glories of Gods and Kings*. Translated by D. Tedlock, commentary. New York: Simon and Schuster.

Trethewey, Natasha. 2006. "Miscegenation." Accessed January 18, 2023. www.shiningrockpoetry.com/miscegenation-by-natasha-tretheway/

Slowing Down the Ethnographic Gaze through Observational Videomaking

Peter Sutoris

Creative Ethnographic Toolkit: Visual ethnography, observational filmmaking, thick description.

Immersion in the surrounding environment and attention to detail are hallmarks of good ethnography. But the pressure for fast research (and fast life) can make slowing down difficult. This prompt encourages creative ethnographers to put the brakes on by experimenting with capturing the uniqueness of a space, a life, or a person through observational videomaking, paying attention to the many choices that go into framing video sequences. It aims to help ethnographers to think of observational videos as a non-verbal way of engaging with ethnography by conveying the intangible elements of the experience of being in the world, like atmosphere, mood, and sensory immersion.

Prompt

1. Take a camera (it can be on your phone or any other camera that can record video), turn it on and look at its display so that you can view the world around you the way the camera sees it. Do this in a place with which you are familiar, i.e., a "mundane," "unexciting," everyday space. Do not look for a subject, do not zoom in or out or make any other adjustments, and do not press the record button. Just stay with the camera's gaze for a few minutes. Do not listen to the sounds around you for now; instead, focus only on the image.
2. Start slowly rotating the camera and moving it vertically and horizontally, exploring the space around you through the lens. Make sure that you only move the hand holding the camera; do not move the rest of your body. Notice how moving the camera changes the images that you see on its display and how using different angles leads to different objects becoming more prominent while others become subdued. Notice how shadows and reflections change when you turn the camera in different directions. Compare these different images with the images that you associate with the space you are in. Is there anything new or different about how the camera views the space from the way you usually look at it?

DOI: 10.4324/9781003365228-14

3. Now, allow your body to move while still holding the camera in your hand and looking at its display. If you were previously sitting, now stand up; if you were standing, now sit down. Try lying down on the floor. Take a few steps in any direction. Turn around. Raise your arm or extend it to one side. Stand on the tip of your toes for a moment. Keep noticing how these movements affect what you see on the camera's display, how different objects come into view while others disappear, how the lighting changes, and how the mood and atmosphere of the images shift as you make these changes.
4. Start paying attention to sound. Locate any sources of sound (people talking, machines humming, wind howling, water flowing, etc.) and place them in the center of the camera's frame one by one. Then, try pointing the camera away from the sources of sound, using some of the framings with which you previously experimented. Look at the images on the camera's display and listen to the sounds around you, reflecting on what gets communicated when the source of a sound is in the frame vs. when it is deliberately left out of the frame.
5. It is time to start recording. Your goal is to take at least three and at most five shots (video clips) that are no more than 60 seconds long combined. These shots should capture the uniqueness of the space you are in (or the person/life you are filming in the space). Take these shots in the order in which you would like them to be viewed by someone who has never been to this space. Before you press the "record" button, you need to make several decisions.

   1) Which camera angles and positions best capture the uniqueness of the space you are in? Which are most effective at making this "ordinary" space seem extraordinary?
   2) Is the uniqueness of the space better captured through a static shot or does moving the camera while recording make more sense?
   3) Do you want to position any sources of sound inside the frame or leave them out? How could this help you to capture the atmosphere and mood around you?
   4) In what order do you want to take these shots?

   Remember, you are not trying to locate a "subject" in the way we usually do when we take photographs or record videos. Instead, you are trying to come up with a simple cinematic language, based on your experimentation with the camera, that helps you to capture something unique about the space you are in.

6. When you are done recording, watch the clips you have recorded. Then, watch them one more time.
7. Write a short reflection (about 500 words) about the experience, focusing on the ways in which the clips you have recorded help you to see this familiar space differently. What did the camera's lens and microphone capture that your eyes and ears could not? Did the camera's vision help you to discover any blind spots you developed in the space due to spending so much time there or due to being on autopilot and not paying attention to the nuances of the space?

How to Extend

8. Go back to the space and record another 3–5 shots but this time, use a professional camera in manual mode. Do not use your phone camera or any easy-to-use camera. Before you record a shot, do not just pay attention to the decisions you made last time; instead, think about how to set up the white balance, what focal length to use, at what aperture to shoot, and where to set the sound levels. Before you press the record button, spend at least a couple of minutes setting up your shot and making these decisions.

   Remember, the point of these extra decisions is not to overwhelm you with the technicalities of operating a camera nor to create a polished-looking video. The aim is to further slow the process and help you to pay more attention to the space you are recording. Having to make these choices means that you have to think about the space in front of the camera in greater detail, paying even more attention to what makes the space unique and how you can capture this uniqueness.
9. If you feel comfortable, show your clips to your peers and ask for their reactions. Show them both your original shots and your second attempt in manual mode. Then, in small groups, reflect on the following questions:
   1) What did the group members think of each recording?
   2) What difference could they see between the two sets of shots?

   Then, reflect on the following question on your own: Did group member responses resonate with your written reflection or did they notice something different about your recordings?

Why This Assignment

The beauty of ethnography is that it is a slow, immersive process. Yet, we live in a time when our attention spans are shortening, we are bombarded with information, images and sounds, and truly being present in the moment is increasingly difficult. How do we create a thick description of a moment if we cannot truly be *in* the moment? The idea of observational videomaking-as-ethnography is to help ethnographers to slow down and immerse themselves in their surroundings, while simultaneously coming up with non-verbal ways of generating thick descriptions of these surroundings. It is countercultural in its slowness and meditative in its deliberativeness.

In my work, I often rely on Rob Nixon's (2011) idea of slow violence: the notion that environmental decay occurs over long timescales, which makes this destruction harder to perceive than the fast violence of events we see in the news every day. I have argued that engaging with slow violence calls for slow methods, such as observational videomaking (Sutoris 2021), but any ethnographic project can benefit from this method, either directly (as in the mode of video-as-ethnography) or indirectly, either as a starting point for reflection or an elicitation device in conversations with interlocutors, similar to the way in which many researchers use **photovoice** (Wang and Burris 1997).

When used as part of a participatory project in which the ethnographer is not using the method themselves but is facilitating its use by interlocutors, it can aid in building relationships and fostering trust while in the field. For example, in my work with young people in India and South Africa, which focused on their imaginations of **environmental futures** (Sutoris 2022), I taught 6-week workshops in which my interlocutors learned to use camera equipment through a series of exercises before making their own observational films. These films not only conveyed their visions of the future and their sense-making of their social worlds but also became starting points for many fascinating conversations. However, it is a good idea for ethnographers to experiment with the method first to gain insights into its potential so they can better guide research participants in their own experimentation.

What to Watch and Read

My introduction to observational filmmaking was the work of David MacDougall, particularly the films in the *Childhood and Modernity* series (Potts 2015), which are a great example of the potential of observational videomaking. The essays in his books *The Corporeal Image* (MacDougall 2006) and *The Art of the Observer* (MacDougall 2022) are also well worth reading, as are Sarah Pink's writings about sensory and visual ethnography (Pink 2015; 2020). The films of Lucien Castaing-Taylor and the work produced at the Sensory Ethnography Lab at Harvard University could also be sources of inspiration.

References

MacDougall, David. 2006. *The Corporeal Image: Film, Ethnography, and the Senses*. Princeton: Princeton University Press.

MacDougall, David. 2022. *The Art of the Observer: A Personal View of Documentary*. Manchester: Manchester University Press. www.manchesterhive.com/view/9781526165367/9781526165367.xml

Nixon, Rob. 2011. *Slow Violence and the Environmentalism of the Poor*. Cambridge: Harvard University Press.

Pink, Sarah. 2015. *Doing Sensory Ethnography*. London: SAGE. https://doi.org/10.4135/9781473917057

Pink, Sarah. 2020. *Doing Visual Ethnography*. London: SAGE.

Potts, Rowena. 2015. "A Conversation with David MacDougall: Reflections on the *Childhood and Modernity* Workshop Films." *Visual Anthropology Review* 31 (2): 190–200. https://doi.org/10.1111/var.12081

Sutoris, Peter. 2021. "Environmental Futures through Children's Eyes: Slow Observational Participatory Videomaking and Multi-Sited Ethnography." *Visual Anthropology Review* 37 (2): 310–32. https://doi.org/10.1111/var.12240

Sutoris, Peter. 2022. *Educating for the Anthropocene: Schooling and Activism in the Face of Slow Violence*. Cambridge: The MIT Press.

Wang, Caroline and Mary Ann Burris. 1997. "Photovoice: Concept, Methodology, and Use for Participatory Needs Assessment." *Health Education & Behavior* 24 (3): 369–87. https://doi.org/10.1177/109019819702400309.

Writing Silence through Ethnography

Intimate or Otherwise

Fiona Murphy and Evropi Chatzipanagiotidou

Creative Ethnographic Toolkit: Poetry, prose, dialogue, personal essay.

> Sometimes our work is talking. Sometimes our work is simply being, experiencing feelings and thoughts we've put so far away we have no words for them. Then, the silence and our breathing allow these feelings to find the shapes and sounds of the words we need.
>
> – Ntozake Shange (2011), Liliane

Silence features largely in ethnographic encounters. Nonetheless, it is very challenging to write silence (or, indeed, about it) and many of us struggle with its role in our work. Thinking with silence can be generative in both conceptual and creative ways. Ana Dragojlovic and Annemarie Samuels (2021, p. 418) ask in their introduction to an important special edition of *History and Anthropology* on silence, "what it means to *trace* silences, and to include traces of silence in our ethnographic representations. What qualifies as silence, and how does it relate to articulation, to voice, visibility and representation?" These questions are key to this exercise.

The prompt in this chapter asks you to imagine a dialogue with an **intimate other** in order to think through the role of silence in our writing and *trace* and *map* its presence. The writing of dialogue can be challenging, but it has many generative possibilities, not least that it is an obvious space to seek and reflect on voice/voicelessness. This exercise also encourages you to consider whether dialogue is the best way of collecting/reflecting anthropological encounters and narratives or, indeed, if it can also produce other silences. Subsequently sharing this dialogue with peers could propel you to examine the nature of thinking with and writing silences through encounters with intimate others. You could also reflect on the ethics of writing silences and intimacies, as well as the question of how discomfort is involved in this endeavour. Such questions have the potential to spark reflections on other kinds of anthropological and creative ethnographic/non-fiction writing, giving this exercise a vitality beyond itself.

Writing from our own intimate experiences with our families and research participants can greatly complexify the writing process. Alisse Waterston (2019, p. 8) tells us that intimate ethnography is "rooted in particular intellectual, cultural,

DOI: 10.4324/9781003365228-15

political, and anthropological currents, intimate ethnography comes when the need to engage larger publics in rethinking and recounting lives lived and experienced is increasingly urgent." Recently, many anthropologists have turned to thinking and writing in this manner; however, writing from intimate, deeply personal encounters often entails the challenge of dealing with the silences that permeate all of our lifeworlds and encounters in different, complex, and sometimes even troubling ways.

Take a look at Fiona Murphy's (2022) short piece "Archives of Removal" in *Otherwise Mag* (www.otherwisemag.com/removal). In this story of her grandfather, she evokes a number of different intimacies between the dead and the living. There are also many silences in this text: generational, intrafamilial, and in the context of the archive vs. political/state narratives. This exercise asks you broadly to reflect on the different types of silences and how they are or are not documented in the text. Ultimately, we would like you to consider whether there could be a broader creative or political objective in writing like this and what the silences within silences would be in this endeavour.

In a group, discuss the following section of Murphy's (2022) text:

> I hesitate to tell my mother what is written on my grandfather's file in full. I realise quickly that this is an unfairness. She has consented to accompany me on this journey. Yet now I find myself reluctant to share in full the wounding words I have uncovered. This is out of a sense of protection for her gentle nature. I decide, however, quite suddenly on a phone call with my parents, to read what I have uncovered. I blurt it out, unplanned and jumbled. There is silence, long and impenetrable, then tears. My father, accustomed to wearing his discontent like a badge, swears at me furiously. A moment of quietude follows. Then, together, we re-read the lines; we make sense, we think about the contexts of production in which the convenient fictions of this file were scripted. We, my mother, father and I, know there is so much more to this story, so I decide to carry on with my search. I do so, however, in full knowledge that I have certainly awoken particular kinds of ghosts.

While discussing your reflections on the piece, also reflect on what Vincent Crapanzano (2008, p. 35) has to say about the presence of silence in ethnographic engagements:

> Silences punctuate all conversations. They may simply be pauses. They define the rhythm of conversation. Aposiopesis, as the rhetoricians refer to silences, mark the genre, conventions, and style of an exchange. As a rhetorical figure silence may be taught as if was by the ancient rhetoricians. Silences may be persuasive, appellative, seductive, suspenseful, or bullying. They may emphasize the significance of what has been or is about to be said. They may suggest the depth or difficulty of an exchange, the anxiety it produces, the possibility of communicative breakdown. They can be threatening. They may be thought

> to reveal the mental and emotional state of the speakers or their evaluation of their interlocutors. The witting or unwitting use of silence obviously varies from society to society, occasion to occasion, individual to individual, speech genre to speech genre.

The full interview on silence between Vincent Crapanzano and Chowra Makaremi (2008) provides an instructive guide on how to think about silence in both the doing and writing of ethnographic conversations.

Prompt

Part 1

Identify an individual with whom you have/had a close relationship, either from your family or your ethnographic fieldwork. You also have the freedom here to think about a fictional character if you are uncomfortable speaking about a real individual. Write a conversation with that individual: a dialogue that centres on the topic of silence. Imagine what silences this person would like to preserve or break. Ask them why? Consider the familial/historical/political weight of breaking certain silences with them through your writing. What could the ethics of this be? Deploy different kinds of writing techniques to convey both intimacy and silence. Ask yourself, what do we risk by writing intimately/an intimate ethnography and what do we gain? (Allow 20–30 minutes for writing and reflection.)

Part 2

Read your dialogue with a peer and ask for their feedback. Consider the following questions (20 minutes):

- Who did you talk to?
- Why did you choose that person?
- Did you find it effective or challenging?
- Did any silences emerge and did you document these silences?
- How did you approach writing intimacy and silence into your dialogue? What writing techniques did you use (including grammar and punctuation)?
- Do you feel there were any ethical issues with the writing choices you made?
- In your experience, is silence the opposite of "voice"?

If you feel comfortable reading your dialogue aloud to your peer, then that is encouraged.

Following on from this peer-to-peer discussion, together write a short summary of your shared discussion and be prepared to discuss this with other groups. (Allow 15 minutes.)

How to Extend: Drawing Silence from Music

Listen to a piece of music that reflects on or evokes silence. Try to draw or photograph what it inspires in you. As you listen to the song, draw lines or shapes that are inspired by the movement of the music or, if you are very artistic, draw with more detail.

In pairs, consider the differences between how images and words/sounds convey social silences and think about how we can translate this into our writing. To help you with this discussion, read the introduction to Tina Campt's (2017) *Listening to images*, whose work is a poetic call to consider images as something more than rhetorical.

What to Read

For general reading on silence, we recommend the following:

Dragojlovic, Ana and Samuels, Annemarie. "Tracing silences: Towards an anthropology of the unspoken and unspeakable." *History and Anthropology* 32, no. 4 (2021): 417–425.

Virloget, Katja Hrobat and Alempijevic, Nevena Skrbic. "Ethnographies of Silence: Introductory Notes." *Cultural Analysis* 19, no. 1 (2021): 1–7.

Seljamaa, Elo-Hanna and Siim, Pihla Maria. "Where silence takes us, if we listen to it." *Ethnologia Europaea* 46, no. 2 (2016).

To think about the role of silence in writing more generally, an excellent text to read is Griffin, Susan. *Out of Silence, Sound. Out of Nothing, Something: A writer's guide*. Counterpoint Press, 2023.

Please also read "Silenced," "Silent Spaces, Forbidden Ground," "History," and "Chapter" in Crapanzano, Vincent. *Imaginative Horizons: An Essay in Literary-Philosophical Anthropology*. University of Chicago press, 2004.

For this exercise, it is also important to consider how to write good dialogue. Please see Chapter 6 "Embrace Good Dialogue" in Ghodsee, Kristen. *From notes to narrative: Writing ethnographies that everyone can read*. University of Chicago Press, 2016.

For an important discussion on intimacy in writing/ethnographic writing, read Waterston, Alisse. "Intimate ethnography and the anthropological imagination: Dialectical aspects of the personal and political in My Father's Wars." *American Ethnologist* 46, no. 1 (2019): 7–19. Consider what Waterston has to say about how this kind of writing provokes a reflection on silence(s) (family silences, historical silences, political silences, etc.).

The question of whether silence(s) should always be documented and analysed by ethnographers is an important one. To think about this, please engage with Chatzipanagiotidou, Evropi and Murphy, Fiona. "Exhibiting Displacement." *Documenting Displacement: Questioning Methodological Boundaries in Forced Migration Research* 7 (2022): 81. In this article, the authors discuss the idea of *methodological dubiety*. Consider what they are evoking with this term with respect to the ethics and practice of documenting and writing different kinds of silence(s). What ethical issues are involved in the concept of methodological dubiety?

What does it mean to give people a "voice" and what political projects have you encountered in relation to this? Are silences always part of silencing processes? To explore this, read and discuss Goldstein, Diane E. "The Sounds of Silence: Foreknowledge, Miracles, Suppressed Narratives, and Terrorism—What Not Telling Might Tell Us." *Western Folklore* (2009): 235–255 and Chatzipanagiotidou, Evropi and Murphy, Fiona. "'Devious silence': Refugee art, memory activism, and the unspeakability of loss among Syrians in Turkey." *History and Anthropology* 32, no. 4 (2021): 462–480.

References

Campt, Tina M. 2017. *Listening to Images*. Duke University Press.

Chatzipanagiotidou, Evropi and Fiona Murphy. 2021. "'Devious Silence': Refugee Art, Memory Activism, and the Unspeakability of Loss among Syrians in Turkey." *History and Anthropology* 32 (4): 462–480.

Chatzipanagiotidou, Evropi and Fiona Murphy. 2022. "Exhibiting Displacement." *Documenting Displacement: Questioning Methodological Boundaries in Forced Migration Research* 7: 81.

Crapanzano, Vincent. 2004. *Imaginative Horizons: An Essay in Literary-philosophical Anthropology*. Chicago: University of Chicago Press.

Dragojlovic, Ana and Annemarie Samuels. 2021. "Tracing Silences: Towards an Anthropology of the Unspoken and Unspeakable." *History and Anthropology* 32 (4): 417–425.

Ghodsee, Kristen. 2016. *From Notes to Narrative: Writing Ethnographies that Everyone Can Read*. Chicago: University of Chicago Press.

Goldstein, Diane E. 2009. "The Sounds of Silence: Foreknowledge, Miracles, Suppressed Narratives, and Terrorism—What Not Telling Might Tell Us." *Western Folklore*: 68(2/3): 235–255.

Griffin, Susan. 2023. *Out of Silence, Sound. Out of Nothing, Something: A Writer's Guide*. Berkeley: Counterpoint Press.

Makaremi, Chowra. 2008. Engaging with Silence Interview with Vincent Crapanzano. Altérités, *Thinking commitment* 5(2): 33–45. ffhal-03034510f

Murphy, Fiona. 2022. "Archives of Removal." *Otherwise Magazine* .

Seljamaa, Elo-Hanna and Pihla Maria Siim. 2016. "Where silence takes us, if we listen to it." *Ethnologia Europaea* 46 (2): 5–13.

Shange, Ntozake. 2011. *Liliane: A Novel*. Picador.

Virloget, Katja Hrobat and Nevena Skrbic Alempijevic. 2021. "Ethnographies of Silence: Introductory Notes." *Cultural Analysis* 19 (1): 1–7.

Waterston, Alisse. 2019. "Intimate Ethnography and the Anthropological Imagination: Dialectical Aspects of the Personal and Political in My Father's Wars." *American Ethnologist* 46 (1): 7–19.

5 Designing Ways to Make Data Sing

Writing Someone Else's Life Story as a Song

Kristina Jacobsen

Creative Ethnographic Toolkit: Songwriting, creative nonfiction, life writing, fairy tales, close listening.

This prompt asks you to share brief life stories, in pairs, and to write a song based on the story shared with you through a series of writing exercises. Going from freewriting to writing a song can be challenging. So this prompt begins with different "warm up" exercises—cluster writing, verse/refrain form, and writing a fairy tale—to provide a variety of rich language the songwriter can draw from to write the final song. Thus, you are writing a song not based on your own story, but on the story *given to you* by someone else. Songs are then shared, in the order of the pairs who exchanged stories.

Learning to listen closely, to pay attention on purpose, and to voice other's stories with attention and care are three of the most important skills we learn as ethnographers when we go into the field. But these skills are also the central domain of the songwriter. In folk, Americana, blues, country, hip hop and many other music genres, telling stories about the lives of other people to evoke empathy is a key part of these genres. When done with attention and care, having our life story refracted back and shared through the voice and life experience of another person can be not only uncanny; it can also be an extremely powerful way of feeling truly heard. In essence, songwriters are saying to the person who gave them their story: "I heard you and I thank you and this is what I understand from your story."

This prompt was inspired by Paul Reisler's songwriting workshop, offered at the yearly Rocky Mountain Song School in Lyons, Colorado. I teach it, once a semester, to students in my Songwriting I and II classes, and also to students in my Creative Ethnography class. While the storyteller gives the gift of their story to the writer/songwriter, the songwriter is also gifting a song back to the storyteller. Utilizing different methods to approach a song, and seeing the intersections between a fairy tale, "real life" and ethnography, can also give the creative ethnographer tools to write more effectively, more engagingly and more persuasively in traditional ethnographic formats such as ethnographic books (ethnographies) as well. For example, writing a fairy tale gives us a sense of space and temporal distance from the story and the subject, which in turn often provides a freedom to

DOI: 10.4324/9781003365228-17

embellish a story in a way that a “real-life” story might not. Some elements of the fairy tale can then be borrowed and brought into the final song.

Prompt

Meeting 1 (in class): 35 minutes (total)

1) **15 minutes:** take 15 minutes and write down three stories about a place, time or event that changed you/transformed you (can be a positive or negative transformation).
2) **15 minutes:** pair up with one other person and share *one* of the three stories with them; while the other person is speaking, listen closely and deeply: don’t take notes, agree or disagree, or try to relate to the other person’s story. Just listen.
3) **5 minutes:** *Directly* after you’ve heard the person’s story, jot down the most memorable ideas /lines/parts of the story. Be sure to do this directly after hearing the story, and don’t overthink it.

On Your Own

Please do each of these exercises, in the following order:

Cluster Writing

Write down one word/idea *from the story you were given* at the top or center of a sheet of paper: choose two synonyms for this word, then choose four synonyms for the four new words, and so on and so forth (see Figure 5.1). While the initial word for the cluster writing will come from the story you heard, the synonyms will be your own words. After you’re done clustering, go back and underline the words that have the most power/charge for you; try to incorporate these into your song. A visual example of what this might look like at the end is provided in Figure 5.1, where I started with the word “cat.” Note also that, at a certain point, I switched from my right hand to my left hand; the latter is the hand I use when I am more in creative “flow” and this is my indication to myself that this process had

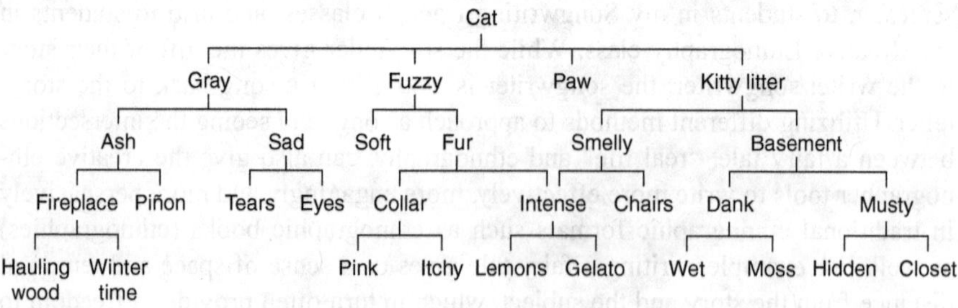

Figure 5.1 Cluster writing.

started. When your clusters become more like sentences and less like single words/thoughts/phrases, you are ready to go to "free associative writing."

Free Associative Writing

Only do this after you've done your clustering and it feels easy and natural. This is "stream of consciousness" writing, where you diligently write down anything and everything that comes to mind. If something especially wild comes to mind, tell the censor to go sit in the corner, and write it down, anyway! (In the end, you will decide what to share and not share with others).

Write a Fairytale

Take the story you heard and write a fairy tale about it. This can be as directly or indirectly related to the actual story as you like. Your fairy tale should start with "Once upon a time" and should be written in the past tense. You are encouraged to be creative and live into the fantastical realm of storytelling, here.

Write a Verse and Refrain

Drawing on the previous writing exercises, write two 4-line verses (ABCB) where lines two and four rhyme.

Meeting 2

In class or on a class discussion board, please share your fairytale, your two verses or both. This allows you and your peers to see the internal workings of what led someone to the song while it is still in the creative process. Offering your peers a window into your own creative process of an unfinished work—something we rarely get to see in other artists—is a generous thing to do!

A Note on Truth and truth in Songwriting and Anthropology

In this prompt, stories are given freely and can't be taken back or retracted. This is very different from how this works in ethnography, where interlocutors are typically welcome, at any stage, to rescind their story if they wish to do so. This means that the story you choose to share should be one you are comfortable giving away, with the knowledge that elements of it will shift in the telling. This also means that you are offering a story, with intention, that you know will be used as the primary "fodder" for a new song. But you are also receiving a story in turn, and creating a song based on what was offered to you. So, this prompt gives us insight and empathy for how it feels when our interlocutors share their stories with us and the sense of vulnerability that accompanies this. The giving of the story, and seeing the ways it morphs through the voice and lived experience of someone else is part of the ethnographic exercise of this prompt. They are given to you by the storyteller as a gift/inspiration to create a song and as such you may take them in whatever direction you want; thus, while your song doesn't need to be "factually" true, it *does* need to feel emotionally true/authentic to the spirit of the story given to you. At the same time, all stories, once they become songs, are also "cowrites," and both persons' names should be listed at the top of the page.

This can be challenging, and it is OK if the song doesn't "land" 100% with your cowriter. This is a key difference between songwriting and ethnography. In ethnography, the facts need to be absolutely correct. We can think of this as "truth" with a small "t." In songwriting, and in the expressive arts more broadly, we have a certain amount of artistic license to filter facts through our own lived experience, dipping into our own sense vaults to flesh out the story using taste, touch, smell, sound, and our kinesthetic and proprioceptive senses. We can think of this as *Truth* with a big "T." But in both contexts, and although the yardstick of measurement is different, there is tremendous pressure to "get it right," and songwriters and anthropologists feel this equally. Telling a story, and the ability to tell someone else's story, in this sense, is sacred.

The **litmus test** in songwriting, then, is about emotional authenticity, rather than the specific accuracy of one single fact and whether it is accurate or not. This is what we might think of as *Truth* with a capital "T" (Cahnmann-Taylor 2003: 33). As Mary Gauthier says, this is the difference between songwriting and journalism, where journalism is "just the facts, ma'am." As songwriter Pat Pattison says, "Never let reality get in the way of truth" (Pattison 2010: 17). The important distinction to understand for this assignment is that sometimes writing a fictional account of a story can honor a deeper truth more accurately than recounting the simple facts of a story. We are *interpreting* someone else's story and *translating* it into a song. Songwriting, and creative storytelling allow us to go to those deeper and more truthful places.

How to Extend: Writing a Song

Write an entire song based on the story you were given. The song should have at least three verses and a chorus that repeats. For inspiration, you may want to incorporate phrases from your cluster writing or your fairytale. If possible, include the chord names directly above the word where they occur in the song.

Select a rhyme scheme for the verses, chorus, and any other sections of your song (for example, ABAB, AAB, or ABxBxA), and follow that scheme for the remainder of your song. Write that rhyme scheme at the top of your submitted lead sheet. Next, *comb through your rhymes,* and make sure that they are really saying what you want them to: avoid forced rhymes at all costs![1]

Select a title for your song. Each verse of the song should be tightly focused around that title. Submit a lyric sheet with a title, your name and the name of the person that shared the story as cowriters below the title, and a copyright date.[2]

Rhyme Scheme Example

For example, in my cowrite, "White Knuckles," written with the English songwriter, Andy Goggin, we chose an AAB rhyme scheme:

She reads Tolkien and **Tolstoy**	A
Married a good **boy**	A
She's a true **believer**	B
Made youngest **partner**	C
And Goldstein & **Gardner**	C
She's an **overachiever**	B

How to Extend: Gifting Your Song Back to the Storyteller

In order of original pairs, thank the person who gave you the story, and share your song with the entire group.

Allow the person who shared their story to be the first to offer feedback and respond. If so moved, they may wish to thank the songwriter who shared their story.

Discuss/share this process of cowriting, as a group. What was it like to hear your story represented through the voice and storytelling of another? What did you learn? What was challenging? How was it different from other songs you've written, either cowrites or on your own?

Notes

1 I suggest consulting https://www.rhymezone.com for rhyme ideas.
2 I also suggest including the following clause in your prompt up front: "All cowrites are 50/50 cowrites, meaning that all song credits are acknowledged as equal and all proceeds from the song, should it be recorded, are shared 50/50."

References

Cahnmann-Taylor, Melisa. 2003. "The Craft, Practice, and Possibility of Poetry in Educational Research." M. Cahnmann-Taylor. *Research News and Comment.*

Gauthier, Mary. 2021. *Saved by a Song: The Art and Healing Power of Songwriting.* St. Martin's Press.

Goggin, Andy and Kristina Jacobsen. 2015. "White Knuckles." *Three Roses.* Kristina Jacobsen.

Pattison 2010. *Writing Better Lyrics.* Ringgold, Inc.

Reisler, Paul. www.paulreisler.com

Songschool, Rocky Mountain. https://bluegrass.com/song-school

Writing Along the Faction Spectrum

Jess Falcone

Creative Ethnographic Toolkit: Fiction, creative non-fiction, poetry.

As an anthropologist, I was taught to collect the truest possible data and let those interview transcripts and fieldnotes dictate the lines and contours of the story. This genre-normative anthropological writing is valuable, but as a writer and ravenous reader of the ethnographic fiction genre, I also yearn to push through the lines, blur them, and scribble deliberately across them. For example, I recently enjoyed *Lissa: A Story of Medical Promise, Friendship, and Revolution* (Hamdy & Coleman 2017), an ethnographic fiction narrative (presented in graphic novel form!) written by two scholars in which fictional **composite characters** (who were drawn from intensive, long-term research work) must negotiate the various medical cultures—breast cancer, organ donation, environmental pollution and disease, etc.—facing them and their families (see also Vidali, Chapter 10, this volume). *Lissa* was an incredibly valuable, albeit genre-bendy, means of representing real sociocultural people and places in an almost entirely fictional manner. When anthropologist Clifford Geertz used the term "**faction**" to refer to creative writing in the social sciences, he was more than a little sarcastic about its value, writing, "It is not clear just what "faction," imaginative writing about real people in real places, exactly comes to beyond a clever coinage; but anthropology is going to have to find out if it is to continue as an intellectual force in contemporary culture—if its mule condition (trumpeted scientific mother's brother, disowned literary father) is not to lead to mule sterility" (1988: 141). While I find his guarded ambivalence about genre-bending a bit stodgy, I concede that we need to be deliberate when we engage in creative play. I prefer to think about faction as a wide range of valuable possibilities from carefully described observations to thoroughly invented make-believe, and in this exercise, I invite you to traverse the "faction spectrum" (Falcone 2020).

Prompt

1. Pick your story. If you are mid-project, pick a scene from your working research project that is interesting to you. Perhaps re-read your fieldnotes from that day.

DOI: 10.4324/9781003365228-18

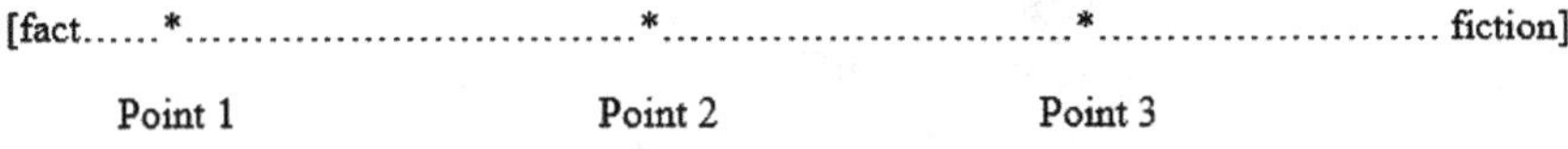

Figure 5.2 Faction spectrum.

If you are not mid-project, then think of an event that you happened to observe in the past few days. It could be a recollection of a religious service, a recent breakfast with friends, a heated class discussion, or something that happened recently that made you smile. [3–5 minutes]

2. Set your intentions. Once you have picked your story, draw a *faction spectrum* (fact–fiction) on a piece of paper and pick three distinct spots on the spectrum. Write down some rules or intentions for yourself as a writer at each point. Feel free to riff off of the example in Figure 5.2 or to set your own rules entirely.

   Point 1: Although my memory (and my fieldnotes) may not be perfect, I will not deviate from them. I will not engage in conscious invention or creative fashioning.
   Point 2: I may change names and a few distinguishing details to protect anyone from recognizing my interlocutors (or friends). I may blur and fudge the edges of the story, but will not actively deviate from the events that took place.
   Point 3: I can freely make up and invent parts of the story, such as descriptions, dialogue, and back story. The story world is mine to shape as I will, but because I did not pick a point even further down the fiction spectrum, I will not deviate from the natural conventions of our observed world (no magic wands, time travel, or aliens).
   [5 minutes]

3. Write across the spectrum. Choose just one expressive genre (prose, poetry, etc.), and then stick to the framing rules that you've set for yourself above. Keeping your chosen story in mind, write three short pieces that are arrayed at the three different points you've chosen for yourself along the faction spectrum. Use a timer, and give yourself at least 10 minutes at each point on the spectrum. [30+ minutes]
4. Reflect. Take a beat and think about how things flowed and what you created. Journal for at least 5 minutes. How did it feel to write across the faction spectrum? What strengths and weaknesses do various pieces have based on the rules of engagement imposed by the position one is engaging with along the spectrum? Did writing along the faction spectrum allow you more insights into the complexities of "making" and "making up"? Which piece is your favorite and why? [5 minutes]

How to Extend

If you are mid-project (paper, thesis, dissertation, book, etc.), write up a short treatise about where you want your project to fall along the faction spectrum. What are your responsibilities, if any, to make that sure your reader understands what genre you are writing in, and to what extent you are taking liberties? What rules of engagement have you set for your project, in these terms? What, if anything, are you fashioning and creating? Do different parts of the writing project sit at different places on the spectrum? How might you explain this to your reader?

How to Extend: Playing with Genre

Play with genre. Arguably the faction spectrum is as important for poets as it is for prose writers. Whichever genre of writing you picked for this prompt, try writing the same story (or a different one, if you prefer) across the faction spectrum through a wholly new genre.

What to Read

The relationship between fact and fiction in writing in the social sciences has been explored at length (Langness and Frank 1978; Narayan 1999; Schmidt 1981), but one way to think through the relationship is to engage with writing that intentionally writes across the faction spectrum. For example, Bruno Latour (1996), Karen McCarthy Brown (2001), and Margery Wolf have each written books that creatively include both fact and fiction; they each clarify which parts of the books are written in a genre-normative manner and which are genre-bending. I took this tack myself in a book chapter, "Maitreya or the Love of Buddhism: The Non-event of Bodh Gaya's giant statue," which danced back and forth around the spectrum (Falcone 2012). Some sections were as close as one can get to pure ethnographic fact: direct transcription. And then—still mostly in the "fact" part of the spectrum, despite the use of pseudonyms—I wrote several genre conventional anthropological sections that laid things out without invention. Sprinkled throughout, I signaled to my readers that they were about to read a creative section (that is, one on the fiction side of the faction spectrum), by prefacing it with the Buddhist phrase, "Thus have I heard." For example, in this section of ethnographic fiction, I narrated the story of the statue as if telling the story to my students in class:

> "Thus have I heard. Recently, a teacher was dwelling in Manhattan –the smaller Apple of the two, the "little Apple," a.k.a. Manhappiness: Manhattan, Kansas– together with a great company of college students who had come from counties in all four directions to take part in a course about culture in the wider world. (It fulfilled a requirement.) They had talked about fieldwork and the ethnographic method in their last class, and now the professor was ready to make good on her promise to discuss her own anthropological research. She flipped on her lapel

mic, and began by telling her students about a great statue that had been planned in Bodh Gaya, and how it had been killed. Murdered, actually" (154).

In the other creative ethnographic fiction sections of that same book chapter, statues could talk and composite characters acted out scenarios that did not happen exactly as described, but all of that art(ifice) was deployed in the service of faithfully relating a true story. In the creative ethnographic fiction sections of my work, statues could talk and composite characters could have discussions that never happened, but all of this was in the service of telling what I maintain was a fundamentally truthful story. When we communicate honestly with our readers about the frameworks we are operating in, even the most genre-bending of pieces has the potential to be deeply, effectively, true.

References

Falcone, Jessica. 2012. "Maitreya or the Love of Buddhism: The Non-event of Bodh Gaya's giant statue." In *Cross-disciplinary perspectives on a contested Buddhist site: Bodh Gaya jataka*, edited by David Geary, Matthew R. Sayers, and Abhishek Singh Amar, 153–171. New York: Routledge.

Falcone, Jessica. 2020. "Genre-bending, or The Love of Ethnographic Fiction." In *Writing Anthropology: Essays on Craft and Commitment*, edited by Carole McGranahan, 212–219. Chapel Hill, NC: Duke University Press.

Geertz, Clifford. 1988. *Works and Lives: The Anthropologist as Author*. Stanford: Stanford University Press.

Hamdy, Sherine and Coleman Nye. 2017. *Lissa: A Story of Medical Promise, Friendship, and Revolution*. Toronto: University of Toronto Press.

Langness, L. Lewis and Gelya Frank. 1978. "Fact, Fiction and the Ethnographic Novel." *Anthropology and Humanism Quarterly* 3 (1–2): 18–22.

Latour, Bruno. 1996. *Aramis, or the Love of Technology*. Boston: Harvard University Press.

McCarthy Brown, Karen. 2001. *Mama Lola: A Vodou Priestess in Brooklyn* (Updated and Expanded Edition). Berkeley: University of California Press.

Narayan, Kirin. 1999. "Ethnography and Fiction: Where is the border?" *Anthropology and Humanism* 24 (2): 134–147.

Schmidt, Nancy. 1981. "The Nature of Ethnographic Fiction: A Further Inquiry." *Anthropology and Humanism Quarterly* 6 (1): 8–18.

Wolf, Margery. 1992. *A Thrice-Told Tale: Feminism, Postmodernism, and Ethnographic Responsibility*. Stanford: Stanford University Press.

Inside the Prose Poem

Using Fresh Metaphors and Similes to Open Up Fieldwork

Adrie Kusserow

Creative Ethnographic Toolkit: Poetry, prose poem.

What is an **ethnographic prose poem**? A piece of writing written by researchers about ethnographic fieldwork in prose having obvious poetic qualities, including intensity, compactness, prominent rhythms, the use of figurative language, metaphor and **simile** and vivid imagery. A prose poem looks like prose but reads like poetry: it lacks the line breaks of other poetic forms but employs poetic techniques, such as internal rhyme, repetition, and compression.

Like many anthropologists, I was looking for the most nuanced ways to represent and understand issues, concepts and people encounter in my research and was particularly drawn to the ways in which metaphors and similes could convey profound subtleties of meaning and bring me to places of fresh insight. What is a metaphor, and what is a simile? A metaphor compares two different things. Something *is* something else. For example: Helen is a walking dictionary. Time is money. A simile compares two different things, something is *like* or as something else. For example: He was as quiet as a mouse. She swam like a fish. A **generic metaphor** or simile is one that has been used over and over and therefore might not evoke as much emotion/insight/resonation in the reader. A generic metaphor has no emotional/conceptual "velcro," it slides off readers' senses because you've heard it a thousand times and all that comes to mind is something stereotypical. For example, My grandmother's folded walker waits beside her like a stiff chair (generic) vs. My grandmother's walker crouches beside her like a praying mantis (fresh). Working with fresh metaphors and similes can also help the anthropologist express and pay more deliberate attention to the many ways culture is embodied in the senses of those we study and attempt to represent for ourselves and others. It allows the anthropologist to intensely focus on the subtle intricacies of body language and non-verbal behavior that are so often evocative of larger socio-cultural and globalizing forces at play. Probing for exact, fresh metaphors and similes is helpful in the process of observation itself and can give rise to aesthetic, less linear ways of thinking about the

DOI: 10.4324/9781003365228-19

field experience, requiring the anthropologist to approach behaviors with all of their senses.

Think of the example: "she swam like a fish." In what other ways could this rather bland simile be turned into a more evocative, detailed, fresh simile that better represents the person you are trying to describe? Imagine a fluorescent light bulb in a room where you are interviewing someone. You could describe it as a lightbulb bright as the sun (generic), or a lightbulb looming above like a screaming planet (fresh). Or when describing a person's black hair, you could say it hung down their back like the mane of a horse (generic), or his glistening ponytail slid like a sunlit black river down his back (fresh). Note how metaphors are piggybacked with sensory qualities and connotations that can then be transferred to the person or place in a way that non-poetic language can't. The elderly walker tucked like praying mantis brings to the reader's consciousness the foreboding protuberant eyes and menacing claws, always clasped as if in prayer. This lends a creepy, scary mood to the situation, as if they (the walker and, by association, its user) are not completely benign in their intent.

Below is an ethnographic prose poem entitled *Stale Refugee*, that arose out of my fieldwork with the Lost Boys of Sudan resettled in Vermont. The Lost Boys refers to the 20,000 children from southern Sudan that fled their homes seeking refuge from the second Sudanese civil war, some of whom were resettled in the US in 2003 (Kusserow 2024). My fieldwork involved focus groups, and semi structured interviews with the Lost Boys in Burlington Vermont, as well as participant observation in their various challenges of resettlement (finding a job, going to school, practicing English) as well as their social gatherings (soccer games, birthdays, home visits, Sudanese of Vermont governance meetings). Through the use of fresh metaphor, I was able to provide the subtle, nuanced and anthropological "thick description" of what had happened to the Lost Boy, Deng, over the years that I knew him. The act of coming up with precise metaphors and similes demands an incredibly rigorous attention and honest approach to human behavior. Vague and **generic** words do not help anthropologists or their readers crawl into the rich, multidimensional places most humans inhabit. Hence, ethnographic poetry is not something that simply reflects an initial ethnographic insight; it is an active ethnographic tool, a deep and refined phenomenological probing, as opposed to a dreamy, distant or sterile musing. Coming up with fresh metaphors often involves using your whole body, every possible sense you have. Often I would sit, in a kind of meditation, focusing on one small ethnographic fieldwork moment, such as playing soccer with the Vermont Lost Boys. Every time my mind wandered, I would come back to the soccer game with every sense I had and try to remember. Sometimes field notes written after these experiences would help jog my sensual memory. The tentacles of the ethnographic poem, through image, metaphor, language, form and rhythm, will enable you to inch even closer to the complex, subtle experiences you are trying to not only describe but understand.

Stale Refugee (written in Winooski, Vermont)

I see him cross the street, hobbling with a cane. Face puffy with opioids. I haven't seen him since the accident, after he dropped out of high school, got hit by a car as he was drunkenly weaving across the street. On disability now.

I pull my car over to say hello in Dinka. *Yikadee!* He pulls his earbuds out, jokes that "no one wants him now… .remember when everyone wanted to talk to us?" They still do, I say, and feeling ashamed, vow to drum up some students to pay him a visit.

It's true. At first they dropped by all the time, the church ladies, the anthropologists, the students, the local reporter. They all left elated, having found something real, like yoga and organic food. But different refugees go in and out of vogue in this town, newspapers want fresh, not stale trauma.

The first Thanksgiving, three families booked him. Leaning hungrily across the long white table, they nibbled at his stories, his lean noble life. Over and over he told them about lions, crocodiles, eating mud and urine, their veins pumping neon fascination, deep in the suburbs, his life flavoring theirs, spicing up supper, really, like a bouillon cube of horror. At the dinner table, the more of what they now called "trauma" he remembered, the more the Americans came alive, with a sad, compassionate glow, a kind of sunset inside them.

He remembers the airplanes belching bags of food from their guts, the dust mushrooming up around a sack of cornmeal as it thudded and slumped over, like a fat woman crying in the sand. As he speaks, he is monitoring what would be of most interest, what will perk up even the boy from his phone. He edits a boring memory out.

When he got off the plane the church ladies took him to a store, bought him fresh sneakers soft and white as wedding cake. The next day he walked through whole aisles of pet food, pictures of cats lounging like kings and queens on their couches.

Now he looks like a too-tall hoodlum, all gold-chained and baggy-trousered. The church ladies give him hushed looks: *we regret to inform you, the path you've taken is not what we had hoped for.* He's channel surfing, listening to Bob Marley, his long legs awkwardly pushed out to each side of the tv. Sudan's moved inside him now, all cramped and bored, sleeping a lot. He cracks another beer, starts to float, the reggae flooding his body. His cousin calls, she needs more money, her son has malaria. She can't afford school fees.

Later, he stumbles drunk into the bathroom. Inside him groggy Sudan flinches at the neon light, paces, then settles in the corner of its den, paws pushing into the walls of his ribs with a dull pain.

The next morning he wakes, stubborn Sudan still shoved up against his ribs, refusing to roll over, into the middle of himself where he can't feel it anymore, into some open place where he ends and a new America finally begins. He wants the old America back, where the freshness of his trauma was sniffed out like raw meat. Rolled in. Chewed in big chunks. He wants to be wanted again, for anything.

Prompt

1) Go through and identify all of the metaphors and similes in the poem, "Stale Refugee." Write each one down.
2) Substitute more generic language in its place and re-read the poem. How does it feel? How does your emotional and intellectual *understanding* of the Lost Boy's situation perhaps shift or change with the input of generic language?
3) Next, take any interpersonal experience you have had with any person in any context, local or international, in the past year and try and describe it with as many fresh metaphors and similes as you can in a prose poem of approximately one double spaced page. For this exercise, please do not try and make the prose poem rhyme. Try to come up with 5–7 fresh metaphors.
4) Now, read this piece aloud with classmates and ask them which similes and metaphors deepen their own understanding of what you were trying to describe. Consider asking your classmates the following questions:

   Were there any places in the writing that were confusing or needed clarification?

   What were the best metaphors/similes in your writing and why?

   How did the fresh metaphors or similes contribute to an in depth appreciation of the cultural, class, gendered, racial or ethnic context of the situation you described?

   What are perhaps some of the sensory qualities in these metaphors that are then subtly taken on/attributed by the person or place in this poem?

   Among those metaphors that classmates selected as the best, in what ways did any of these provide resonant meaning about the sociocultural environment of the person you are describing?

   Aside from metaphors, where else in the writing is there resonant meaning conveyed (that which might convey information about the cultural, class context in which this interaction took place?)

5) Finally, after consulting with your peers, work on a more polished final draft based on their feedback.

How to Extend

Keep a small journal with you at all times and write down the fresh metaphors and similes that come to you at traffic lights, while waiting for someone, while hiking, people watching, musing, baking, sitting in class, or any other activity. Don't assume that you will remember them later on. Experience has taught me that fresh metaphors and similes are often evanescent leaps of the imagination, recognition, and connection and they are hard to pin down and remember long after they have passed through your mind.

What to Read/Listen To

For an introduction to prose poetry's key characteristics and discussions of many historical and contemporary prose poems, I recommend poets and scholars Paul Hetherington and Cassandra Atherton's book *Prose Poetry: An Introduction* (2020).

I recommend you explore poets who write prose poems so that you can really get a sense for how imaginative, evocative and boundary breaking the prose poem can be!

I also suggest reading Ray Gonzalez (2009), Mary Oliver (1994; 2012), Bruce Weigl (2021), Charles Simic (1989), Russell Edson (2022), Renato Rosaldo (2019), Charles Rafferty (2021), Claudia Rankine (2014), and Berlant and Stewart (2019).

Finally, you can find one example of ethnographic prose poems in my recent book *The Trauma Mantras: A Memoir in Prose Poems* (Duke University Press, 2024).

References

Berlant, Lauren and Stewart, Kathleen. 2019. *The Hundreds*. Durham, NC: Duke University Press.

Edson, Russell. 2022. *Little Mr. Prose Poem: Selected Poems of Russell Edson*. Rochester, NY: BOA Editions, Ltd.

Gonzalez, Ray. 2009. *Cool Auditor*. Rochester, NY: BOA Editions, Ltd.

Heatherington, Paul and Atherton, Cassandra. 2020. *Prose Poetry: An Introduction.* Princeton: Princeton University Press.

Kusserow, Adrie. 2002. *Hunting Down the Monk.* Rochester: BOA Editions, Ltd.

Kusserow, Adrie. 2013. *REFUGE.* Rochester: BOA Editions, Ltd.

Kusserow, Adrie. 2024. "Stale Refugee" in *The Trauma Mantras*. Durham, NC: Duke University Press 41–42.

Kusserow, Adrie. 2024. *The Trauma Mantras*. Durham, NC: Duke University Press.

Oliver, Mary. 1994. *White Pine*. Boston: Mariner Books.

Oliver, Mary. 2012. *Swan*. Boston: Beacon Press.

Rafferty, Charles. *A Cluster of Noisy Planets*. Rochester, NY: BOA Editions, Ltd.

Rankine, Claudia. 2014. *Citizen: An American Lyric*. Minneapolis, MN: Graywolf Press.

Rosaldo, Renato. 2019. *The Chasers*. Durham, NC: Duke University Press.

Simic, Charles. 1989. *The World Doesn't End.* New York: Ecco.

Weigl, Bruce. 2021. *Among Elms, In Ambush*. Rochester: BOA Editions, Ltd.

6 Entering the Field Site: Space and the Non-Human

Seeing the Field, Landscapes, and Non-Human Life in Places of Inquiry

Creating Empathy and Writing from a Picture

Kristina Jacobsen

Creative Ethnographic Toolkit: Songwriting, poetry, writing with the senses, building visual observation skills.

How do we tell the story of a life, whether our own or another's? Using a photographic portrait as the entry point and inspiration for a creative writing exercise, this prompt encourages creative ethnographers to tell a life story with nuance and depth through a song or poem. In songs and poems, the challenge is to write expressively yet economically: every line "counts." Identity, placemaking, storytelling as a cultural narrative, and place and social hierarchies can all be explored using this prompt. This prompt allows creative ethnographers to ground theoretical constructs within the narrative details of everyday life and can provide unique access to and understanding of these larger ideas, preparing the way for understanding the self as this relates to social theory, storytelling, and the arts.

Prompt

Find a picture of a person that interests you. This could be a loved one, a family member, a research participant, or a complete stranger. The picture *should be a portrait* and focus closely on the face. Write about this portrait without using grammar, punctuation, or rhyming. Write in as much detail as possible, engaging all of your senses (taste, touch, smell, sight, sound, body, movement, etc.) as viscerally as you can. What do you see in the photo? What is communicated through the eyes, body language, face, or movement? What do you want your audience to know about the human in the photo and what essential details do people who can't see the photo need to know in order to see what you see?

Now, go back to this freewriting and circle or underline the parts that feel the most alive to you. I call this the "juice." Which parts of your freewriting feel the truest, rawest, or most authentic to what you observe in the photo? Those are the parts (which can be just single words or phrases!) that you want to carry forward into the next step. Next, decide on a story or memory that you'd like to relate through your song or poem, based on the picture you selected. This story can be factually true or

DOI: 10.4324/9781003365228-21

created by you. Either way, the story or memory should feel emotionally authentic for you as the writer and for your audience when they listen to it as well.

Then, shape this into a poem or song lyric, selecting the parts from your freewriting that you underlined and that felt rich or alive to you. The song or poem does not *have* to rhyme, but each verse or section should have its own focus and idea. If you *do* decide to rhyme, do not sacrifice what you want to say for the sake of the rhyme and avoid rhyming each line! A good resource for how to avoid "forcing" a rhyme is www.rhymezone.com. Also think about the rhythm (meter) of the syllables in each line and try to be consistent from one line to the next. Decide on a title for the poem or song.

For full credit, your poem or song should invoke/identify at least two different senses and identify a who, what, where, or when. Remember, you want to show, not tell! The title of your song or poem should also directly relate to the central theme of your work.

Read or perform the song or poem (or share a recorded version) with your peers and bring a version of the photo that inspired you to share with them.

As you complete this assignment, consider further turning on your writerly senses by following the journaling assignment below at the same time.

How to Extend: Paired Journaling Assignment

Select five photographic portraits and write about one image each day for at least 20 minutes (set a timer!). The only rules are to write whatever comes to mind, keep your pen moving, and *tell the censor (we all have one!) to go sit in the corner.* Please avoid rhyming at this stage. Write for at least *five days* (write these down in your journal log) or write *every* day if you're inspired enough!

Some websites and artists that I recommend for finding vivid portraits (both photography and painting) include:

Rob Amberg (region: Appalachia): www.robamberg.com/galleries
Wendy Ewald (region: Appalachia): https://wendyewald.com
Will Wilson (region: Navajo Nation): https://willwilson.photoshelter.com/index
Shonto Begay (region: Navajo Nation): www.tomalexanderphotography.com/photogallery/gallery41/
Francesca Corriga (region: Sardinia, Italy): www.instagram.com/francesca_corriga/?hl=en

How to Extend: Shaping Your Lyrics or Poem into a Song

Can you imagine a melody that could fit your lyric or poem? Try humming something, without worrying about chords or notes, and record a few versions in the voice memo app on your phone. Or can you imagine a chord progression (i.e., the chords that are played under a song on an instrument)? Now, see if you can try pairing these things together with your writing. When pairing lyrics to music/

a melody, consider consulting these resources to help to align the scansion of your lyrics to the rhythm and melody of your music.

If you are beginning with the lyric: www.musicnotes.com/now/tips/art-lyric-writing-match-lyrics-melody/
If you are beginning with the melody: www.youtube.com/watch?v=oVtfjoa_d1E

Finally, your song can be written on your own or collaboratively with one of your peers. This process, known as cowriting, can work especially well if one of you is more skilled in lyric writing and the other is more skilled in music.

For full credit, your poem or song should invoke/identify at least two different senses and identify a who, what, where, or when. All cowritten songs should include a title, copyright date, and the full names of all collaborators. The title of your song or poem should also directly relate to the central theme of your piece.

Why This Assignment

How do we tell the story of a life, whether our own or another's? Rural identities (Stewart 2007; Ching and Creed 1997), placemaking (Basso and Feld 1996; Williams 1973; Gupta and Ferguson 1997), storytelling as cultural narrative (Stewart 1996), and place and social hierarchies (Bourdieu 1984) can all be explored using this exercise.

What to Listen To

One song of mine was inspired by a prompt created by the Chicago songwriter Steve Dawson. My song is called "Inez" and it tells the story of a **Diné** woman who was my supervisor when I worked as a ranger at the Canyon de Chelly National Monument. Inez was, and remains, one of my primary friends and was a key entry point into Diné life for me as a non-Diné Anglo woman.

Inez, big smile, crooked teeth
White T-shirt and a Ranger's watchful eyes
Foster parents in Brigham City
Stolen generation, black hair and white lies

Another song, which was cowritten with the Swedish singer–songwriter Lina Horner, was inspired by two photos of different migrant mothers: one photo was of a mother from the Oklahoma dust bowl, taken by photographer Dorothea Lang; the other was a stock photo of a "nameless" woman and child who were refugees from Syria fleeing to Sweden. The song is called "No Man's Land."

Verse 1
Covered head
Cried-out eyes
Firm hand
Comforts the child at your side
Temporary home
Strange new city
People all around, Amina,
Yet you're all alone.

Pre-Chorus: *A Swedish suburb*
Wasn't what you planned
But here you are, now,
In a no man's land

Chorus: *I won't pretend*
To know what you've been through
But as I look at your picture
I'm trying to
No, I won't pretend
To know what you've been through
But I want you to know
I see you

Finally, some other songs that tell the story of a life with nuance, breadth, and depth include John Prine's portrayal of aging and the isolation of elders in "Hello in There" (1971) and Gretchen Peters' portrait of a waitress in "Five Minutes" (2010).

I've got five minutes to sneak a cigarette
Five minutes to myself
Back behind the screen door of Andy's luncheonette
And I ain't got time to worry 'bout my health

My boss Andy says I'll smoke myself to death
Andy he reminds me some of you
Back when you were Romeo and I was Juliet
West Texas Capulet and Montague

References

Amberg, Rob. 2022. www.robamberg.com/galleries

Basso, Keith. H. and Steven Feld., and School of American Research. 1996. *Senses of Place.* Santa Fe: School of American Research Press.

Begay, Shonto. 2022. www.tomalexanderphotography.com/photogallery/gallery41/

Bourdieu, Pierre. 1984. *Distinction: A Social Critique of the Judgement of Taste.* Translated by Richard Nice. Cambridge, MA: Harvard University Press.

Ching, Barbara and Gerald. W. Creed, eds. 1997. *Knowing Your Place: Rural Identity and Cultural Hierarchy.* New York: Routledge.

Corriga, Francesca. 2022. www.instagram.com/francesca_corriga/?hl=en

Ewald, Wendy. 2022. https://wendyewald.com

Gupta, Akhil and J. Ferguson James. 1997. *Anthropological Locations: Boundaries and Grounds of a Field Science.* Berkeley: University of California Press.

Jacobsen, Kristina and Lina Horner. 2017. "No Man's Land." Released as a single track. https://soundcloud.com/kristinajacobsenmusic/no-mans-land-1?utm_source=clipboard&utm_medium=text&utm_campaign=social_sharing

Jacobsen, Kristina. 2015. "Inez." *Three Roses.* Three Roses Music. Accessed March 6, 2023. https://open.spotify.com/track/7n8ilqUwvhU8bBzs1KM0HU

Lang, Dorothea. 1936. "Migrant Mother." www.artsy.net/article/artsy-editorial-fateful-roadside-led-dorothea-langes-migrant-mother
Peters, Gretchen. 2010. "Five Minutes." *Hello Cruel World.* Circus Girl Music.
Prine, John. 1971. "Hello in There." Atlantic Records.
Stewart, Kathleen. 1996. *A Space on the Side of the Road: Cultural Poetics in an "Other" America.* New Jersey: Princeton University Press.
Stewart, Kathleen. 2007. *Ordinary Affects.* Durham: Duke University Press.
Williams, Raymond. 1973. *The Country and the City.* Oxford, UK: Oxford University Press.
Wilson, Will. 2023. "Talking Tintypes." https://willwilson.photoshelter.com/index/G0000n_hiXQrBXN

Writing Space and Place

Paul Stoller

Creative Ethnographic Toolkit: Memoir, creative non-fiction, descriptive placemaking.

An artful ethnography can bring ethnographic spaces and places to life. It can give readers a sense of locality, which is one of the greatest gifts that ethnography brings to the world. How can writers use words to describe the smells, tastes, sights, sounds, and textures of a landscape, wall, road, house, or room? For me, like novelists, poets, and memoirists, anthropologists should aim to be writers who try to describe spaces or places as if they were alive, with feelings and memories. To do this, writers should attempt to let the sights, smells, sounds, and textures of a space/place dictate how they describe it (see Basso 1996; Feld and Basso 1996; Casey 1993; Stoller 1997). This technique borrows from the great 20th century artist Paul Klee's technique of opening his being to the forest and painting it to "**break out**." In this painterly style of describing ethnographic spaces/places, it is important to highlight salient features. It is also important to imagine what a particular room, house, tree, or pathway has witnessed. When I recently observed the majestic baobab[1] tree (see Figure 6.1) that grows next to the Institute of African Studies at the University of Ghana, Legon, I wondered what history that tree had witnessed.

Sensuously setting an ethnographic scene can captivate readers, compelling them to keep turning the pages. Here are some examples in which writers use the senses to evoke spaces and places. Consider how Agee and Evans (1941), the authors of *Let Us Now Praise Famous*, describe a sharecropper's "house" in this palpable description of life in rural Alabama during the American Depression.

> Every few minutes George would get up and open the door a foot or so, and it showed always the same picture; that end of the hallway mud and under water, where the planks lay flush to the ground; the opposite wall; the open kitchen; blown leaves beyond the kitchen window; a segment of the clay rear yard where rain beat on rain beat on rain beat on rain as would beat out the brains of the earth and stood in a bristling smoky grass of water afoot high... (Agee 1941: 365)

DOI: 10.4324/9781003365228-22

Figure 6.1 The baobab tree (photo by Paul Stoller).

A more contemporary example of sensuous ethnographic scene-setting comes from Badkhen (2018) and her work of creative non-fiction called *Fisherman's Blues: A West African Community at Sea*, in which she establishes the boundaries of space and place. Follow how Badkhen describes the sea at dawn near the city of Joal, Senegal's largest artisanal fishing port.

> Dawn spills astern: lavender, violet, golden. Capillary waves gently scale the ocean all the way to the horizon. Winds clots low fog. The *Sakhari Souare* glides at full throttle west-southwest, rolls over lazy six-foot swells. The shore's low skyline of baobab, eucalyptus and doum palm flashes in the light, sinks into the sea. Its bruised cumulus vanishes, too. Black against the banded east, a seabird, an early riser, falls out of the fog and scoops something out of the water and banks away. The pirogue's[2] six crew balance spreadeagled on the thwarts and on the foredeck, dig their bare soles into the slippery wood, lean into one another, watch the sea for fish. (Badkhen 2018: 1–2)

Here is one example from my own ethnography of Songhay spirit possession, called *Fusion of the Worlds* (Stoller 1989), in which I attempt to craft in prose what filmmakers call an establishment shot, which spatially sets the locale and tone of a film or ethnography.

> Clack! A sharp sound shattered the hot, dry air above Tillaberi. Another clack, followed by a roll and another clack-roll-clack, pulsed through the stagnant air. The sounds seemed to burst from the dune that overlooked the secondary school of the town of a thousand people, mostly Songhay-speaking, in the Republic of Niger. The echoing staccato broke the sweaty boredom of a hot afternoon in the hottest town in one of the hottest countries in the world and, like a large hand, guided hearers up the dune to Adamu Jenitongo's compound to witness a possession ceremony. The compound's three-foot millet stalk fence enclosed Adamu Jenitongo's dwellings: four straw huts that looked like beehives. At the compound's threshold, the high-pitched whine of the monochord violin greeted me. Inside, I saw the three drummers seated under a canopy behind gourd drums. Although the canopy shielded them from the blistering Niger sun, sweat streamed down their faces. Their sleeveless tunics clung to their bodies; patches of salt had dried white on the surface of their black cotton garments. They continued their rolling beat. Seated behind them on a stool was the violinist, dressed in a red shirt that covered his knees. Despite the intensity of the heat and the noise of the crowd, his face remained expressionless as he made his instrument "cry." (Stoller 1989: 1)

This final example is from Lucas Bessire's (2022) gripping ethnography/memoir about the depletion of water resources on the high plains of western Kansas.

> After fifteen years, the land matched my memories of it. I recalled precisely the vault of space, the circled sky the most dominant feature and the sun a physical

weight. Grids of stubble that rotate every half-mile, from corn to wheat to sorghum to corn. Each field a parable about boys who became men by learning the plow every inch, by knowing what not to know, by never learning or by never coming back.

The road dead-ends at the break of the now dry Cimarron River, where the tablelands fall abruptly to a ribbon of short-grass nestled in a river bend with sage and sand hills rising to the south. Here stands the Little Rock House. Named after century-old concrete walls and corrals, it was once my great-grandfather's cattle camp. It is where I spent most of my adolescent summers and it is where my father returned to live out his years amid broken flints and buried bison bones.

The sensuous description of place and space is a key ingredient in the recipe for an artful ethnography. One of the greatest gifts that ethnography brings to the world the evocation of sense of place, which can help readers to understand the conditions in which people live and how those conditions impact their everyday lives.

Prompt

Select a space or place that is meaningful to you. It could be a house, a particular room, a building, a wall, a streetscape, a garden, a river, a lake, an ocean beach or shoreline, a tree, a field, or a landscape. Visit this space or place, either in person or in your mind's eye. Imagine that this space or place is alive. What memories or feelings does your place evoke? Jot down a list of features that constitute this special place. Using this list, write a descriptive passage. Write short sentences in the **active voice**. Use a thesaurus to vary your word choices. Try not to describe everything; just focus on the salient features (sounds, textures, smells, colors, etc.) that create palpably meaningful impressions to evoke the majesty of the space or place. Your text can focus on a memory or a place, or both. Aim for a total word count of 250–500 words.

How to Extend

Your descriptive essay should evoke at least two different senses and identify how your chosen space or place embodies a feeling or memory. Showing how a place or space evokes a feeling and/or memory is better than telling. Show your drafts to a peer and ask for their and then, after revising your text, write a final version of the piece.

Establishing place is a key ingredient in recipes for ethnographies that remain "open to the world." Use the techniques introduced in this exercise to write about the majesty of space and place in future works. These techniques will help to make the work more accessible to readers and compel them to keep "turning the pages."

Notes

1 Baobab trees have thick spiney trunks, produce fruit that is used in savory sauces, and grow quite tall. They are widespread throughout West Africa.
2 Pirogue: one of a variety of small boats, particularly dugouts and West African canoes.

References

Agree, James and Evans Walker. 1941. *And Now Let us Praise Famous Men.* New York: Houghton Mifflin.
Badkhen, Anna. 2018. *Fisherman's Blues: A West African Community at Sea.* New York: Riverhead Books.
Basso, Keith. 1996. *Wisdom Sits in Places.* Albuquerque: University of New Mexico Press.
Bessire, Lucas. 2022. *Running Out: In Search of Water on the High Plains.* New Jersey: Princeton University Press.
Casey, Edward. 1993. *Getting Back into Place: Toward a Renewed Understanding of the Place-World.* Bloomington, IN: Indiana University Press.
Feld, Steven and Keith Basso. 1996. *Senses of Place*. Santa Fe, NM: School of Advanced Research Press.
Stoller, Paul. 1989. *Fusion of the Worlds: An Ethnography of Possession Among the Songhay of Niger.* Chicago: The University of Chicago Press. www.google.com/search?client=firefox-b-1-d&q=fusion+of+the+worlds+pdf
Stoller, Paul. 1997. *Sensuous Scholarship.* Philadelphia: University of Pennsylvania Press.

Attending to Animal Stories

Listening for Lines

David Syring

Creative Ethnographic Toolkit: Interview, poetry.

Ethnographers would be hard pressed to find a cultural context that doesn't include animals. However, the ways in which cultures value animals and the non-human relative to human life are less obvious. When people engage with animals, whether as companions, helpers, food, wildlife, spiritual guides, or something else, we always have something to say about them. Speaking about animals also offers great insights into the values and beliefs that are at play within a given cultural world. Ethnographic writing frequently reduces cultural expressions to dull prose. But when people speak of animals, they often come alive, engaging sparks of art, wit, myth, and more.

This exercise invites you to analyze a human dialog about animals. If you are a student and have permission to conduct interviews, you could record and analyze an exchange with someone in your class. Otherwise, you could interview a family member or friend. Then, I invite you to re-listen to the interview and shape what you hear into poetry. If you are unable to arrange an interview with someone, consider analyzing examples from the public domain (for example, a video from TikTok or another publicly accessible media platform) or one of the videos on the "Nature & Animals" playlist on the YouTube channel "The Great Big Story."

Prompt

Part 1: The Conversation

Identify an individual to talk to about their relationships to animals in general, or perhaps a specific animal. This could be a friend or family member who works with animals, someone who has a pet, or a community member engaged in a larger project. Arrange to meet for a conversation.

Begin by inviting the person to tell you a story about how they originally came to pay attention to animals/the animal in a meaningful way. Ask if you can record the conversation. If permission is given, then record the entire conversation on your phone or another easily accessible recording device. Otherwise, plan to take

DOI: 10.4324/9781003365228-23

detailed notes, either by hand or on a computer. It is also crucial to expand on your notes after the event using your memory. We often remember a lot more upon reflection following a conversation: use that recall well, as ethnographic work is only as good as the records that we create of what we learn!

Your task as the ethnographer in this conversation is two-fold: (1) understand the cultural context, i.e., the ways in which people make, do, and feel as shared experiences; (2) invite specific stories. This means you must *listen*, both for general background and the nuance and texture of specific experiences.

Listen for **pitch** and pauses, such as when the person's voice rises with excitement or when they pause to gather a thought before speaking. These are often cues that can help us to discern the significance of their story. After the person has shared their general thoughts, ask them to expand on one or more of those moments of excitement. Ask follow-up questions to gather more detail. Ask if their story raises any curiosities for them. Initiate a discussion, encouraging the person to reflect on the meanings that they see in their own stories.

End the interview when you and your interlocutor (see the introduction of this book) are both satisfied with the conversation. Interviews can be as brief as a few minutes or they can stretch on for longer times, depending on the rapport that develops. Rapport is a feeling of connection and trust between you and the people you are working with. Ethnographers, as human beings working with other human beings, frequently depend on developing these connections in order to do our work. Often, physical cues can reveal when a conversation is over. You may notice that eye contact becomes sparser or that one of you becomes fidgety. Keep in mind that you will need to listen to your interview several times in the next part of the project, so even a 15-minute conversation could yield sufficient material for a successful project.

Part 2: Re-Listening/Re-Engaging

If you were given permission to record, listen to your recording several times. If you were unable to record, your task is a bit more challenging as you will need to develop your notes more fully. I think of each listening as a separate event, each with different emphases. For each round, jot down notes as you listen. If you do not have a recording, use a similar process to read through and expand the notes you took during the conversation.

First Listen: Seeking Insights into Broader Questions

Here are some questions to ask yourself:

- What's the big picture here?
- How is this person's life tangled up with those of animal others?
- What can you interpret about the significance of animals within the cultural context from which your interlocutor speaks?

Second Listen: Seeking What is Characteristic for This Person's Words

Here are some questions to ask yourself:

- What can you discern about why animals were what the person was most excited to talk about?
- What made their story unique and engaging for you as a listener?
- Can you attune to specific elements of the speaker's voice? i.e., their cadence, tone, repeated words, or the use of metaphor or simile to tell their story.

Third Listen: Listening for Lines

Write out specific vivid words or phrases that the person said. Your goal is simply to record the vitality of the person's storytelling in written form.

NOTE: While you can create a **transcription** of the conversation, I find that re-listening to the actual speech of the person keeps me grounded in the conversation and reminds me that whatever I create must be accurate to the person's identity, thoughts, and manner of speech.

Part 3: Shaping the Text

Now, begin looking for lines of poetry in the stories that your interlocutor shared. The idea is to draw out dynamic ways of speaking and thinking that are unique to that individual. You are looking at how you can draw attention to the core thoughts and experiences of your interlocutor. You can try different ways of breaking their speech into bite-sized lines to emphasize what you interpret as significant. Your goal is to help your reader to slow down and begin to understand what the person thinks is important about their relationship with animals. If a full-length poem seems more than you can or want to make from the person's words, you could instead create a poetic fragment using a few lines that you find interesting and fun to play with, poetically and linguistically.

Reflection Questions

Here are some questions you could use to reflect on your own work or the work of others who complete this project:

1) What aspect was the most vivid in the story that was shared?
2) What felt accurate? Why?
3) What did you learn from creating your piece of writing or reading someone else's writing?

My Example

Stories of animals that my friend and collaborator Benigno Cango shared during our fieldwork in Saraguro, Ecuador, led to a poem (Syring 2020), which was embedded as part of an essay for *Anthropologica* on human–non-human relations. I found that a simple reporting of Benigno's words in blocks of prose did not do justice to the excitement that he exhibited when talking about the small, golden figurines of animals that people in his community sometimes find from the Incan past. Considering Benigno's words with an engaged openness and listening for potential lines of poetry in his stories made the process feel more alive. This made me pay close attention to Benigno's description of the **animacy** of the living landscape. Here, I share two excerpts from my three-part poem that was written from my translations of his spoken Spanish, which was recorded in a video. For the full poem, see the original publication.

1: Benigno Tells a Story "*propia de mi*"

I had the cow and calf over in this part of my land.
Every day, I came to see the animals.
One afternoon I brought the cow to drink
from the river. I found a tortoise,
about this size, like a *tomate de arbol*.[1]

And I said to myself, 'This tortoise, is it alive or dead?'
I touched the leg of the tortoise … the leg was like marble.
It was marble.
I put it in my pocket.

I arrived at the house and I said,
'Look, Anita, I've brought a tortoise.'
Anita said, 'What do you mean?'
I put it on the table. It looked like a tortoise.
Shell with segments, exactly like a tortoise.

I asked my grandmother. My grandmother said,
'It's made of gold.'

In the final section of my poem (see the excerpt below), I experimented with poetic form by adding a hemistitch structure (which is essentially a broken line with a gap in the middle), so that the final section of the poem can be read both across and down:

3: Hearing the Stories Both Down and Across

I found a golden … snake that moved into dry grass
turtle on the bank … below our feet as we went
where I lead one cow … down the mountainside
to drink each morning. … light shimmering on the stream.

How to Extend

If you have some experience with writing poetry and a knowledge of poetic forms, see if you can assemble your favorite lines into an entire poem. Perhaps you could experiment with the hemistitch form to try to find multiple ways to communicate ideas in the same lines? Try different poetic techniques, including line breaks, enjambment, repetition, and so on to see what resonates with what the person said. Try *lots* of ways of structuring the words on the page. The goal is to do more with the text than conventional prose blocks. After all, people don't really speak in paragraph structures.

Note

1 Tomate de arbol: a small tree (Solanum betaceum) that bears plum-sized, oblong fruit that is commonly eaten in juices and sauces in Ecuador and elsewhere. Benigno grows these in his gardens and greenhouses.

Reference

Syring, David. 2020. "Golden Animals: A Lyric Essay on Animacy and Resilience." *Anthropologica* 62(1): 196–200.

7 Language

We Are What We Speak

Translingual Poetry and Scholarship

Melisa Cahnmann-Taylor

Creative Ethnographic Toolkit: Poetry, literary and ethnographic translation.

"Translingual," "translation," "translanguage," and "transgender" are all terms that embrace the Latin root "trans," which is a prefix denoting fluidity and things that "cross" boundaries and disrupt dualistic, binary norms. The term "translingualism" has replaced previous terms, such as bilingualism and multilingualism, to draw attention to new repertoires of exposure, integration, and fusion among diverse languages and cultures. Poetry is the perfect location to explore the dislocation, hybridity, and precarity associated with moving between, across, and within more than one language, culture, religion, ability, and/or nation state.

I have identified three different ways in which more than one language, or **code**, appear in translingual literature that can be helpful for the ethnographic study of translingual communities. These movements invite readers to write and play with more than one language within a text.

1. Direct translation
2. Remixing and reimagining
3. Happy accidents

Direct translation, the act of writing that appears in one code being interpreted into a different code by a translator and may be the most common occurrence of more than one language appearing in a single text. Consider the bilingual edition of Neruda's (2004) odes as an example where the Spanish and English languages are treated separately, with the source language poem being followed by its translation. A fluent Spanish–English translator and editor worked with me on poems that I originally (mostly) wrote in English to interpret them for a Spanish-language audience. Currently, I am translating the work of the Mandarin language poet Nianxi Chen into English in collaboration with the bilingual Mandarin–English scholar–poet Kuo Zhang (e.g., Cahnmann-Taylor and Zhang 2023a; 2023b). The experiences of reading translated creative work, having my creative work translated, and translating another's poetry have offered unique and complementary insights into how words mean different things across languages and how meaning can still come to be shared with great attention to dialogic interpretation.

DOI: 10.4324/9781003365228-25

In translingual literature, we also see the **remixing** and **reimagining** of old forms, with writers taking old, formal poetry conventions (e.g., the English "sonnet," the French "villanelle," the Malay "pantoum," the Italian "sestina," the Japanese "tanka," the Persian "ghazal," etc.[1]) and using those structures for poetry in another language or another cultural moment of human experience. Remixing old forms can also include the invention of new forms, such as Jericho Brown's creation of a "duplex" poetry structure in which he merges the structures of the sonnet, the ghazal and the blues, crafting urban, African American experience with lyrical innovation (discussed in this interview). Natasha Trethewey used the Malay *pantoum* structure for her poem "Incident"[2] to reconstruct the incident of a cross burning on her childhood lawn in Mississippi. Below are the first two stanzas and the last stanzas from "Incident." Notice how the first and third lines in stanza one (S1, L1, and L3) become the second (L2) and fourth lines (L4) in the final stanza (S5). Writing about childhood in the segregated South as a child of mixed-race parents, the *pantoum* form helps Trethewey to look forward and look back at this racist "incident" by repeating lines that came before and adding new ones that reappear later from different perspectives on how families and communities tell and re-tell stories.

We tell the story every year—
how we peered from the windows, shades drawn—
though nothing really happened,
the charred grass now green again.

We peered from the windows, shades drawn,
at the cross trussed like a Christmas tree,
the charred grass still green. Then
we darkened our rooms, lit the hurricane lamps.

.....
When they were done, the men left quietly. No one came.
Nothing really happened.
By morning all the flames had dimmed.
We tell the story every year.

Remixing old forms can also include reimagining translingual novelties and inventions. The bilingual Arabic–English writer Dujie Tahat (2020) illustrates this reimagination in his poem "Salat to be read from right to left." In the following excerpt from the longer poem, notice how he imports an English language poem into Arabic structure by asking readers to read the English words from right to left, as Arabic script is read.

[adhan]
messages Facebook me sends uncle My
does translator Facebook .understand barely I
.ج with starts One .images to apply not

amo ,you love I writes He

Finally, translingual poets also encounter ***happy accidents***, noticing the markedness of so-called "errors" in and between languages and bringing the experience of second-language acquisition to readers' attention, even those who are monolingual. In my own study interviewing US adults who were studying Spanish in Mexico, I introduced myself as an ethnographic poet, observed Spanish classes for tourists, and interviewed adult language learners, asking them "When, if ever, have you felt misunderstood in your second language (Spanish)?" I compressed those many interviews into the following lyric poem (Cahnmann-Taylor 2016: 15).

When You're a Retired American Studying Spanish in Mexico and
After Six Months Can Barely Order Something Off a Menu
(Cahnmann-Taylor, 2016, p. 15)

Chances are you've said *I'm pregnant* when you meant
I'm embarrassed,
fuck a bus
when you wanted to *catch it*,
or *vaginas*

instead of "páginas" to describe an art book's pages.

Odds are you've boozed these errors,

loosened the alveolar ridge,

that ineffable tongue flap

that probably made all the difference

when you lacked that packed *poncho,*

exact *pesos*

or translations for the dose, the punch line,

the bus route, the landlord, the speedy

vowels garbled into the phone you answered and fat

chance you sent the right words back,

misreading ingredients,

hunting for ATMs. Filthy footed, fed

up with it all, you tangled in a carnival of outlets,

sickened from taco cilantro,

broke human likenesses

with a stick. You risked time
reduced to mere numerals,

a few verbs that evaporated
like desert water. Raw
as the bed- frame wood that men
back-holstered up missing cobblestones,
you startled like patron saint firecrackers
outside a sleepy weeknight
wooden door. But when you creaked,
wide-awake, to blue mornings, you exposed
like a rare book's ink sensitive pages, as if damage
mattered less to you than a small, braided fist of cheese.
Whey spilt, you inevitably unraveled, turned question marks
upside down until tart tamarind tasted sweet.

Prompt

Begin by generating a list of moments when you have felt misunderstood or been witness to misunderstandings across more than one language or variety of language (e.g., using youth slang and being misunderstood by an elder or using a second language for buying a bus ticket or another transaction and not being fully understood). By remixing and reimagining form, build a poem that helps to narrate the incident using more than one language. You can recall and/or conduct research on other failures, mistakes, and misunderstandings that have come about through error.

Work with your notes and try to write them in a verse form like the villanelle. The villanelle is a complex, traditional form originally from France that can generate an impression of simplicity and spontaneity. It is characterized by 19 lines divided into 5 tercets and a final 4-line stanza, using only two rhymes (rhyming lines are indicated by "A" and "B"). I have provided a map of the structure below, where you can see how the 3-line stanzas repeat the first (A1) and third (A2) lines in each subsequent stanza and use the same rhyming sound as the second line (B) throughout. The final stanza, unlike the others, contains both A1 and A2 and has four lines. When I write a villanelle, I often write the first 3-line stanza and use this map to help me to flesh out what remains to be written in the poem. This may seem confusing, but once you come up with two "A" lines for the first stanza, you have the foundation for the rest of the poem.

Stanza 1: A1 B A2
Stanza 2: A B A1
Stanza 3: A B A2
Stanza 4: A B A1
Stanza 5: A B A2
Stanza 6: A B A1 A2

Lines 1 and 3 become strands that are woven throughout the poem in a complex pattern, resembling a refrain since each line is repeated three times.

Refrain 1 (R1) = line 1 = lines 6, 12, and 18
Refrain 2 (R2) = line 3 = lines 9, 15, and 19

Caution! It is much more interesting if you can change the lines to avoid exact repetition. Notice how poets change the "repeating lines" slightly in the examples below.

What to Read

I believe it's easier to understand how to write a villanelle by reading exemplary models of this form, such as "Do Not Go Gently Into that Good Night" (Dylan Thomas), "The Waking" (Roethke), "Parsley" (Rita Dove), and my favorite, Elizabeth Bishop's "One Art." To read about a poet's take on the relationship between form and meaning, I suggest Annie Finch's (2007) book on forms and Mary Oliver's (1998) book on meter.

Why This Assignment

There are many ways to integrate translations, remixing, and happy accidents into your own creative ethnographic writing. This prompt invites you to play with a combination of these approaches and feel the power of forms that come from other languages and cultures. This prompt also helps writers to appreciate the relationship between form and meaning in any genre of writing. The constraint of working within different forms often impacts and informs what a writer is able to say. Much like songwriters (see Jacobsen, Chapter 3), poets writing in form also use www.rhymezone.com to help to generate options for exact and **slant rhymes**. **Exact rhymes** have the same number of syllables and exact rhymes (e.g., bat and cat or cable and fable). Slant rhymes are inexact, but may have **assonance** (different consonant sounds but similar vowel sounds, e.g., crush and lunch), **consonance** (different vowel sounds but similar consonant sounds, e.g., crush and crash), or different syllable counts with exact rhymes in the final syllable (e.g., capable and fable). Exploring slant rhymes can help to energize a contemporary poem's music and offers many more interesting options than exact forms. Exploring rhyme, meter, and form, among other writing constraints, can help writers to broaden their craft from writing what they already know to writing for sound, music, and the not yet known. Engagement with form can help to generate new, unexpected thinking and discoveries.

How to Extend

Now that you've tried a villanelle, why not try writing fieldwork notes within the constraints of a 14-line (rhyming) sonnet (either Shakespearean or Petrarchan) or any of the other formal verse forms. You may wish to learn the structure of a poetic form that is new to you and try it out. I suggest trying a traditional form, such as the *pantoum* or *villanelle*, or a newly innovated form such as the "duplex" discussed earlier. You could try to map out the structure in advance of writing the poem. In addition to forms already discussed, I encourage readers to look to a wide variety of Western and non-Western verse structures, such as the quintilla from Spain, tanka from Japan, jueju from China, and ghazal from Persia. Finally, I also find working within the constraint of matching syllable counts, or "syllabics," to be generative of new thinking. For example, notice how Michael Water's use of 10 lines with 10 syllables each draws attention to the sartorial dynamics of gender in his poem "The Wedding Dress."

Notes

1 For definitions of these poetic forms, please consult www.poetryfoundation.org/learn/glossary-terms

2 See the full poem here: www.vqronline.org/incident

References

"About English Jueju." n.d. www.ou.edu/cis/research/institute-for-us-china-issues/us-china-cultural-issues/newman-prize-for-english-jueju/about-english-jueju

Cahnmann-Taylor, Melisa. 2016. *Imperfect Tense*. San Pedro: Whitepoint Press.

Cahnmann-Taylor, Melisa, and Kuo Zhang. 2023a. "From Records of Explosion: Poems by Nianxi Chen, Translated from Chinese by Melisa Cahnmann-Taylor and Kuo Zhang, with an Interview by Mihaela Moscaliuc – Plume." *Plume*. August 1, 2023. https://plumepoetry.com/from-records-of-explosion-poems-by-nianxi-chen-translated-from-chinese-by-melisa-cahnmann-taylor-and-kuo-zhang-with-an-interview-by-mihaela-moscaliuc/

Cahnmann-Taylor, Melisa and Kuo Zhang. 2023b. "Chen Nianxi – A Portfolio of Poetry – Translated from the Chinese by Melisa Cahnmann-Taylor and Kuo Zhang – Tupelo Quarterly." *Tupelo Quarterly*. August 1, 2023. www.tupeloquarterly.com/translation/chen-nianxi-a-portfolio-of-poetry-translated-from-the-chinese-by-melisa-cahnmann-taylor-and-kuo-zhang/.

Finch, Annie. 2007. *A Formal Feeling Comes: Poems in Form by Contemporary Women*. Cincinnati, OH: Wordtech Communications.

Neruda, Pablo and Lawrence Ferlinghetti. 2004. *The Essential Neruda: Selected Poems*. San Francisco: City Lights Books.

Oliver, Mary. 1998. *Rules for the Dance: A Handbook for Writing and Reading Metrical Verse*. Boston: Houghton Mifflin Harcourt.

Poetry Foundation. 2006. "Wedding Dress by Michael Waters | Poetry Foundation." www.poetryfoundation.org/poems/49224/wedding-dress.

Poetry Foundation. n.d. "Salat to Be Read from Right to Left by Dujie Tahat | Poetry Magazine." *Poetry Magazine*. www.poetryfoundation.org/poetrymagazine/poems/152125/salat-to-be-read-from-right-to-left

Trethewey, Natasha. 2006. "Miscegenation." Accessed January 18, 2023. www.shiningrockpoetry.com/miscegenation-by-natasha-tretheway/

Writing a Song in an Endangered Language

Sara Snyder Hopkins

Creative Ethnographic Toolkit: Songwriting.

Because *endangered* languages often have few first-language speakers, opportunities for learners of those languages to practice speaking are often limited. As such, conversational fluency is unattainable for many. Writing simple songs in endangered languages allows learners to creatively engage with the languages without the pressure to demonstrate conversational competence. Songwriting can generate new understandings of pronunciation, grammar, and cultural uses of the target language. This prompt encourages you to apply tools from linguistic anthropology and ethnomusicology to explore songwriting as a device for language acquisition and cultural expression.

Prompt

Identify an endangered language that you would like to use to write a song. If you are studying a language, you can draw on what you already know in that language. Or you can visit websites such as www.endangeredlanguages.com/ and www.elararchive.org/ to find audio recordings in endangered languages from around the world. Choose a topic you would like to write a song about. If you are completely new to your language, keep it relatively simple. Nouns, such as the names of colors, numbers, body parts, and animals, are often good material for beginners. More advanced language students can choose more complex vocabulary items or grammatical structures (see below). To the best of your knowledge, choose a topic and words that are unlikely to be offensive, particularly if you plan to share your song in public.

Next, choose a known melody that you feel comfortable singing. Simple folk songs and nursery rhymes that are already familiar to you are ideal for this assignment, such as "Twinkle, Twinkle Little Star" (which is itself a borrowing from the French folk song "Ah, vous dirai-je, Maman"). You can hear a version online in the endangered Tlingit language (Sealaska Heritage Institute 2019). Be aware of any copyright restrictions on your chosen melody when sharing any

DOI: 10.4324/9781003365228-26

recordings you make via social media. In the US, songs written before 1926 are generally in the public domain. Copyright laws vary internationally.

Now, write down several words or phrases in the target language that you have learned. If you are new to the language you have chosen, you may need to familiarize yourself with how the sounds of that language are written. If the orthography is very different from your own, you may wish to represent the sounds as best you can using a writing system you already know. You should listen to audio recordings of the words you are using. Do not go solely by written words for this activity.

Say the phrases you have written aloud and then document where the syllabic stress falls. Certain sounds have more weight or length when you say them. You can do this using any method you like. For instance, you could capitalize or underline the stressed syllables, as in the following examples:

the **DUCK SWIMS** on the **RI**ver
the <u>duck swims</u> on the <u>ri</u>ver

Egwoni **A**da**WO'A** ("He is swimming on the river" in Cherokee)
<u>e</u>gwoni <u>a</u>da<u>wo</u>'<u>a</u>

UP a**BOVE** the **WORLD** so **HIGH LIKE** a **DIA**mond **IN** the **SKY**.
up a<u>bove</u> the <u>world</u> so <u>high like</u> a <u>dia</u>mond <u>in</u> the <u>sky</u>.

Now, listen to your chosen melody and listen for ***melodic stress***. If you are familiar with "Twinkle, Twinkle Little Star," for instance, you can hum the melody and hear how some parts have more emphasis than others. You can notice that the syllabic stress of the words in "Twinkle, Twinkle" align with the melodic stress.

Turning to your song, try to line up the spoken stress of your words with the melodic stress. You now have a pleasing song phrase. Next, see if you can make your list of words or phrases fit your chosen melody with the stresses aligned. You may need to add or take away words to complete the entire melody or choose to create additional verses so you can sing through the melody more than once to use all of your lyrics.

How to Extend

When it comes to songwriting, repetition is your friend. Those with more experience in the target language may consider what is *poetic* in that language. Some languages rhyme and some do not, for instance. A rhyme invites listeners to notice the sounds of the words in addition to their meanings. Other poetic devices include onomatopoeia, alliteration, consonance, and the repetition of words or phrases.

Those with a moderate grasp of grammatical structures in the target language can conjugate phrases to create *parallelism*, which is a form of repetition. **Grammatical parallelism** exists when two or more phrases share the same or similar structures, like in the following examples:

I bought a cat.
I bought a dog.
I bought all the animals,
And brought them home.

Repetition and parallelism are quick ways to create additional verses (strophes) for a song, as illustrated by the "Cherokee Mask Song"[1] I composed using phrases from Cherokee speaker Myrtle Driver, which was elicited by Hartwell Francis at the Kituwah Preservation and Education Program. The verb root is shown in bold so that you can see how parallelism works by changing one or two components of a word or phrase while keeping the rest of the structure.

Verse 1

Agw**agvdula**	I'm wearing a mask.
Ts**agvdula**-tsu?	Are you wearing a mask?
H**agvdula**ga.	Put on a mask!

Verse 2

Ugvdula	He's wearing a mask.
Sdagvdula-tsu	Are you two wearing a mask?
Sdagvdulaga	You two put on a mask!

Parallelism is a great way to help yourself and others to remember different conjugations and grammatical concepts. In the Cherokee song example, a person who learns the song can learn several different conjugations and phrases related to wearing masks. It also teaches you how to add a question marker ***morpheme*** to ask a question.

If you are fortunate enough to work with a first-language speaker of your target language, you can ask them for help in creating parallel phrases using conjugations. You may consider recording the speaker on your phone or with an audio recorder so that you can listen to it again later (but always ask permission!). If the speaker is musically inclined, they may even be able to help you to develop your song.

Adding Gestures

Are there actions that could help to demonstrate the meaning of your song? In the *Cherokee Mask Song*, you can point to a single individual when singing "are you wearing a mask" and then point to two people when you say "are you two wearing a mask?" Finger plays are also great for telling stories and visualizing the content of songs. For younger children, lateral dance moves for songs can aid in remembering words and melodies.

Why This Assignment

> *Part-whole, parallelism, irony, outcry, proverb, and enigma suggest the incredible richness and sheer quantity of figures that writhe within language, waiting to be exploited or working on their own* (Friedrich 1986: 29).

Linguistic anthropologists recognize that poetry and songs are formed from the patterns of everyday speech (Tannen 1987; Fox 2004). In songwriting, we "play" with language to find poetic moments in seemingly mundane words or phrases. This can help a language learner to begin to *feel* their target language in creative ways. Songwriting as a form of speech play is a good method for investigating grammatical structures through repetition and parallelism, which aid in language acquisition (Cahnmann-Taylor and Hwang 2019). Cook (2000) notes that grammatical parallelism "isolates units, and shows the repeated structure operating with different components and with increasing complexity. The very act of repetition also allows greater time for processing, and creates a generally more secure and relaxed (because it is more predictable) atmosphere which may aid receptivity" (30). Songs can also be helpful mnemonics and teaching devices and have been used as such by cultures across the globe. Songwriting can also be a window for observing cultural uses of language. Using songwriting to explore the poetic features of a language opens the door for you to observe how people engage with poetic forms to negotiate or push back against inequalities of social power (Bauman and Briggs 1990; Briggs and Bauman 1992; Feld et al. 2004).

From an ethnomusicological perspective (Blacking 1973), this exercise draws attention to the ideology (and reality) that just as all humans have language, they are also universally musical and capable of producing musical expressions. Choosing to sing in an endangered language is a powerful symbol and is used as a practice of perseverance and revitalization for communities that have faced cultural repression and loss (Vallejo 2019). Songs are especially useful to learners because they operate outside of the problematic metrics of competency and fluency. In the context of language loss, this activity invites learners to develop affective (or feelingful) connections to an endangered or heritage language through which they may not yet be able to communicate in other ways.

What to Listen To

The original children's song *The Five Senses*, which I cowrote with my colleague Ellen Rainy Brake (Brake and Hopkins 2016), demonstrates the use of repetition and grammatical and thematic parallelism within a strophic song structure. The song teaches the concept of the five senses, which is a standard for elementary education. It repeats the grammatical construction of affixing a morpheme to the name of body parts in Cherokee to indicate whose they are. You can see the morpheme *tsi* underlined below. This indicates that it is "my" body part. What can you infer about the *di* prefix that occurs before the *tsi* in verses 1–3[2]? You can incorporate gestures when singing the song by using or pointing to the relevant body parts in rhythm to the music.

Verse 1	
Tsigowtisgo, ditsiktoli (x3)	I see, my eyes
Gvti ditsiktoli	Using my eyes
Verse 2	
Gatvgisgo, ditsileni (x3)	I hear, my ears
Gvti ditsileni	Using my ears
Verse 3	
Gasvnige, ditsiyesadv (x3)	I touch, my fingers
Gvti ditsiyesadv	Using my fingers
Verse 4	
Gakvnadv tsingo gvti (x3)	I taste[3], using my tongue
Gvti, tsingo gvti	Using, using my tongue
Verse 5	
Akiwisvgo, tsiyvsoli (x3)	I smell, my nose
Gvti tsiyvsoli	Using my nose

Notes

1 https://soundcloud.com/tsalagiseli/cherokee-mask-song-demo

2 The *di* makes the body part plural.

3 The word used for taste actually means something akin to "it is made clear to me." Taste is not a native sense category in Cherokee because it is considered an attribute of food items, not the sensory experience of the person eating them. Another way that the concept of taste is expressed in Cherokee is "gadelo'osga ugisdi nusdv" (I am discovering what is food-like).

References

Bauman, Richard and Charles L. Briggs. 1990. "Poetics and performance as critical perspectives on language and social life." *Annual review of Anthropology* 19: 59–88.

Blacking, John. 1973. *How Musical Is Man?* Seattle: University of Washington Press.

Brake, Rainy and Sara Hopkins. 2016. "Five Senses Song." https://soundcloud.com/tsalagiseli/five-senses-song

Briggs, Charles L. and Richard Bauman. 1992. "Genre, Intertextuality, and Social Power." *Journal of Linguistic Anthropology* 2(2): 131–172.

Cahnmann-Taylor, Melisa and Yohan Hwang. 2019. "Poetic habits of mind in TESOL teacher preparation. *Language and Education* 33(5): 399–415.

Cook, Guy. 2000. *Language Play, Language Learning*. Oxford: Oxford University Press.

Feld, Steven, Fox A. Aaron, Porcello Thomas, and Samuels David. 2004. "Vocal Anthropology: From the Music of Language to the Language of Song." In *A Companion to Linguistic Anthropology,* edited by Duranti Alessandro, 321–345. Oxford: Blackwell Publishing Ltd.

Fox, A. Aaron. 2004. *Real Country: Music and Language in Working-Class Culture.* Durham: Duke University Press.

Friedrich, Paul. 1986. *The Language Parallax: Linguistic Relativism and Poetic Indeterminacy.* Austin: University of Texas Press.

Sealaska Heritage Institute. January 17, 2019. *Twinkle, Twinkle Little Star in Tlingit* [Video]. www.youtube.com/watch?v=oECfhf7AyKE

Tannen, Deborah. 1987. "Repetition in Conversation: Toward a Poetics of Talk." *Language* 63(3): 574–605.

Vallejo, M. Jessie. 2019. "Revitalising Language through Music: A Case Study of Music and Culturally Grounded Pedagogy in Two Kanien'ke: Ha (Mohawk) Language Immersion Programmes." *Ethnomusicology Forum* 28(1): 89–117.

Lyrical Storytelling and Finding Voice

Steven Alvarez

Creative Ethnographic Toolkit: Bildungsroman poetry, narrative poetry, fieldnotes, thick description.

A ***bildungsroman*** is a narrative that focuses on the spiritual and educational growth of a character from youth to adulthood. We can see this recognizable narrative in novels, films, songs, and, of course, poems. When considering the growth of a character over a series of poems, it is easy to imagine how the lyricism of verse can enhance elements of the story. Further, *bildungsroman* narratives present a frame for understanding how significant events impact how individuals see themselves. They can acknowledge the transformation in how individuals perceive and understand the social world from child to adult. Building on this idea, in this prompt, we focus on micro-fiction stories about how writers "came of age" and when they first felt like their voices mattered to adults.

In preparation for the writing prompt, it would be helpful for you read *The Poet X* (Acevedo 2018) and *Long Way Down* (Reynolds 2017), which are two young adult novels in verse that depict characters coming of age in two different contexts. *Long Way Down* focuses on a young man named Will and his dilemma of either avenging the murder of his brother or disrupting a cycle of toxic masculine violence. In contrast, *The Poet X* tells the story of fifteen-year-old Xiomara as she navigates high school, religion, love, and family life, all while finding her passion for spoken word poetry. Both of these books use familiar language in poetic ways to tell compelling and relatable stories and can also be used as models for composing short, poetic texts. While studying these novels, participate in the low-stakes poetry exercises modeled after spoken word verse and poems that are presented in this prompt. For the writing project, you will be able to draw from this content to modify your pieces into longer stories. The number of poems used to tell these stories varies; for example, I use nine poems for the example assignment.

Those who are attentive to the possibilities of writing verse can study and practice the aspects of line breaks, structuring through stanzas, and meter variations. *The Poet X* and *Long Way Down* both offer examples of these poetic elements, which can be read and studied in the context of a novel. Because *The Poet X* (Acevedo 2018: 287–88) narrates the story of Xiomara becoming a spoken word poet and finding her voice through her verse, the poems in the novel reaffirm the power of lyrical performance.

DOI: 10.4324/9781003365228-27

[. . .] "Wassup, X! Write anything new?"
And I know that I'm ready to slam.
That my poetry has become something I'm proud of.
The way the words say what I mean,
how they twist and turn language,
how they connect with people.
How they build community.
I finally know that all of those
"I'll never, ever, ever"
stemmed from being afraid but not even they
can stop me. Not anymore

As the protagonist Xiomara comes to find confidence in her voice while also paying attention to the craft of her words and even experimenting with the form of her poems as the novel progresses, you also have the opportunity to think about taking chances with your verses while studying how to craft a narrative. For this reason, I find *The Poet X* to be a perfect model text for studying the *bildungsroman* while also being a perfect critical reading text to help you to make creative projects of your own design. Imitation and drawing inspiration from model texts encourages us to further explore of aspects of character, identity, place, and growth in bildungsroman poems. These explorations, in turn, benefit from us writing about our communities and with places which we closely identify, both creatively and critically.

Prompt

With *The Poet X* and *Long Way Down* as your mentor texts, imitate the structure of a bildungsroman story in verse to write your own "coming-of-age" tale in nine poems. Write nine poems that explore the aspects of character, identity, place, conflict, and growth in your story. Invent a character, tell the story of this character's coming of age, and practice using some of the elements of crafting poetry and stories that we have looked at so far. Each poem must be at least one page long, but no more than two pages (i.e., a total of 2000–2200 words when single-spaced typed). Also include a final reflection about the project, identifying which aspects of *The Poet X* and/or *Long Way Down* you brought into your own creative work.

To begin, make a list of three different moments when you felt your voice "came of age." Then, narrow these down to the story you want to focus on for this sequence (though save that list for potential later projects!). Once you have your focus, try to think of three scenes you could portray that "show" you growing up and use these as the basis for generating additional related scenes to support the action. Or, alternatively, make a list numbered 1–9. In this list, try to break up your story into a sequence of chronological events. As you order the events, bear in mind that there should be a story arc to this narrative and, ideally, there should be room for the resolution toward the end of the list. This list of nine events can form the basis for a narrative poem. As you flesh out this sequence of events, it is important to include elements of dialog, staying true to how you speak **colloquially**, as in the poetic styles of *The Poet X* and *Long Way Down*.

Example

I offer a single bildungsroman poem of my own from a longer poetic narrative project titled "la jefa." "La jefa" means "the boss" in Spanish, but it is also a **colloquial** word Mexican and Mexican American people use to refer to their mothers. In this poem, I zoom into a time in my life when I questioned how much my parents could protect me, in the sense that there were "professionals" with degrees whose words were more powerful than those of my folks, especially my mother. The poem also explores aspects of how my education, including poetry, distanced me from my parents and also from my roots.

"la jefa"
(Alvarez, unpublished)

la jefa smiling her gummy smile smiling
w. all her soul smiling that smile
into me my gums
those gums those teeth
my teeth she raised me
she bore me
la jefa wants to be smart for me closes her eyes
for me
uses big words in English to please me
knowing that reminds me she needs me to listen
& as i turned her away
shut her mouth & nodded anti-depressant specialist lectured
la jefa seeming attentive lifted her head that loyal jefa
wd never let her babies—
understanding no scientific jargon
of brain impulse restriction & imbalance
dependence
el jefe asleep next to her
he's the only genuine one in my family fought her eyes falling
wanting me to see she can be one of those
educaos she'll fight her accent
prove to those who she sd were better than her
who were never beaten by their ex-lovers
battered by their heritage
who don't remain silent as
stones
who can see things in words who are better than most
mexicans who don't have excuses to
cry

who don't have to clean
offices at nights who don't have to
care for the children of others to live she obeys to send her boy to school
to be one of those educators

la jefa sez i'm better than her but i'm not
la jefa's real i'm not
la jefa's better her smile she hurts
her wrinkles on the back of her neck hurt her old knees hurt & buckle
wrinkles around her eyes
her fist she cannot clench
hurts

once
after work after tagging along w. her to the D.E.S. first cleaning
job
she had she searched the bottom
of her bolsa
for change bought me a dilly bar from dairy queen pack
of pall malls & bottle of coors for el jefe at triangle drive-thru liquor
& nothing for
herself
more than once she forgot herself

la jefa told my hermana one day
she wuz afraid of me because i make her words not hers that i can
twist English into evil that my education distances us
reverses the power & admiration
that everything i sey is smart to my advantage

yet my words fail
to go home go to resent blood
go to old eyes brown
mirrors reflecting me
white

& for that i say fuck poetry

Why This Assignment

This bildungsroman project asks you to focus on your voice and how you felt heard or unheard by adults as you aged into young adulthood. From there, you can begin to narrow in on the elements of how your language(s) and communities impact, and sometimes conflict with, how you perceive your personal growth. Examining the transformative possibilities relating to language and adulthood offers an inroad for creative projects that allow you to think critically about your own lived experiences. Ethnographic inquiry is a vital methodology for researchers, writers, and poets that enables them to observe the cultural practices of individuals and groups, which also underpins the reflexive practices of writers who craft researched, expressive compositions that rhetorically appeal to audiences in academia and beyond. Telling a story offers a critical and creative way of approaching a narrative with attention to language. As I briefly mentioned before, I use nine poems in this prompt, but feel free to modify this number or start with a smaller number and build up to writing additional poems to further flesh out your story over time. No matter the number of poems, the point of writing narrative poetry in this manner is to weave the telling of tales with the musicality of language to enhance the crafting of stories.

In their ethnography of a student poetry group *Writing Instruction in the Culturally Relevant Classroom*, Maisha Winn and Latrise Johnson (2011) offer two ideas about students becoming ethnographers. Winn and Johnson write, "students can be involved in participatory action projects such as examining 'spatial location and demographic trends' in their community [. . .] and study the linguistic practices of others through close listening" (p. 71). Creative writing genres, such as memoir, poetry, and fiction, can also become expressive outlets, especially when you research, listen, and learn with and from the communities with whom you engage in inquiry. This kind of work can lead you to uncovered knowledge about local demographics and represent the voices of communities, in particular racially (and linguistically) minoritized communities. It also contributes to increasing awareness of social and cultural contexts and works to build confidence, voice, and valuable research experiences.

What to Read and How to Extend

The novel in verse *The Poet X* (Acevedo 2018) is a beautiful example of a coming-of-age story told through poems. It is about a young Dominican woman finding her voice in poetry. Studying this book and using it as a model for your poetry would be useful, not only because it is written in a way that is accessible but also because it is relatable in terms of the themes, such as questioning religion, bullies, puberty, sexual harassment, bilingualism, and more. The novel also focuses on how the heroine Xiomara becomes the Poet X and finds her voice as a slam poet at New York City's famous Nuyorican Café.

I often turn to slam poets in my courses because their performances often leave students feeling that poetry and music have a closer relationship than expected, particularly hip hop lyricism. For over a decade, Button Poetry's YouTube channel (2011) has offered a plethora of performance poetry for people to enjoy and learn from.

Finally, my own book *Community Literacies en Confianza: Learning from Bilingual After-School Programs* (Alvarez 2017) offers ideas for how you can approach, engage with, and partner with different cultural communities to design creative and culturally sustaining pedagogies that productively engage those with different literacy abilities.

References

Acevedo, Elizabeth. 2018. *The Poet X.* New York, NY: HarperCollins.

Alvarez, Steven. P. 2017. *Community Literacies en Confianza: Learning from Bilingual After-school Programs.* Urbana, IL: National Council of Teachers of English.

Button Poetry. 2011. Youtube. Accessed February 16, 2023. www.youtube.com/c/ButtonPoetry

Reynolds, Jason. 2017. *Long Way Down.* New York, NY: Atheneum.

Winn, Maisha. T. and Latrise. P. Johnson. 2011. *Writing Instruction in the Culturally Relevant Classroom.* Urbana, IL: National Council of Teachers of English.

8 Our Bodies, Our Selves

Interrogating the Ethnographic Body, Kinship, and Food During Fieldwork

Temporality and Embodied Experience

Nomi Stone

Creative Ethnographic Toolkit: Poetry, embodiment, temporality, phenomenology, writing through the senses.

We (ethnographers and students of anthropology) and our interlocutors in the field all live within bodies and within time. Representing the texture of that embodied temporality, with its perceived dilations and accelerations and its knots and fissures, is essential, especially if we take a phenomenological approach to our work. That is, we focus on "conditions of experience and how such conditions shape what and how it is to be human in any given context" (Throop and Jarrett 2021). One tool at our disposal to emphasize time in poetry is the line break. In a poem, a line is a unit that exists relationally and in context: it is always in tension with the sentence. By manipulating the charged relationship between these two rhythmic units, we can enact and perform time itself, its ongoing stream and even its ruptures, and indeed, the very texture of being alive. In this exercise, we'll first do a close reading of line breaks that achieve this and then try our own hand at this craft tool, using our own fieldwork or life experience.

In James Wright's (1990) poem, "A Blessing" we witness a gentle exchange between the speaker and two ponies, one of which nuzzles his hand. Notice how in the first half of the poem, each sentence is folded in half at the break of the line, a measured pace.

Just off the highway to Rochester, Minnesota
Twilight bounds softly forth on the grass.
And the eyes of those two Indian ponies
Darken with kindness.
They have come gladly out of the willows
To welcome my friend and me.

The poet Dana Levin describes the line as "a unit of experience," where *enjambment* "enacts the drama and pace, of feeling and thinking through" (2011). In Wright's poem, as each sentence folds in half, the world releases itself incrementally but regularly, stepping into sight: Sentence one, *Step:* Just off the highway to Rochester, Minnesota; *Step* Twilight bounds softly forth on the grass. Sentence two, *Step:* And the eyes of those two Indian ponies; *Step* Darken with kindness. In

DOI: 10.4324/9781003365228-29

this movement, first, we see the eyes; then, their gentleness. First the ponies come out of the willows, then they welcome the speaker and his friend. Event unfolds, perception unfolds—and all, gently, as if approaching an animal.

And then the poem changes, reminding us how the line's relationship to time allows us to expand and contract into *feeling itself*. Quite suddenly after five sentences folded in half or nearly, we come to this section of the poem, which describes the ponies:

> "They bow shyly as wet swans. They love each other.
> There is no loneliness like theirs."

Here is the slowing to a point, its aching brightness within three discrete sentences, which each tell the reader to *stop, to look:* "They bow shyly as wet swans." *Stop:* "They love each other.// There is no loneliness like theirs." Each sentence-moment is saturated with that fullness. There, the line makes a kind of tenderness in our gaze that changes the quality of time's unfolding.

My teacher Jim Longenbach created a taxonomy of different kinds of lines, reminding us that there is no hierarchy among lines: there isn't one better than the other. The key here is that different kinds of lines make a system of contrasts, pressing up against each other. There is the **end-stopped line**: self-explanatory enough: it is a line that is self-enclosed by its own closing punctuation. Wright's last two lines are end-stopped: "They love each other./ There is no loneliness like theirs." Such lines are good for declarative statements or question moments in poems. Then there is the **parsing line**: it is a line that fluidly follows the syntax of the poem, breaking at natural pause points for the breath. The first five sentences of the poem are all demarcated by parsing lines. The final kind of line is an **annotative line**, which means it works against, in opposition to the syntax. Namely, the poet annotates or makes a comment on the sentence by severing it in an unusual place. This can often create a more jagged pacing or moment of rupture. Wright has one pivotal annotative line in the poem, at the very end.

> "Her mane falls wild on her forehead,
> And the light breeze moves me to caress her long ear
> That is delicate as the skin over a girl's wrist.
> Suddenly I realize
> That if I stepped out of my body I would break
> Into blossom."

The speaker approaches the pony, he touches her ear, and the moment generates a flood in him: "Suddenly I realize/ That if I stepped out of my body I would break/ into blossom." This moment of seeming to transcend the body works on two levels: first the self "breaks"—that is, seems to be wounded or annihilated—and then with the break of the line itself, the self instead *breaks into blossom*, becomes new. These two registers remain in the poem: an ecstatic shattering and blooming, the way one only transcends the body through the body itself.

Prompt

Now, it's your turn. Start with a free-write in prose. If you have done fieldwork before, write a moment in your research where first you noticed your surroundings with great detail and then something surprised you. If you haven't done fieldwork yet, pluck a moment from your own life where you observed something interesting. Write with as much concrete, sensory detail as possible. What did you hear, smell, see; how did these experiences register in your body?

After you have written at least 300 words, either longhand or typed, underline the sentences you think are the sharpest, most sensory, and most musical: the sentences which seem to contain the heat or the crux of the affective, embodied moment you describe. Choose at least six sentences.

Rewrite those sentences in a new paragraph. Look carefully at the sentences which remain. How did you experience those moments? Did your experience of time seem to gallop forward or stand still? Did you experience shifts? Use the discussion above as a *guide* to use your intuition on which kinds of line-breaks would be effective for different moments of experience. Next, break the sentences into lines. In your exercise, use at least one parsing line, one end-stopped line, and one annotative line to turn your six sentences into a poem.

Remember, and *this is key:* there is no static formula for what any given kind of line-break means or does. Each poem will create its own tensions and possibilities. Line-break might create forms of time, but it also might do innumerable other forms of work. It might create moments of sliding between identities, of feeling either contained or off-kilter.

What to Read

In my poem "The Quadrant" (2014), where Middle Eastern role-players enact war for training soldiers in mock villages in the US, I use line-break in varying ways: to mark shifted states and to note moments of emphasis. The first line-break in the poem works to demarcate the entry into a dream-state or an unnerving liminality (or groping back toward the world), as role-players simulate war: "Climb/ in, climb out of the little black square." Then, in the first prose poetry verse of the poem, I break on the preposition *in*, a choice meant to emphasize the claustrophobic enclosure of the simulations: "The village rises into form amidst the pines. Cows and goats stand unstunned in/ the forest." A few lines later, I break on the pronoun "they" to emphasize a military logic that bifurcates "we" from "they:" "At the beginning of the exercise, the soldier students are told half-truths. They/must stabilize who and why." In my poem "The Soldier Takes the Anthropologist to the Shooting Range" (2019), I use line-break to show the disjuncture of a queer Jewish anti-war speaker doing fieldwork with the military: "The round so splits her: nerve/root/where/ to take cover, in this field of copper teeth?" In this poem, I use line-breaks not only at the line level, but also at the lexical (word) level—that is, slash marks *within* the line itself, to create a sensation of both disorientation and severed self. Different kinds of line-breaks create a dynamic system of contrast in a poem, an aliveness to meet our listening. Give yourself room to experiment and play.

How to Extend

And another mode of writing that you might find inviting for moving into sensory and affective terrain (but this time without the line-breaks) is flash ethnography, short self-enclosed bursts of prose that create a world of experience. Check out the online anthology of flash ethnography (2020) that I co-curated with the anthropologist Carole McGranahan. Happy writing!

References

Levin, Dana. 2011. "Where It Breaks: Drama, Silence, Speed, Accrual," in *A Broken Thing: Poets on the Line*, edited by Emily Rosko and Anton Vander-Zee. Iowa City, IA: University of Iowa Press, 148–151.

Longenbach, James. 2018. *The Resistance to Poetry*. Chicago: University of Chicago Press.

Stone, Nomi. 2019. "The Soldier Takes the Anthropologist to the Shooting Range," "Shock: War Game," and "The Quadrant," in *Kill Class*. North Adams, MA: Tupelo Press.

Stone, Nomi and Carole McGranahan. 2020. "Flash Ethnography: An Introduction." In *Flash Ethnography*, edited by Carole McGranahan and Nomi Stone, *American Ethnologist* website. October 26, 2020. https://americanethnologist.org/features/collections/flash-ethnography/flash-ethnography

Throop, Jason and Zigon Jarrett. 2021. "Phenomenology," in *The Open Encyclopedia of Anthropology*. Accessed February 16, 2023. www.anthroencyclopedia.com/entry/phenomenology

Wright, James. 1990. "A Blessing." *Poetry Foundation Website*. Reprinted from Wesleyan University Press. Accessed February 16, 2023. www.poetryfoundation.org/poems/46481/a-blessing

Cultivating Appetite

Food, Travel, and Communing through Food

Kristina Jacobsen

Creative Ethnographic Toolkit: Creative nonfiction, foodwriting, travel writing, writing through the senses, eating in community, arriving.

How do we cultivate our own relationships with food, home, and community? This writing and eating prompt asks creative ethnographers to select and write about a memorable encounter with food and describe it in as much sensory detail as possible. Then, ethnographers are invited to step back and think and write about the broader social contexts and cultural meanings behind their chosen food encounter. Why was this moment so significant? How was the taste of the food intermingled with your social or cultural experience? By the end of the written description, we want our readers to be open to eating the food that we are describing and be curious and open about the place where we ate it. In other words, we are aiming to cultivate our readers' appetites, even for foods that they thought they never wanted to try. As an optional extension to this prompt, encourage your peers to bring along the food described in the prompt for a potluck dinner.

Travel is often documented and made memorable through the foods we eat, and food can be an especially powerful medium for storytelling. Similarly, our relationships with home and other places are often sutured, renewed, or severed through our relationships with food. Food, and the anthropology of food, is closely tied to place and concepts of culture, identity, and self. How can we write using descriptive language that is fully alive and can conjure up the experience for someone far away who has not eaten the same food in the same way? What we crave, and what we consider to be delicious, is highly dependent on how we are socialized into ideas of food, taste, craving, comfort, and "home." Foods, on their own, are not intrinsically "delicious" or "disgusting." In Sardinia, Italy, my friends say that to live and eat well (*mangiare come si deve*), you need to have at least one long, multicourse lunch a week, which is eaten at a leisurely pace, preferably on a Sunday afternoon surrounded by family or friends and preferably including generous amounts of locally produced wine. When I lived as a guest on the Navajo Nation and taught at a university "off-rez" (off the reservation) many hours away, each time I recrossed the reservation border to return home, I would pull over at the convenience store in Leupp, Navajo Nation, to purchase a bag of hot Cheetos as

DOI: 10.4324/9781003365228-30

I re-entered the Diné part of my world. My re-entry ritual into place and home was tightly bound with a snack: a food defined in a working-class context as a special treat and in a more middle-class context as "junk food," but a food that nonetheless ritualized my return each week.

Prompt

Part 1

Think back to a favorable and memorable encounter you had with food. Were you traveling? Were you at home at your auntie or grandma's house? Did you sit across from a complete stranger or did you sit beside a loved one? Was it a warming meal, a snack with an incredible crunch, an exquisitely flavored beverage, or something indescribably different? What were the textures of the food and what made it notable? What were the flavors, smell, and context in which you ate it and who were the people you were surrounded by?

Describe this food using the present tense and include as much detail and invoke as many of your senses as possible (taste, touch, smell, sight, sound, body, movement, etc.). Convey the mood of the moment. Then, situate it geographically and culturally. Where did this food experience take place? What was its cultural context? Were you in a new country, town, or state? Were you in a familiar home or at a kitchen table you love to eat at? In other words, what *made* this experience with food so memorable? Your readers should know how much you loved this food not by you stating that you loved it, but by your handling of the details. Your goal is to write persuasively.

Now, return to your initial piece of ethnographic creative non-fiction and do some research on the food that you described. Without changing the tone of your writing, incorporate 2–3 relevant facts about this food and its history into your draft. By the end of your piece of writing, you want your readers to be ready to eat the food you've described. You also want them to be curious and open to learning more about the place where you ate it. In other words, you want to cultivate your readers' appetite, even for a food that they thought they never wanted to try.

Part 2

Exchange your draft with a peer and focus on the following questions:

1. Does the piece make you hungry? Why/why not?
2. Does reading the piece make you want to visit the place, memory, or moment that the writer speaks about? Why/why not?
3. Which senses are specifically invoked (by the author) and evoked (in the reader)?
4. What specific words or turns of phrase make this piece believable? Be as specific as possible.

5. What choices in words (diction) or grammar (syntax) could the writer consider using to render this story or passage more believable or make it come alive?
6. Is there anything else you'd like to add as peer reviewer?

Part 3

Revise your draft based on the feedback provided and then submit your first and second drafts together, including a paragraph discussing the changes you made.

For full credit, your piece of creative non-fiction should include a detailed description of the food experience using at least three senses. Your choice of words (nouns, verbs, adjectives, and adverbs in particular) should directly reflect the mood that you're aiming to convey. Your piece should include a description of the texture of the food, 2–3 facts about the food, and a specific geographic place, whether that is a place you call home or one in which you are/were a guest. Your piece should have a who, what, where, and when. Finally, your piece should have a title that directly relates to the central theme of your work and is grounded in the narrated experience of your piece.

What to Read

One example of the interconnection between food and social context can be seen in a piece by food writer Margo True, in which she describes her arrival in New Delhi, India, through food.

> *One warm, moon-bright evening about ten years ago, I was standing in a square beneath the majestic bulk of the Red Fort in New Delhi, transfixed by what I was eating. The shy street-vendor behind one of the dozens of carts parked there had just handed me, fresh and hot from a pot of bubbling oil and carefully stacked inside a newspaper cone, several tiny, golden puffs. I put one between my teeth and bit down. Instantly the frail crust gave way, flooding my mouth with cool, cilantro-flavored water spiked with chili. It was great fun, like popping edible balloons. I remember what a surprise it was—and how well it characterized my experience of traveling in India. Practically everything about India surprised me, and my senses felt flooded nearly all the time. In the witty little 'pani poori' I ate that night—for it surely seemed to me they'd been created by a cook with a subtle sense of humor—I found an expression of all three* (True in Sterling ed. 1996: 1).

In the example above, note the descriptive word choices that Sterling uses specifically to convey joy and surprise, such as: bubbling, popping, golden puffs, fresh, hot, frail crust, cool, cilantro-flavored, and spiked with chili.

In another example, the filmmaker and adventure travel writer Barbara Banks describes a road trip through rural Tibet in her piece "A Tibetan Picnic."

Meanwhile, Phurbu has poured the black tea into the wooden churn, and hooks his leg around it as a brace. He adds a knife-blade full of yak butter and a small handful of salt, then with the gesture that is rhythmic and graceful and practiced a thousand times over, he churns the sö cha, or butter tea, regular as a metronome. The tea is poured, thick as cream and the color of caramel, back into the black kettle, its smoky flavor interwoven with the scene of melted yak butter. Phurbu reaches over to the twig that Shamba had brought back from the river and fits it into the spout, a perfect strainer. Our cups are ready, always ready for tea: there are silver-lined traditional wooden tea owls alongside plastic thermal mugs, and the kettle is lifted time and again—no cup gets drunk to the bottom before being refilled, and the broth mixture is warming from deep within (Banks in Sterling ed. 1996: 23).

A final example was inspired by the year I spent living as a Fulbright artist and scholar on the Italian island of Sardinia and is taken from my blog, www.ethnographicsongwriting.com.

In Santu Lussurgiu (OR), I lived just 40 minutes from the Mediterranean sea. Each Sunday, I would hop in my gray Opel Corsa, put my dog in the hatchback, and drive up and out of the hollowed-out volcano where the village lay and drive over, around and down to the sea. After a brisk walk together along the white sea cliffs with the Mediterranean macchia crunching underfoot (low-growing, aromatic plants that grow only on the Mediterranean), the lingering perfume of 'elicriso' and 'ginepro' (juniper) in the air, I would luxuriate in a meal at a restaurant on a bastion looking out to sea. Red geraniums decorated all the window boxes, contrasting strikingly against the brilliant aquamarine of the sea, smooth like plateglass. And each Sunday, it was the same: 'spaghetti alle vongole con bottarga' (spaghetti with fresh baby clams and bottarga, a type of buttery, powdered fish roe) and a glass of semi-sweet Vermentino, a chilled white wine produced in the northern part of the island. The mix of tender clams, parsley, garlic and olive oil with the buttery flavor of the bottarga on the al dente spaghetti, combined with the crisp coldness of the first sip of white wine with a very slight sweetness in the finish, remains one of my sharpest sense memories of place and of Sardinia. Eating this meal alone in the most social of places felt even more decadent: on an island where most meals are eaten in the company of others—and something I did frequently—eating a meal by myself, alone with my own thoughts and savoring every morsel, felt rebellious and raucously liberating (it still does). During these meals, Sardinia was sinking into my bones and my senses at a visceral level. Now, she is a part of my sensory DNA.

The same techniques can be employed in songs. For example, consider the ways in which the senses and appetite are invoked by songwriter Lyle Lovett in his classic love song to a small Texas town "This Old Porch."

And this old porch is like a steaming, greasy plate of enchiladas
With lots of cheese and onions and a guacamole salad
And you can get 'em down at the La Salle Hotel in old downtown
With iced tea and a waitress and she will smile every time

How to Extend: Potluck Dinner

After completing this prompt, encourage your peers to bring along a sample taste, texture, smell, sliver, or dish to share with each other. Your offering can relate directly to the food described in your essay or, if that would be difficult to obtain, you can simply choose a dish that brings you a similar sense of joy or other emotion when you eat it. Enjoy these samples as a friendly potluck dinner and food celebration. Whatever you bring, keep it simple: don't let it be a source of stress and keep your contribution within your financial means. As your peers eat the food that you brought, you can take additional fieldnotes, noticing and documenting their responses to your dish.

References

Jacobsen, Kristina. n.d. "Ethnographic Songwriting," Accessed February 6, 2023. www.ethnographicsongwriting.com

Lovett, Lyle. 1986. "This Old Porch." *Lyle Lovett.* Curb/MCA Records.

Sterling, Richard, ed. 1996. *Food: True Stories of Life on the Road.* San Francisco, CA: Travelers' Tales, Inc.

True, Margo. 1996. Introduction. In *Food: True Stories of Life on the Road*, edited by Richard Sterling. San Francisco, CA: Travelers' Tales, Inc.

Artful Scholarship with Interview Data

Melisa Cahnmann-Taylor

Creative Ethnographic Toolkit: Performance, poetry, literature review, interviews, reflexivity, humility.

Conducting an ethnographic interview can be an artful practice. Interviews are "a conversational meeting with at least one other self" (Skinner 2012), which provide a way for stakeholders in the topic at hand (also referred to as interlocutors or study participants) to reflect upon their views and experiences. Not only does the researcher gather and make sense of these stories (DeMarrais 2004) but they can also make change and be changed by the process of thoughtful questioning and deep listening.

There are many challenges to interviewing practice, many of which are discussed thoroughly in Skinner's (2012) book and cannot be addressed here. My attention is focused on artful innovations in interviewing, including performance and poetry. For example, Deena Pollack's (2006) *Listening Out Loud* technique is a way to "embody listening as an antidote to *knowingness*" (104, original italics), which she refers to as a "handshake with history… [that is] all the more tender and resplendent yet for not knowing what happens from here" (103). Creative ethnographers using poetic and performative transcription can seek what artist Anna Deveare Smith (1994) refers to as the music in language when those interviewed open up beyond the rehearsed, feel-good stories of the self to "the very moment that the smooth-sounding words fail us…where 'character' lives" (xxxi). To interrogate complexity and move away from acceptable, political, or rehearsed language, Smith (2023) suggests using three open-ended questions:

1. Have you ever come close to death?
2. Do you know the circumstances of your birth?
3. Have you ever been accused of something you did not do?

I have used variations on Smith's questions to understand the complexities of race and language between the United States and Mexico (Cahnmann-Taylor 2016). One of the most significant questions in my poetic inquiry was to ask about a time when participants felt misunderstood in their second language (a version of question #3 above). The answers to this and other interview questions became a series of verse and performance poems that bear witness to the complicated relationship U.S.-born Americans have to the Spanish language and to their own possibilities for

DOI: 10.4324/9781003365228-31

bilingualism. More recently my focus has shifted, attending to what I refer to as **trans/scripts**, "compressed renderings of original transcripts that utilize techniques from poetry and the dramatic arts (e.g. theatre scripts) to highlight emotional 'hot points' and heightened language from the original discourse in our data" (Cahnmann-Taylor et al. 2009: 2548) to understand issues of tension regarding language, race, and religion. Scholars, too, can become prey to oversimplification of deeply polemic issues that involve our fieldwork, from different points of view on climate change (do we or do we not need stronger environmental legislation?), gender identity (is gender fixed at birth or a fluid, lifelong choice?), national borders (to what extent should borders between nations be closed and protected by military, e.g. between the US and Mexico, between Israel, the West Bank, and Gaza?) among many other complicated subjects. The artful interview is our tool to defy simplification and amplify complexity. Inquiry and analysis of many polemic topics can move us away from seeing any one side as flawless or heroic and provide deeper insight to human intersectionality.

Turning to ethnographic interviewing of hotly debated political issues can leave scholars, artists, and audiences with more complicated and nuanced understandings, presentations and performances of histories and perspectives. Smith's (1994) work on US race relations, Loomer's (2019) play, "Roe," concerning the abortion debate, and Ibrahim Miari's (2023) exploration of relations between Israel and Palestine, are just a few examples of the ways in which research-informed art expands rather than oversimplifies difficult topics.

I often use trans/scripts to inform scholarship and artmaking (Cahnmann-Taylor, 2016; 2017; 2022), most recently in response to wars between Israel and Hamas that took place in May 2021 and more violently on October 7, 2023. Modeling on Stevens' (1954) notable poem, "13 Ways of Looking at a Blackbird," I entitled the performance poem, "Eighteen Ways of Looking at Property" to reflect a fraction of divergent perspectives and their origins. Here are the first 7 of the 18 stanzas in the poem:

Eighteen Ways of Looking at Property
(Melisa Cahnmann-Taylor, 2022)

I.
Chai (חי) is Hebrew for "life"
which is also the number 18 because it's the sum
of *chet* (8) and *yud* (10). As a result, Jews frequently make gifts
in multiples of $18.

II.
A peculiarity.
The quality of being proper.
A possession.
Shares or investments in land.

III.
I am of three American minds, like a country
in which Arabs, Jews, and Palestinians
all want peace.

IV.
By thirteen years old, I was invested,
a *Mazel Tov* bond at 4% return.
Thirty years later, a letter
from the Ministry of Finance called it:
"ABANDONED PROPERTY."
According to the State of Israel, the bonds are still available.

V.
"The historic preservation movement is all-too-often defined by 11th-hour reactions to impending loss. It seems to be human nature to only act when threatened."

VI.
"If statehood rests on the oppression of others,"
said the progressive educator, "we should all be 'Diaspora Jews.'"
"But," she said, "don't quote me on that. If they knew how I felt
about Israel, I'd lose my Sunday school job."

VII.
A Palestinian friend in the U.S. has pretended, for years,
to be married to a woman. "Arabs are stoned to death for less."
While visiting, he posted a photo eating *kunafeh* and *halvah.*
with his twenty-year-old cousin who promised a day before,
throwing bottle rockets at Israeli soldiers,
to dance in the afterlife with dozens of women.
He's since been shot dead.

To read stanzas VIII – XVIII, visit the online poem at https://lilith.org/2022/04/poetry-eighteen-ways-of-looking-at-property/

Prompt

The 18 part poem excerpted above was informed by online and in person debates among anthropologists as well as those in my university and personal communities. The first part of this prompt asks you to identify a topic about which you feel passionately, and about which people in your personal and/or professional communities do not share the same opinion. Find interviews online from diverse perspectives, especially those different from your own, which may be found on television, audio podcasts, YouTube channels, etc. Listen for any question the interviewer uses that has something in common with Smith's (2023) questions listed above: are there any similarities? Identify any other questions you feel invited answers that were unexpected or where there was an observable shift in body language or tone.

Selectively **transcribe** up to one minute of text from across the length of the entire interview (e.g. selections transcribed need not be consecutive). The transcription should be of selections that you believe are most resonant with that person's character and experience. Then try to trans/scribe this text into ten lines of a poem with no line having more than 20 syllables and/or as a dramatic monologue lasting no more than 60 seconds. Write a title that gives readers information about the context for this poem.

How to Extend the Prompt with Data

If you are already working on an inquiry project, consider the focus of your study. Then follow this three part prompt.

Part 1

Identify which aspects of your study entail deep divides, conflicts, or even intolerances, those you learn about in the context of the study and those you may hold yourself. Craft a version of Smith's (2023) questions above. For example, in discussion with Jewish and Palestinian educators living in the US, I have asked: "What are the circumstances of your understanding of the war between Israel and Palestine?" and "Have you ever been accused of being anti-Muslim or antisemitic?" Include these questions in 3–7 interviews with those who hold divergent views on the given topic (making sure to have **institutional review board** approval for your research and **consent forms** signed by participants). Be courageous. Talk less and listen more. Write notes about what you heard just after the interview. Then, transcribe the interview word for word. Notice not only *what* is said but *how*: where the singing or music changed in a person's voice, where you yourself faltered or struggled to ask the next question, or where your interlocutor hesitated (breath pause). Highlight those moments.

Part 2

Once you have a completed transcript, tease apart the most resonant sections of text using a script. Using roman numerals I through V, write 10 lines for each of these five stanzas. You may set yourself some or all of the following constraints:

1. Each stanza must reflect a different voice or perspective on the same issue.
2. Each stanza must have no more than 10 lines.
3. Each line must have no more than 20 syllables.
4. Each stanza must include at least one color and one physical object or body part.

The above four constraints are intended to give some formal structure to the ways in which you represent much longer interview transcripts and guide choices in the ways you trans/script the most resonant understandings.

Part 3

Return to these five stanzas. Are there any words that are often repeated? Go to your university or public library to access the Oxford English dictionary. Look up one of the words and explore what are companion words for this concept? What words come before or after it in the dictionary. Write another 1–3 stanzas that meditate on that word alone and its varying meanings.

Why This Assignment

There's a famous excerpt from Williams' (1962) poetry that captures the intersections between art, news, social science, and politics. These are the most famous lines often excerpted from "Asphodel, That Greeny Flower" that I find useful for answering the "why" of our endeavors with art and science.

It is difficult
to get the news from poems
          yet men die miserably every day
                    for lack
of what is found there.

In the context of the creative ethnographic interview, these lines acknowledge that while it may be difficult, perhaps impossible, to get traditional "scholarship" from artful interviews, the practice may save us from academic misery. Without art, there is often no heart, no feeling, and/or fear that anything close to the personal or aesthetic can contaminate scholarly objectivity. The arts, when engaged with rigor, integrity, diversity of perspective, and specificity, can bring us closer not farther from objectivity. The best use of social science and artistic tools is to find ways to make sense of the insensible and express what may otherwise be unsayable.

I have observed graduate students and colleagues engage miserably in academic tasks for lack of the arts in scholarly pursuits. Those of us who begin investigations with passionate curiosity and connection to our subjects, are often dulled rather than animated by disciplinary conventions. Politics, especially when harnessed by social media, can overwhelm scholarship leading to a dangerous one-sidedness of perspective. While politics simplifies argument, the arts amplify complexity: the latter is in much better service to ethnographic endeavors than the former. As Blumenfeld-Jones (2018) wrote: "Art-making is the exploration of questions for which there are no easy or obvious answers, revealing the human complexity of our situation and addressing the confusions amongst which we all, inevitably, live."

What to View, Listen To, and Read

View Smith's (2023) discussion of her approach to capturing music and character in an interview, her book (Smith 2000), script (Smith 1994) as well as her numerous roles on television. Then attend to all the marvelous interviewers available on your favorite podcasts, from Terry Gross, Maria Hinojosa, Damon Young, Imara Jones, Ezra Klein, Julia Dreyfuss, and others. Notice the fluidity and order of what they ask, when, and how they frame their questions. Attend to resonant images and words and their various meanings.

References

Blumenfeld-Jones, Donald. 2018. "Wild imagination, radical imagination, politics and the practice of arts-based educational research (ABER) and scholartistry." In *Arts-Based Research in Education*, edited by M. Cahnmann-Taylor and R. Siegesmund, 48–66. New York: Routledge.

Cahnmann-Taylor, Melisa. 2016. *Imperfect Tense*. San Pedro, CA: Whitepoint Press.

Cahnmann-Taylor, Melisa. 2022. "Eighteen Ways of Looking at Property." *Lilith (selected by Alicia Ostriker).* https://lilith.org/2022/04/poetry-eighteen-ways-of-looking-at-property/

Cahnmann-Taylor, Melisa, Mariana Souto-Manning, Jennifer Wooten, and Jaime Dice. 2009. "The Art & Science of Educational Inquiry: Analysis of Performance-Based Focus Groups with Novice Bilingual Teachers." *Teachers College Record* 111: 2535–2559.

Cahnmann-Taylor, Melisa. 2017. "'I'm Not Talking to You' 'You Don't Have to!' Trans/scripting the Bland-Encinia Case." *Pedagogy and Theatre of the Oppressed Journal* 2 (2). Available at: http://scholarworks.uni.edu/ptoj/vol2/iss1/2

DeMarrris, K. 2004. Qualitative Interview Studies: Learning through Experience. Mahwah: Erlbaum.

Dowd Hall, Jacquelyn and Della Pollack. 2005. *Remembering: Oral History Performance*. Palgrave Macmillan.

Eisner, Elliott. 1985. *The Educational Imagination: On the Design and Evaluation of School Programs*. New York: Macmillan.

Loomer, Lisa. 2019. *Roe*. New York, NY: Dramatists Play Service.

Miari, Ibrahim. 2023. In-Between (play). Downloaded from https://ibimiari.wixsite.com/website/contact

Pollock, Della. 2006. "Memory, Remembering, and Histories of Change: A Performance Praxis." In *The SAGE Handbook of Performance Studies*, edited by D. Soyini Madison and Judith Hamera, 87–105. Thousand Oaks, CA: SAGE Publications. doi: 10.4135/9781412976145.n6

Skinner, Jonathan. 2012. *The Interview: An Ethnographic Approach*. New York: Routledge.

Smith, A. 2000. *Talk to Me: Listening Between the Lines*. New York: Random House.

Smith, Anna Deavere. 1994. *Twilight Los Angeles, 1992: On the Road: A Search for American Character*. New York: Anchor.

Smith, Anna Deveare. 2023. "How are Language and Identity Connected?" *Big Think*. Downloaded on October 19, 2023. www.youtube.com/watch?v=D5pu47-iQ8E&t=311s

Stevens, Wallace. 1954. "Thirteen Ways of Looking at a Blackbird." In *The Collected Poems of Wallace Stevens*. New York: Alfred A. Knopf, a division of Random House, Inc.

Williams, William Carlos. 1962. *Pictures from Brueghel and Other Poems by William Carlos Williams: Collected Poems 1950–1962*. New York: New Directions.

9 People, Places and Performance

Ritual, Religion, and Visualities

Production Values in Practice

William Lempert

Creative Ethnographic Toolkit: Videomaking, videography, observational skills, freewriting.

This prompt aims to provide practical experience in identifying, analyzing, and enacting ethnographic media values of production. Production values are a product of the ways we become socialized into visual, audio, and experiential film worlds. In filmmaking, anthropologists past and present, continue to balance the tension between mainstream documentary film production values (Nichols 2017) and the value systems of those engaged within ethnographic projects (Aufderheide 2007). While Hollywood films are often described through the language of "high" or "low" production values, what these entail is usually taken for granted as inevitable and objective. This activity promotes an active understanding of how production values represent specific aesthetic and moral sensibilities set within a worldview. Through three prompts, this activity has students (1) analyze a value in a personally resonant film, (2) create a short video with a partner that expresses that value, and (3) reflect on the process after viewing an ethnographic film.

Production values are simply those prioritized in the production of media making. Beyond those of Hollywood, there are many others that filmmakers around the world prioritize, including community building, dignified processes, and youth media training. Ethnographers have debated the value of media in anthropology since the earliest film work by Margaret Mead and her contemporaries (Heider 2006). Over decades, many anthropologists have come to understand media as capable of transcending the limits of written language (MacDougall 2006). Through the practice of "shared anthropology," Jean Rouch (2003) was an early innovator who reimagined the boundaries of ethnographic media and authorial control for both ethnographers and research partners.

The increasingly collaborative and dialogical tradition of ethnographic media has flourished in recent years. This is exemplified by projects such as *Phone & Spear: A Yuṯa Anthropology* (2019) by the Miyarrka Media art collective, which includes Aboriginal Australian media makers and anthropologist Jennifer Deger. Their work gestures toward a model of ethnographic media production that "does not simply analyze relations, [but] seeks to make them" (56). In other words,

DOI: 10.4324/9781003365228-33

contemporary media anthropologists are exploring how relationship building and collaborative thinking emerge through mediamaking itself.

Prompt

Part 1 (approximately 30 minutes)

We are going to do some writing and will move fairly quickly through multiple sections. Do not worry about whether you feel completely finished within each, just move fluidly between them. The goal here is about the process more than the product.

Watch the opening 5 minute scene from *In Her Own Time*, a 1986 ethnographic film engaging an Orthodox Jewish community in Fairfax, California, which centers the value of solace in relation to anthropologist Barbara Myerhoff's battle with cancer.

Now, take a deep breath and imagine a favorite film from when you were in grade school. Quickly picture the most vivid scene you can remember from that film and, with your eyes closed, play it in your mind over the next minute.

For a few minutes, write about this scene. Rather than tracing the story, describe the sensory details that you find most compelling, however small they might seem. *Try to show and not tell.*

Take another few minutes to reflect on why you selected this scene. Emphasize your connection to this film and how the scene makes you feel.

For a few more minutes, identify and write about one value that you think makes this scene particularly compelling. Do not choose a cinematic or aesthetic value, but rather a human quality (e.g. patience, redemption, deception, etc.). This value may reveal something about what you find moving in an ethnographic sense. Or, you might identify a value that you find you do not personally share, which would also be interesting to explore here.

Next, take 10 minutes and share what you have written with a partner. Keep in mind that the person you are sharing with will be your collaborator in Part 2 of this prompt. Take turns going through your responses.

Part 2 (approximately 40 minutes)

Overview: In the second part of this prompt, you will make a brief video that aims to evoke the production value you identified from the previously discussed movie scene. You will do this with a partner using one of your phones, aiming for a running time of approximately 1–2 minutes. Do not worry about your videomaking experience. The goal here is simply to learn through practice. Just do your best with your current level of technical familiarity.

First, freewrite for 5 minutes on at least one specific idea for expressing your scene's value in a short video. Remember that the video will consist of only one continuous clip of a minute or two, without any editing. While planning, consider your environment. Can you move beyond the room you are in or even go outside? How will you deal with sound interference? Try to center the philosophy that constraints are your friend when doing creative work and that necessity is the mother of invention!

Next, share these video ideas with your partner. Over 10 minutes, pool your creativity to develop a plan for making the video. Make sure that whatever your final collective video plan is, it centers both of your identified values. They may connect or contrast. Use that relationship to fuel your creative process.

You now have 15 minutes to put your plan into action! Although you are shooting a single continuous scene, you may attempt it multiple times. As with other aspects of this quick video production, you have a tight constraint around time. This is often the case for ethnographic mediamaking. Use this constraint to help you lean into your intuition as you adapt throughout the process. Do not worry about small mistakes or what you might have done differently. Above all, your goal here is to consider ways in which compelling human values can be expressed and communicated through mediamaking. Pay close attention to your time and return to the room by the end.

After this, get into groups of four that include two partner pairs. Before discussing your video, watch both of them and try to guess what values the other group was attempting to convey. Then reveal them, and in about 5 minutes discuss challenges in the process and what you might have done with more time and resources to develop the video further.

Part 3 (15–40 minutes)

In the last part of this prompt, watch part or all of *Number our Days*, Barbara Myerhoff's 1983 Oscar winning half hour ethnographic film. Released a decade before *In Her Own Time*, it engages the same Orthodox community, though conveys quite different values. As Myerhoff describes in the introduction, this was a project that emerged from her deep self-reflection on the purpose and subject of ethnographic media. Depending on class circumstances, any of the following three scenarios will work well: watch (1) just the beginning and concluding 5-minute sections in class, (2) the entire film in class, or (3) the entire film individually before the next class.

After viewing, write about the following two questions for 5 minutes: How would you describe the human production values of this film? Are these values important to you, or might you have emphasized others?

Over 5 minutes, discuss your written responses in your previous group of four, making connections to your videomaking experiences from the Part 2.

Finally, have a few volunteers summarize key takeaways from their final small group discussion.

Why This Assignment

This set of activities aim to provide practical experiences in analyzing, enacting, and reflecting upon the values in media. They aim to help students identify the values that are featured in their favorite media, and consider if these are values they share and wish to promote. This prompt aims to promote the active understanding of how production values become socialized, aesthetic, and moral sensibilities, helping students to more deeply engage with ethnographic and non-Western produced media, and increasing their awareness in consuming and considering media.

What to Read/Watch

Read Dowell's (2021) publicly available Video Production Handbook. This is an excellent and concise distillation of how to practically create an ethnographic interview video.

Explore the online digital version of *Phone & Spear: A Yuṯa Anthropology*. As a digital version of their book by the same name, it provides vivid inspiration on emerging possibilities of collaboration and ethnographic media forms.

Watch the short video *Documentary and Ethnographic Film: What's the Difference*. This introduces some of the nuance between documentary and ethnographic media.

How to Extend

For a deeper engagement, I suggest that you extend their filming period by 20 minutes, so that they can slow down and be even more deliberate in their process. If some students indicate further interest, I would recommend that they engage Kristin Dowell's (2021) *Video Production Handbook* and *The Bare Bones Camera Course for Film and Video* (Schroeppel and DeLaney 2015).

References

Aufderheide, Patricia. 2007. *Documentary Film: A Very Short Introduction*. Oxford: Oxford University Press.

Dowell, Kristin. 2021. *Video Production Handbook*. Washington DC: Smithsonian Center for Folklife and Cultural Heritage.

Heider, Karl. 2006. *Ethnographic Film*. Austin: University of Texas Press.

MacDougall, David. 2006. *The Corporeal Image: Film, Ethnography, and the Senses*. Princeton: Princeton University Press.

Miyarrka Media: Gurrumuruwuy, Paul, Jennifer Deger, Enid Gurunulmiwuy, Warren Balpatji, Meredith Balanydjarrk, James Ganambarr, et Kayleen Djingadjingawuy. 2019. *Phone & Spear: A Yuṯa Anthropology*. London: Goldsmiths Press.

Myerhoff, Barbara and Lynne Littman. 1983. *Number Our Days*. 29 min. Direct Cinema.

Myerhoff, Barbara and Lynne Littman. 1986. *In Her Own Time*.

Nichols, Bill. 2017. *Introduction to Documentary, Third Edition*. Bloomington: Indiana University Press.

Rouch, Jean. 2003. *Ciné-Ethnography*. Translated by Stephen Feld. Minneapolis: University of Minnesota Press.

Schroeppel, Tom and Chuck DeLaney. 2015. *The Bare Bones Camera Course for Film and Video*. New York: Simon and Schuster.

Creative Sensory Ethnography through Group Songwriting

Naomi Sunderland

Creative Ethnographic Toolkit: Group songwriting, poetry, sensory ethnography.

This activity draws together practices of sensory ethnography and creative group songwriting in ways that will ideally allow you to connect with others and share stories about what it feels like to experience shared places and events from diverse bodies, perspectives, and standpoints. In anthropology and social sciences research approaches, sensory ethnographers are notable in seeking to understand what it "feels" like—including embodied sensory, emotional, and intellectual experiences—to inhabit spaces, places, and events from diverse individual and shared perspectives (Sunderland et al. 2012). Anthropologists such as Sarah Pink (2011) developed sensory ethnography as a methodology for studying the ways our bodies, senses, and cultural and social backgrounds shape our individual and shared lived experience of places, spaces, and events. More recent work has used sensory ethnography in combination with creative methods to offer deep and rich understandings of how diverse people and communities experience places, spaces, and events (Chenhall, Kohn, and Stevens 2020; Ginsburg 2018).

In my experience as a mixed heritage First Nations health researcher, singer-songwriter, and community music facilitator, creative ethnographic processes blend incredibly well with "sense-bound" approaches to songwriting that encourage songwriters to create vivid images and metaphors of places and experiences through their songs (Jacobsen 2017; Pattison 2012), which in turn offer listeners a chance to listen "with their whole bodies," i.e., to get a vicarious sense of what the songwriter is experiencing and communicating (Mathews and Sunderland 2017). Sense-bound songwriting can also offer accessible ways for people who have experienced traumatic events to reconnect with their body and senses, which can be an important aspect of trauma healing (Atkinson 2002; Harrison, Jacobsen, and Sunderland 2019).

I have combined sensory ethnography with group songwriting as a way of eliciting and sharing rich stories about shared places and experiences, often in intercultural and First Nations settings. In that work, I have found that it's important to be sensitive to the dynamics of trauma that people might have experienced, especially when asking people to consciously inhabit their body and talk about shared

DOI: 10.4324/9781003365228-34

or individual sensorial experiences (Sunderland et al. 2023). Hence, in this prompt, I share tips on ways that you can be sensitive to trauma in your work and provide some suggestions for further reading. I hope that this prompt helps you to become aware of how sensory, embodied, and emplaced storytelling can highlight how sensory engagement with the world shapes our experiences in more and less visible ways. In my experience, sensory ethnographic and trauma-informed group songwriting can be a powerful tool in arts-led community development (e.g., through storytelling and shared understanding), co-research in intercultural settings (e.g., using music making as a connecting process), and participant-led self-advocacy (e.g., through sharing stories and messages that participants most want to express to audiences).

Prompt

Students are invited to undertake a small group process that involves cowriting a shared song about sensory experiences of a place or event. The activity guides you through a process of identifying and sharing individual stories and experiences in order to form an overall song about the diverse and/or shared ways in which a group of songwriters may experience the same place or event. In doing so, students are creatively and collaboratively exploring and gathering stories about how sensory experiences of place can shape and be shaped by shared cultural, social, and political dynamics that affect individuals and communities (Pink 2011; Sunderland et al. 2012). I have included a range of example songs and further readings at the end of this prompt that you can use to deepen your understanding of the processes and potential outcomes of this activity.

To complete this task, students will need to work in small groups or pairs to:

1. Establish a sense of shared comfort and connection with your songwriting group.
2. Identify a shared sensory-rich topic for storytelling and songwriting.
3. Undertake activities that "turn up," or activate and heighten, your senses as you explore a chosen topic.
4. Use collaborative songwriting practices to translate embodied sensory experience into songs.

Step 1: Establishing Connection and Comfort in Groups

Students first need to establish connection and comfort in their group in order to support the creative and collaborative process. Establishing connection and comfort is a key element of trauma-informed practice in any setting (Atkinson 2002; Sunderland et al. 2022). Connection and comfort can be facilitated in many ways and should adapt to cultural and other forms of shared and individual diversity: we do not all experience connection or comfort in the same way. It is important that students know all activities are *optional* and that they have power to adapt and make decisions for themselves.

I have been taught to establish connection and comfort in groups by First Nations teachers and elders in my communities who specialize in healing intergenerational trauma and through engaging with literature on trauma-informed practice in community arts and arts-health (Atkinson 2002; Sunderland et al. 2022). You can find some great practical resources for creating connection and comfort, such as the International Centre of Art for Social Change's principles for facilitating group dialogue (Goldbard n.d.). Examples of processes that I use to establish connection and comfort while adhering to First Nations cultural and trauma-informed protocols for meeting and creating connections include:

- Asking all group members to introduce themselves, where they are from, and their cultural heritage.
- Suggesting shared protocols for collaborating, such as respecting confidentiality, avoiding disruption, and speaking mindfully (see Goldbard n.d. for definitions of these protocols and other ideas), and asking participants if there are other protocols that they would like to add.
- Establishing a buddy system where participants have the option to pair with someone in order to debrief. I typically encourage group participants to choose their own buddies, but teachers can help with matching participants into buddy pairs if needed. Again, respecting individual choice and agency is important.
- Discussing go-to techniques that students can use to self-regulate strong emotions (e.g., deep breathing or taking a walk outside). It can be helpful to ask students if they want to share any self-regulating and calming techniques that they already find effective. Teachers may also want to model some new techniques with the group, such as a basic breathing meditation. The aim of discussing these techniques is to encourage everyone to practice agency in self-regulating as needed if they feel any level of unpleasant emotional activation because of the songwriting activities. We can never guarantee that shared spaces are going to be completely comfortable for all students, but we can encourage self-regulation and agency through promoting voice, choice, and access to grounding techniques (Sunderland et al. 2022).
- Reassuring students that being out of their comfort zone can be an incredible experience, but that they will choose how much they move into new things.
- Working with external advisors, such as community elders, counselors, or social workers, in order to identify who students can speak to if they feel overly conflicted or upset.

You may like to come up with your own processes in your small group that match your context. Remember, key aspects that support connection and comfort include adaptability, inclusion, choice, respect, and shared power.

Step 2: Identifying a Sensory-Rich Topic

In this step, students can identify a shared sensory-rich topic for storytelling for their group, "turn up" their senses, and ask themselves how it *feels* to experience the chosen place or event. In their small groups, students should choose a shared topic that each person has experienced directly. They can reflect on their diverse individual experiences of that place or event and share stories to discover if there are similarities or differences with others' experiences. This highlights the divergent and shared sensorial experiences of places and events, which can be incredible fodder for creative ethnographic research.

Examples of topics/questions to prompt storytelling for sensory ethnographic songwriting include:

- What does it feel like to be in a place you regularly visit, such as a cafeteria or public transport?
- What does it feel like to be in a local food market?
- What does it feel like to experience a first date?
- What does it feel like to experience a place that feels most like home?
- What does it feel like to experience a place that feels least like home?
- What does it feel like to participate in a major cultural holiday or event?
- What does it feel like to be in a place that is very different from where students live?
- What does it feel like to be a member of a particular geographical or cultural community?
- What is the potential social, cultural, and political significance of those feelings?

Trauma-Informed Tip: To maintain comfort and connection, remind students that they are not required to disclose personal stories or memories and that everything is a choice.

Step 3: Turning Up the Senses: Warm-Up Activity

Students now need to "turn up the senses" so that they can create songs that sensorially and meaningfully depict chosen places and events.

Class warmup activity: As a warmup for "turning up the senses," students can reflect on what it feels like to be where they are now, i.e., the classroom or online meeting room. Invite students to sit still or move around the room or neighborhood together in a mindful fashion while asking themselves what smells, tastes, textures, sounds, sights, and feelings are associated with being there? If doing this indoors, the activity can be quite brief, e.g., 3–5 minutes of noticing and then 15 minutes of sharing back experiences with the group. If doing guided walks outside, I recommend allowing approximately 15 minutes for walking and then 15 minutes for sharing back experiences with the group. Teachers may like to facilitate guided sensory walks in person, point out sensory experiences, and invite (do not require) students to do the same. After conducting that mindful embodied observation, invite students to share a brief story about what it felt like to be in that place. Encourage experimenting with rich ways to describe felt sensations and mindful embodied observations that use words, colors, sounds, metaphors, similes, and so on.

Examples of ways to creatively and mindfully describe individual and shared embodied sensorial experience are provided in songs previously generated using versions of this activity. I include lyrics and online links for two songs below and encourage you to read the lyrics and listen to the music and sound components in order to get a full sense of the storytelling that can emerge.

Spirit of Santo co-written by local music ensembles in Espiritu Santo, Vanuatu (Banban Bamboo Band et al. 2016). Listen and watch at: www.youtube.com/watch?v=XTV1HDwgyTI

Verse 1:
I come, I come from the Island, I come from the water I come from the village to sing
I come, I come from the mountain when the spirit of Santo, is calling for me

Chorus:
Feel the spirit of freedom, feel the spirit of love
Cool water on warm skin rain on the palm leaves smiling hello
Feel the spirit of laughter feel the spirit of love
The spirit of Santo, the spirit of home

Verse 2:
Blue, on the champagne white beaches, breathing the air of the forest that makes me feel free
Sweet like the smell of vanilla, this green island home is the place where my soul longs to be

Bridge:
Welcome is what we say
Welcome here we say
Welcome is our way
Welcome here today

Chorus: [Rap]
The spirit of freedom the spirit of love the spirit of love
Cool water on warm skin rain on the palm leaves
Smiling hello
The spirit of laughter the spirit of love
The Spirit of Santo the spirit of home

New Skies Above co-written by refugee musicians in Turku, Finland (Albano et al. 2018). Listen at: https://research-repository.griffith.edu.au/handle/10072/390282

Verse 1 – spoken word
Life, life, life, it's what you make it
Everyday everyday everyday it's a struggle
Everyday everyday is a new day

OK December 4, I will never forget
My sister and I outside of a police station
All my life I hated the police
But here I am praying to see a police car
It's 4 degrees out here, cold as hell
I feel pain in my legs, my hands about to freeze
I can barely move oh I wish I could have a coffee now
Bad memories come to my head
Will somebody come to rescue us?
I don't know
Can you relate?
A big word but it feels like an empty space
It's like a theatre when everyone is anxious to clap

Chorus 1 – sung
Clap hands
Suddenly this is my everyday
Clap hands
Go to a meeting and beg to stay
She's mad
no answer there when I call her phone
So sad
tired of fighting I buy a rose
[spoken word]
That's it, I'm going to take the first bus and disappear outta here
Oh no, the bus doesn't work
It's like the universe is saying to me...
Stay

Verse 2 – spoken word
Hey yah wah the best day of my life
Me and my sister got the best news today
I'm breathing a different air now
I meet my father
We've been living separate lives
He gives me a hug
I watch my baby boy
This is the moment I always dreamed of when I was a boy
Hey yah wah the whole night is a festival
And now I have a reason to smile
Bridge – sung
It's the smell of the coffee
It's your cinnamon smile
It's a feeling of freedom
I haven't felt for a while
A long walk to the ocean

To make new stars above
My baby Suma is rising
Our generation of love

Chorus 2 – sung
Clap hands
I can't wait for the sun again
Clap hands
The smell of the coffee and cinnamon
Clap hands the noon is dark and the night is light
Clap hands
I walked all the way to see this sight
Clap hands
Here is the place we call our home
Clap hands
[spoken] Now, we have a reason to smile

Step 4: Sensing and Storying Group Song Topics

Next, students can work in groups to mindfully and sensorially experience and story their topic. Students may want to visit a real place in order to do this or simply remember a place or event *with their whole bodies.*

Students should work in small groups to:

- Reflect on what it feels like to experience the place or event that they have chosen as their songwriting topic. Sit still or move around in a mindful way and ask yourself what are the smells, tastes, textures, sounds, sights, feelings and embodied memories and stories associated with that place or event?
- Students can use optional non-verbal capturing of sensorial experiences, e.g., poetry, photography, sketching, soundmaking, etc., but remember to *stay tuned into* your body and senses if doing this.
- Students invite (do not force) members of their group to share a short story and creative artifacts (optional) about what it felt like to be in their place or event. Students should try to use rich ways to describe felt experience and observations. **NB Those stories form the basis of collective song writing. Students should therefore capture the group's shared stories** by notetaking on a whiteboard (where possible) or by audio recording. Notetaking can be done by a facilitator/teacher if the class is small or working as a single songwriting group, or student groups can nominate one person to take notes and facilitate sharing.

Trauma-Informed Tip: As part of trauma-informed practice, students and teachers can adopt nervous-system-regulating activities (such as deep breathing and walking outside) if anyone in the group remembers a place or event that brings up unpleasant sensations. If strong emotions emerge during storytelling, students and teachers can invite the group to continue breathing and wait for the storyteller to indicate how they would like to proceed. If group members are experiencing strong unpleasant memories, students and teachers may need to share a "release" activity (such as stretching or jumping to music) at the end of this session to release tension from the body. They can also promote group connection and comfort by encouraging group members to connect with a buddy for a debrief and offering information on people who can be contacted if any unusual upset emerges.

Step 5: Convert Sensory Stories into Songs

The final step requires students to co-create a group song using the group's sensory stories. This is intended to combine students' individual stories in order to reflect whatever diversity or similarities are shared in storytelling about experiences of the chosen place or event.

- If there are musicians present, consider ways to capture and evoke the sensorial experiences shared in musical accompaniment, melody, and sound. Start by tuning into the embodied sensorial memory again and singing or playing sounds that emerge organically from the memory.
- If there are no musicians present, students can verbally sound out the experience of the event or place, e.g., with spoken word, electronic beats and instruments on devices, oohs, ahhs, clapping, tapping, and singing. Students should improvise and "jam" together until something starts to gel into a melody or sound bed that can carry stories in accompanying lyrics.
- Step down option: If creating music for a song is far out of the comfort zone of some students, they can consider writing a multiverse poem instead.
- Students should harvest and combine the most memorable experiences, words, and phrases from the group's recorded stories in order to form verses and choruses for the song or poem.

Songwriter's Tip: A basic popular music song structure that I often use consists of verses and choruses. You will hear this structure used in the song referenced earlier *Spirit of Santo* (Banban Bamboo Band et al. 2016). The same structure can be applied to poems. For example:

1. Verse 1 grabs the listener's attention, introduces the topic, and sets the scene for the story.
2. Chorus provides a memorable lift to the song and emphasizes key messages or themes.
3. Verse 2 deepens the topic and gives more information.
4. Chorus typically repeated verbatim from the first iteration.
5. Verse 3 or bridge may introduce contending information and provide summary lessons/advice. Often uses different musical accompaniment.
6. Chorus typically repeated verbatim from the first iteration.
7. Chorus typically repeated verbatim from the first iteration.

An important aim in all aspects of sensory ethnographic songwriting is to encourage audiences to *listen with their whole bodies*, i.e., *invoking* ***their*** senses. Students should consider how their song can create a memorable multisensorial listening experience that conveys a thick and rich account of what it felt like to be in the place or event.

Trauma-Informed Tip: Students should adapt the songwriting and lyrics to manage potential triggers and needs. For example, students can support each other to shift the assignment and resulting song in ways that are workable for them based on how they are feeling each day.

How to Extend

Students often benefit from sharing their songs, in whatever form they have ready, with others in class. This can be in the form of a song circle, in which groups present or perform their song in live or basic recorded form (e.g., on their own devices).

Audience members (other students) can be encouraged to offer feedback to each group on what stood out the most in the song and how it made them feel.

The song circle can be used for peer and teacher grading of song outputs. It can also be a useful precursor to students recording their songs in basic form for submission and grading, if that is desired.

Examples

Here are some examples of songs written using this group songwriting prompt:

- *Spirit of Santo* song co-written by local musical ensembles on Espiritu Santo Island, Vanuatu, with two researchers (Sunderland and Graham) as facilitators: www.youtube.com/watch?v=XTV1HDwgyTI.
- *Motalava Come to Me* song co-written by residents on Motalava Island, Vanuatu, with two researchers (Sunderland and Graham) as facilitators: https://sway.office.com/seCbGCDy3mJ5uIcJ?ref=Link&loc=play.
- *New Skies Above* cowritten by refugee musicians in Turku, Finland, with three researchers (Sunderland, Jacobsen, and Harrison) as facilitators: https://research-repository.griffith.edu.au/handle/10072/390282.

What to Read

These stimulus readings provide scope and background to sensory ethnographic and creative research approaches that inform the prompt.

Harrison, Klisala, Jacobsen, Kristina, and Sunderland, Naomi. 2019. "New Skies Above: Sense-bound and Place-Based Songwriting as a Trauma Response for Asylum Seekers and Refugees." *Journal of Applied Arts & Health* 10, no. 2 (July): 147–167. https://doi.org/10.1386/jaah.10.2.147_1

Goldbard, Arlene. n.d. "Holding Space: Some Principles of Facilitating Group Dialogue." *International Centre of Art for Social Change*. Accessed September 13, 2023. https://icasc.ca/resource/holding-space-some-principles-of-facilitating-group-dialogue/

Jacobsen, Kristina. 2017. "Songwriting as Ethnographic Practice, or How Stories Humanize." In *Arts-Based Research in Education: Foundations for Practice*, edited by Melisa Cahnmann-Taylor and Richard Siegesmund, 115–127. Routledge.

Pink, Sarah. "Situating Sensory Ethnography: From Academia to Intervention." In *Doing Sensory Ethnography*, 7–23. SAGE. https://oss.adm.ntu.edu.sg/19s1-dv3003-tut-g01/wp-content/uploads/sites/3599/2019/08/1-Pink_doing-sensory-ethnography.pdf.

Sunderland, Naomi, Bristed, Helen, Gudes, Ori, Boddy, Jennifer, and Da Silva, M. 2012. "What Does It Feel Like to Live Here? Exploring Sensory Ethnography as a Collaborative Methodology for Investigating Social Determinants of Health in Place." *Health & Place* 18, no. 5 (September): 1056–1067. https://doi.org/10.1016/j.healthplace.2012.05.007

Sunderland, Naomi, Stevens, Fiona, Knudsen, Kate, Cooper, Rae, and Wobcke, Marianne. 2022. "Trauma Aware and Anti-Oppressive Arts-Health and Community Arts Practice: Guiding Principles for Facilitating Healing, Health and Wellbeing." *Trauma, Violence, & Abuse* 24, no. 4 (October): 2429–2447. https://doi.org/10.1177/15248380221097442

References

Albano, Xavier, Djamiww, Naomi Sunderland, Vanessa Garrido, Fouad Ibrahim, Rosa Rantanen, Ahmed Zaidan, Nora Al Zubaidi, Raad Obaid Al Zubaidi, Kristina Jacobsen, and Klisala Harrison. 2018. "New skies above." University of Helsinki Open Repository. https://helda.helsinki.fi/items/8e21bb0f-88e7-44f9-a835-2115858b990b

Atkinson, Judy. 2002. *Trauma Trails, Recreating Song Lines: The Transgenerational Effects of Trauma in Indigenous Australia*. Melbourne: Spinifex Press.

Banban Bamboo Band, Water Music Ladies, NCYC youth band, Phil Graham, and Naomi Sunderland. 2016. *Spirit of Santo*. YouTube video, 3:42. Accessed September 14, 2023. www.youtube.com/watch?v=XTV1HDwgyTI

Chenhall, Richard, Tamara Kohn, and Carolyn S. Stevens. 2020. *Sounding Out Japan: A Sensory Ethnographic Tour*. London: Routledge.

Ginsburg, Faye. 2018. "Decolonizing Documentary On-Screen and Off: Sensory Ethnography and the Aesthetics of Accountability." *Film Quarterly* 72, no. 1 (September): 39–49. https://doi.org/10.1525/fq.2018.72.1.39

Goldbard, Arlene. n.d. "Holding Space: Some Principles of Facilitating Group Dialogue." International Centre of Art for Social Change. Accessed September 13, 2023. https://icasc.ca/resource/holding-space-some-principles-of-facilitating-group-dialogue/

Harrison, Klisala, Kristina Jacobsen, and Naomi Sunderland. 2019. "New Skies Above: Sense-Bound and Place-Based Songwriting as a Trauma Response for Asylum Seekers and Refugees." *Journal of Applied Arts & Health* 10, no.2 (July): 147–167. https://doi.org/10.1386/jaah.10.2.147_1

Jacobsen, Kristina. 2017. "'Songwriting as Ethnographic Practice' or How Stories Humanize.'" In *Arts-Based Research in Education: Foundations for Practice,* edited by Melisa Cahnmann-Taylor and Richard Siegesmund, 115–127. New York: Routledge.

Matthews, Nicole, and Naomi Sunderland. 2017. *Digital Storytelling in Health and Social Policy: Listening to Marginalised Voices*. London: Taylor & Francis.

Pattison, Pat. 2012. *Songwriting Without Boundaries: Lyric Writing Exercises for Finding Your Voice.* Des Moines, Iowa: Penguin.

Pink, Sarah. "Situating Sensory Ethnography: From Academia to Intervention." In *Doing Sensory Ethnography*, 3–24. Los Angeles, London, New Delhi, Singapore, Washington DC: SAGE. https://oss.adm.ntu.edu.sg/19s1-dv3003-tut-g01/wp-content/uploads/sites/3599/2019/08/1-Pink_doing-sensory-ethnography.pdf.

Sunderland, Naomi, Helen Bristed, Ori Gudes, Jennifer Boddy, and M. Da Silva. 2012. "What Does It Feel Like to Live Here? Exploring Sensory Ethnography as a Collaborative Methodology for Investigating Social Determinants of Health in Place." *Health & Place* 18, no. 5 (September): 1056–1067. https://doi.org/10.1016/j.healthplace.2012.05.007

Sunderland, Naomi, Fiona Stevens, Kate Knudsen, Rae Cooper, and Marianne Wobcke. 2023. "Trauma Aware and Anti-Oppressive Arts-Health and Community Arts Practice: Guiding Principles for Facilitating Healing, Health and Wellbeing." *Trauma, Violence, & Abuse* 24, no. 4 (October): 2429–2447. https://doi.org/10.1177/15248380221097442

War and Witness*

Ather Zia

Creative Ethnographic Toolkit: Poetry, observation.

*Trigger Warning: This exercise includes discussing and reflecting upon situations of war, violence, and abuse.

How does one witness sites and locations objectively, especially if the situations have been observed closely and are infused with violence, armed or otherwise? This task serves an ethnographer in two ways: honing the art of "poem making" and generating theoretical moorings through deeper engagement with space and surroundings of one's field of research.

As a born and bred Kashmiri, I have closely witnessed the war in Kashmir, a Himalayan region between India and Pakistan. Later in life, from 2008 till 2014, I did my doctoral fieldwork in the region. Witnessing the "**Line of Control**" (LOC), or the ceasefire line that exists as a de facto border between Indian- and Pakistani-administered Kashmir ended up as a formal academic essay in the *American Quarterly* (Zia 2019a) and a contest-winning poem titled "i.will.cross" in *Sapiens* (Zia 2020b). The academic essay and the poem pivot around the LOC and the complications it produces in Kashmiri people's lives, their responses and the politics that governs them. The rendering of this witnessing for two different audiences and genres is never deliberate on my part but a natural compulsion, one that serves the goals of a public facing anthropology and ethnographic poetry.

The poem "i.will.cross" (Zia 2020b) is located at the site of LOC. One of the world's most densely militarized frontiers, the LOC is so heavily surveilled that it is even visible from space. This poem embodies the viewpoint of a **Kashmiri militant** who intends to cross this line. A militant is a non-state Kashmiri Muslim combatant who has taken up arms against the Indian government. As a lover of *azadi*, or freedom and independence, the militant as a speaker in the poem pursues what Kashmiris have been clamoring to do for over the last 72 years: to unify the region and freely travel between divided Kashmir. The people living around the LOC suffer because families and communities have been bifurcated since 1947. Since 1989, when the resistance movement against Indian rule began, the situation has

DOI: 10.4324/9781003365228-35

been grave. More than 100,000 people, both combatants and noncombatants, have been killed in Indian counterinsurgency operations. Crossing the LOC is illegal and dangerous, and many Kashmiri militants have been killed while trying to do so.

I chose to render the poem in the voice of a Kashmiri militant for several reasons. The most important is that a militant's voice is largely missing from the narrative of Kashmiri struggle, even though their armed struggle is central. The militant is only seen through "acts" of armed resistance and never seems to have a real say even about their own motivations. This poem reveals the militant, not just as a combatant, but also as a lover and protector of his homeland. The act of crossing the LOC has been criminalized by India, who call crossing an "act of terrorism." Thus, the militant's insistence that "i.will.cross" becomes an iconic call. The refrain of crossing in the voice of a militant is to evoke the legitimacy, longing and love connected to the desire to have freedom from India.

As a Kashmiri anthropologist and an ethnographer-poet, I see my role as "akin to holding a wound—a wound that is simultaneously in the body of the other" (Zia 2020b) and reflected in my own body. A poem can reach into the spaces where bearing witness pours beyond the borders of "objective" observation, where reason seeks to escape measured words and emotional constraints. Thus, an ethnographic poem becomes a moment of participant observation, where there is an empathy, an experiencing, and a witnessing; a feeling and conveying of another's life. Translating the field is a dual labor—providing witness as a professional and as a dreamer, who is uninhibited by formalities of the discipline of anthropology or society in general. Thus, I insist that as an ethnographer-poet, what you write about becomes a double responsibility, as an ethnographer and ethnographer-poet.

"i. will. cross."

my love,
i am at the line of control—
inching—
tonight, the moon is graying
the darkness—perfecting itself
or so i hope—
the breeze is weakening
like the old tyrant's hand
i. will. cross.

my love
senses are crammed—
bright, blinding searchlights, again—
i might as well be visible from space
barbed wires, drones, electric fences,
empty bottles of liquor. i taste blood.

guns, lights, smoke.
coughing, cursing, soldiers, dogs—
and
i see the dark beauty of our moonlit meadows
your perfume on the other side is a paradise
i. will. cross.

my love
waiting to hold you has been such a joy
how many lines will i have to cross?
or infiltrate, as they say?
i mind no more—
i. will. cross.

my love,
i fear this year's snow will again be sparse
our thirst will only grow, i should not wait.
i am a lover who is labeled a terrorist anyway
i. will. cross.

my love,
i will always be in love
with your ***wadiyan***[1]
your wildflowers. your wilderness.
and winds that say my name.
and your waterfalls.
wading in growing puddles of blood
i. will. cross.
i. will. cross.
i. will. cross.

Prompt

This exercise urges you to think about countries engaged in war as well as day-to-day struggles in which battlefields may be both literal and figurative. Thus, the idea of war is not limited only to a violent military battle but can include situations of daily strife, resistance, and conflict in culture. You can base this prompt on any formal fieldwork that you have done in or outside your home country, or, if you have not conducted any formal fieldwork, this exercise can be done based on the informal observation of relevant situations around you. To do so, you might conduct focused observation of public events, houselessness, or drug abuse in your vicinity. Wherever you are doing your observing, be sure to ask permission to take photos or record anyone's voice, and be sure to keep your own and other's in mind while doing so.

This exercise is based on three steps I have used in my own poetic and ethnographic work. Step 1: meditate and reflect. Step 2: read a poem. Step 3: write a poem. Type, length and rhyme scheme of the poem is up to you.

Step 1: Meditate and Reflect (Conjuring the War)

- Find a quiet space, settle, and allow yourself to meditate and reflect on your field of research or a relevant place such as your home, neighborhood, city, or a special community of practice.
- What kind of conflict or violence permeates this place? Is it domestic or political, is it connected to social marginalization, racial tensions, houselessness, armed violence, state terrorism, human rights violations, war, surveillance, militarization, or something else?
- Breathe deeply, then ask yourself: why did your mind and heart go to this place?
- Note everything that is happening around this situation that exists. How do you feel about it?
- Take some time to recall words that resonate with the memory of this place. Do any people, things, or other artifacts come to mind vis a vis this situation and why?

Step 2: Read a Poem

Read the "i.will.cross" poem (Zia 2020b) or listen to it as a recitation by the author in the journal, or also as a song with one of the editors (Zia and Jacobsen, 2022); this collaboration is discussed in the Kashmiri literary magazine *Inverse Journal* (Amjad 2022).

Step 3: Write a Poem

- Write a poem about the location/place/situation you conjured. What do you see? Recreate the feeling, sights, scene; capture the smellscape and soundscape. Show us everything around you; describe thickly. You are free to channel a voice you deem fit to render the poem.
- Reveal why your mind went to thinking about this place; how is it important to your work, if at all? It is OK if you do not have a ready answer for this!
- Do you recall any words or phrases connected to your chosen location? If so, write them down! These can be words drawn from colloquial use or any other words of interest.

Your poem should hold the reader's hand and take them on a tour of your emotional topography or landscape of this place. While recollection is mechanical, the poem should be dreamy or focused on the fantastical elements of the experience you are describing. Having a title is optional. Your poem should be laden with thick and lyrical description, self-reflexivity, and a nuanced understanding of what you see.

How to Extend

For students who are more familiar with social theory, you might ask yourselves: Does your rendition of the place feel rooted in a certain social theory or framework of knowledge?[2] Think about the connections to anthropological canon, if any, and weave that into your poem.

What to Listen To/Read

You are encouraged to read the poetry from ethnographer poet Renato Rosaldo's (2013) book *The Day of Shelly's Death* (this volume, Chapter 12) where he describes "antropoesía" as bridging the cultural and social scientific fields of poetry and anthropology. You are also encouraged to read the poet, Mary Oliver (1994), who is known for her sharp observation of the natural world. In a favorite poem by her titled "Wild Geese" she lifts to lofty imagination the simple routine of a flock returning to their nest creating an achingly beautiful hope inspiring one to love the world we live in and be compassionate to oneself. Both poets offer examples of the witness and rendition of everyday life that poetry provides to announce "your place in the family of things" (Oliver 2004: 15). Additionally, for more of my opinion about writing poetry as an anthropologist, you can read/listen to my interviews in the links given in the bibliography section.

Notes

1 Wadiyan—valleys/meadows in the Kashmiri language.
2 This can be any framework you've encountered in your readings and studies that you might find useful. For example, semiotic theory, practice theory, Marxist theory or arts-based research methodologies (among many, many others) are all "theories" you might apply to this exercise.

References

Majid, Amjad. 2022. "Music Feature: A Song by Kristina Jacobsen, inspired by Ather Zia's Poem 'i. will. cross.' + Exclusive Interview with the Two Professors." *Inverse Journal* 3/27. www.inversejournal.com/2022/03/27/exclusive-musical-feature-a-song-by-kristina-jacobsen-inspired-by-ather-zias-poem-i-will-cross-includes-extended-interview-with-the-professors-and-relevant-links/

Oliver, Mary. 1994. *A Poetry Handbook.* Boston: Mariner Press.

Oliver, Mary. 2004. *Wild Geese.* Tarset [England]: Bloodaxe Books.

Rosaldo, Renato. 2013. *The Day of Shelly's Death: The Poetry and Ethnography of Grief.* Durham: Duke University Press Books.

Zia, Ather. 2019a. LoC: The Line "out" of Control in the Region of Kashmir. *American Quarterly* 71 (4): 1037–1043.

Zia, Ather. 2019b. "Ethnographic Poetry: A Conversation with Ather Zia." https://allegralaboratory.net/ethnographic-poetry-a-conversation-with-ather-zia/

Zia, Ather. 2020a. "What does Anthropology Sounds Like: Poetry?" *Anthropod.* https://culanth.org/fieldsights/what-does-anthropology-sound-like-poetry
Zia, Ather. 2020b. "i.will.cross." Sapiens www.sapiens.org/culture/line-of-control/
Zia, Ather and Kristina Jacobsen. 2022. "I.will.cross." https://on.soundcloud.com/QBuwV

Part III

After the Field

Readers and contributors have explored many different genres of artmaking in this book. Hopefully, it has been an enriching, scholarly, generative, and fun process! But how do creative ethnographers translate their work back into social science research and quantifiable data? Conversely, how can you translate social scientific data for broader, non-academic audiences? In other words, what happens *after the field*, in the liminal, betwixt-and-between moments when you are neither in the field nor fully home? The prompts in the final portion of this book (Section III) encourage us to dig into these questions.

Chapter 10 invites us to explore the different ways we code, or list and quantify, our research data in public fora. Vidali's prompt invites creative ethnographers to explore issues of social or political import via pencil and paper, creating mural sketches to communicate our findings with broader audiences. Reid's prompt invites us to code research interviews at a very granular level, walking us through how to translate data into collaborative ethnographic songs intended for a listening public. Pirie invites us to consider the affordances of mask-making and composite characters.

The prompts in Chapter 11 approach these questions from a variety of unique and creative angles. Hammond encourages us to think about the ways in which data are generated through sound-recording processes and how we can most effectively communicate the experience of being in a particular place at a particular moment in time through a sound recording. Demetriou offers us ways to sift through our fieldnotes to dig into the deeper questions of what our research is really about and what we want to say about it, offering a series of short, guided writing exercises to help us to "write to discover what we truly want to say." Phillips and Vidali offer us an expansive definition of the *archive* in order to explore it ethnographically, asking creative ethnographers to craft ethnographic exhibits that communicate their research findings to a broader public. Moretti has us exploring and pondering the *afterlife* of our fieldwork and the unanswered questions with which we often leave the field. Beginning with a recurring phrase that has stayed with us from the field, creative ethnographers are invited to explore **poetic prose** as a mode in which we can texture, layer, and communicate the complexities of our fieldwork experience.

DOI: 10.4324/9781003365228-36

Chapter 12 offers prompts from two anthropologists who have been deeply influential for ethnographers and aspiring scholartists over recent decades. Both prompts offer insights into creative representations of ethnographic fieldwork that capture both thinking and feeling in social science inquiry. These prompts are also uniquely intimate and vulnerable, acting as models of how we hope that you, as creative ethnographers, will approach your own scholartistry in future. Behar offers three short writing prompts that encourage creative ethnographers, in various ways, to develop and deepen empathetic listening and storytelling skills, an approach Behar describes as "ethnography that breaks your heart" (Behar 1996; 2022). Inspired by his own poetic inquiry approach in *The Day of Shelly's Death* (2014), Rosaldo invites us to explore **antropoesía**, or verses informed by ethnographic sensibility, by taking a moment in our lives or fieldwork and, beginning with ourselves, spinning it out from different angles. In this way, creative ethnographers can write from both the center and the margins of an experience in first, second, and third person, playing with differing points of view and positionalities in the process.

The editors of this book contribute narratives of their own creative ethnographic experiences in Chapter 13. Jacobsen explores how a gap year in her academic ethnomusicology studies helped her to explore singer–songwriter opportunities more fully and arrive at a place where she could give herself permission to both make artful scholarship and scholarly art. Cahnmann-Taylor remembers her first poetry experiences with scholartist mentors and considers a future where the study of the arts and social sciences will be more fully integrated. This closing chapter is an opportunity to reflect on past journeys and imagine our ways into creative ethnographic futures that include arts-based research, research-based art, and creative practices for mentorship and instruction.

10 Creative Approaches to Social Science Data

Representing Ethnographic Insights through Mural Sketches

Debra Vidali

Creative Ethnographic Toolkit: Drawing, mural composition, form-meaning relations, non-linear representation, public communication.

Public murals use large wall areas to celebrate community, express viewpoints, document events, and portray the human condition. Most public murals are dynamic and multivocal. They invite the eye to move across regions of the wall to discover different meanings. Words and images in murals often resonate with words or images that are already circulating in popular culture, community conversations, or ongoing public debates.

Prompt

Part 1

Think of a current issue or event that interests you. Or, if you are already doing ethnographic research, think of a theme that is represented in your research. If you could create a dynamic mural to express what is going on, what would you portray? Develop a rough sketch of your mural. You can hand draw your mural on an 8.5" x 11" sheet of paper or you can create it digitally. Think of using a combination of words and images. Think of using different areas of your page to depict different events, sub-themes, or viewpoints. Don't worry if you have messy areas of composition or bad hand drawing skills. You can even use stick figures. This is not about producing artistic work or a finished product. It is about experimenting with the power of visual communication to represent ethnographic insights. For inspiration and ideas, see Figures 10.1–10.5 and the readings at the end.

Part 2

Write an 800 word reflection on these questions:

- What is the title of your proposed mural?

DOI: 10.4324/9781003365228-38

- Where would it be located? Why?
- What themes and insights does your mural convey?
- How do the words and images in your mural resonate with words or images that are already circulating in popular culture, community conversations, national debates, or international arenas?
- If your mural is based on your ethnographic research, explain the connections.
- Are different voices and viewpoints represented? Or one common perspective?
- Are different things going on in different areas of your mural? What? Why?
- What do you want people to feel, do, or learn after seeing your mural?
- Explain some of your design choices. For example: "the face is in the center, larger than any other item, because that is the focal point," or "the writing is in big blocks to indicate shouting or an urgent situation," or "I use the color green for the background to indicate hope and new growth."

How to Extend

Extend your written reflection with a more detailed response to the last question. For example, how do shapes, proportions, and placements inform the meanings in your mural? Is there balance, imbalance, symmetry, or distortion? Add a 400-word extension to your written reflection explaining how your mural captures ethnographic insights differently and perhaps even more powerfully than conventional written ethnography.

Why This Assignment

Visual inquiry and documentation have long histories in anthropology (Grimshaw 2001; Pink 2021). Increasingly, anthropologists are deploying visual inquiry practices in fieldnote production and multimodal projects (Atalay et al. 2019; Bonanno 2019; Taussig 2011). This prompt asks you to think of murals as collages of ethnographic data and multivocal argumentation. Students experiment with (a) presentation of voices, experiences, and events in non-linear formats and (b) visual depictions of ethnographic insights. You can sharpen their anthropological thinking and analysis as they reflect on the human condition and ongoing events as fields of dynamic relations. For example, one can represent the experience of cancer diagnosis and treatment as shaped by the pharmaceutical industry, genetics, bureaucracy, and environmental toxins (see Figure 10.1, from Hamdy et al. 2017). Even a single person's experience can be represented as a field of voices, influences, and contrasts, as shown in Phoebe Einzig-Roth's drawing for her interviewee "Minnie," a COVID-19 long hauler (Figure 10.2). A hand-drawn map of a continent or community depicts a field of relations. Jemila Mussa's mural sketch, for example, shows an African woman's tears forming the River Nile as diamonds and other resources are squeezed from the continent (Figure 10.3). Students can design murals that are mirrors back to the community. For example Olivia Bautista's *Nuestra Ciudad: Los Angeles* (Figure 10.4) shows how street

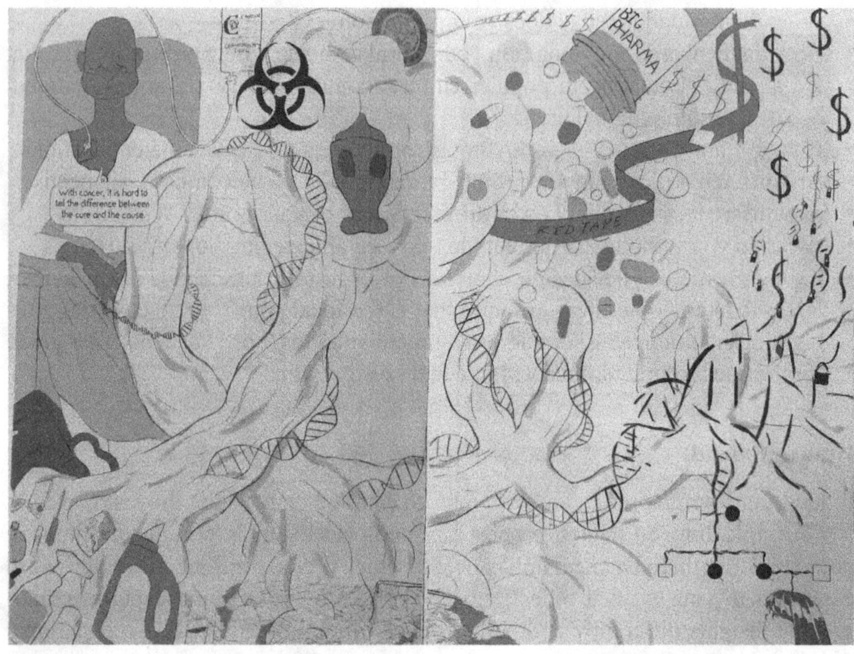

Figure 10.1 Splash page from Hamdy et al. (2017, pp. 130–31). Used with permission of the University of Toronto Press.

signage, tattoo art, and pathways from farm labor to education define Chicano experiences in Los Angeles.

With this assignment, students at any level of artistic ability can creatively play with drawing techniques. Students can also learn about and be inspired by related genres of visual communication such as graffiti, graphic novels, and comics. The fundamental idea that form can carry meaning is a valuable lesson. It can be applied in mural creation, as well as future creative ethnographic projects. You can make choices about the sizes of images and their placement within murals and use these choices to communicate specific ethnographic insights and analyses. For example, a human hand that is bigger than an entire continent conveys the immense power of external forces in Mussa's version of Africa (Figure 10.3). A vertical sequence of images can be used to convey hierarchy or status, as in Mikail Albritton's placement of images for jobs on the mural's right side (Figure 10.5).

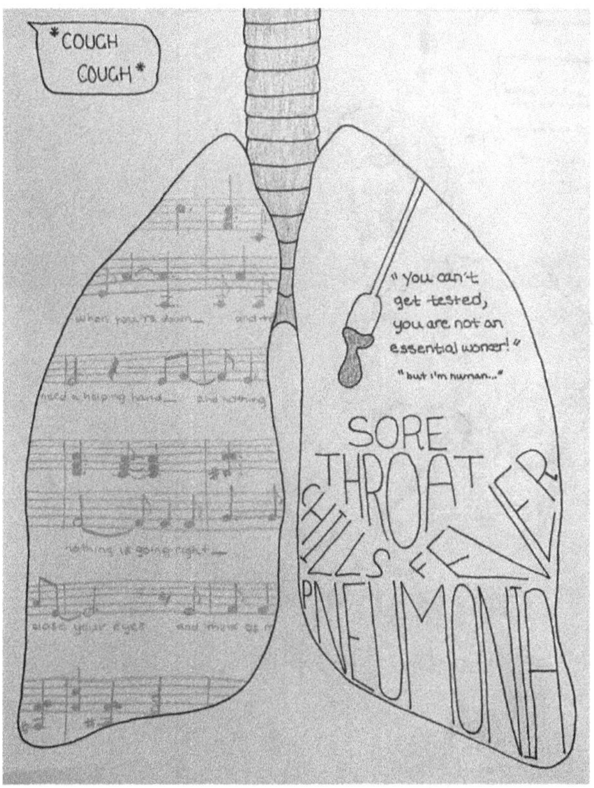

Figure 10.2 Minnie by Phoebe Einzig-Roth (2020). Used with permission of the artist–ethnographer.

What to Read and How to Extend

For inspiration, consider Figures 10.1–10.5 and also look at the splash pages and murals on pages 84, 134–135, 235, and 239 of the book *Lissa: A Story About Medical Promise, Friendship and Revolution* by Hamdy et al. (2017). Also look at Magaña 2022, the special online issue Atalay et al. 2019 and the website *Graphic Medicine*. For further reading on drawing techniques, graphic novels, graffiti art, and visual lexicons, see Causey (2016) and McCloud (1994). In addition, students may want to learn more about style writing, graffiti art, and public murals through

Figure 10.3 *Unheard Voices* by Jemila Mussa (2020). Used with permission of the artist–ethnographer.

artists on Instagram, such as Kevin Bongang (@bongangart), H. J. Parsons (@h_j_parsons), and Lisa Quine (@lisa_quine).

NOTE: Figures 10.2–10.5 were produced in Vidali's "Experimental Ethnography" course at Emory University during Fall 2020.

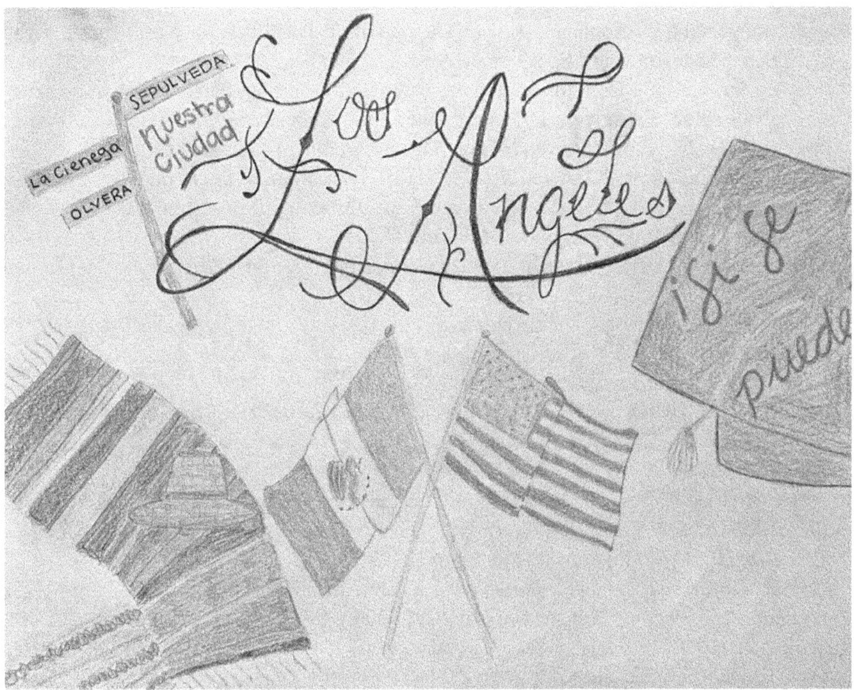

Figure 10.4 *Nuestra Ciudad: Los Angeles* by Olivia Bautista (2020). Used with permission of the artist–ethnographer.

Figure 10.5 *The Economy of Progress* by Mikail Albritton (2020). Used with permission of the artist–ethnographer.

References

Atalay, Sonya, Letizia Bonanno, Sally Campbell Pirie [as Galman], Sarah Jacqz, Ryan Rybka, Jen Shannon, Cary Speck, John Swogger, and Erica Wolencheck. 2019. "Ethno/Graphic Storytelling: Communicating Research and Exploring Pedagogical Approaches through Graphic Narratives, Drawings, and Zines." *American Anthropologist* online. Accessed Jan 25. www.americananthropologist.org/ethnographic-storytelling

Bonanno, Letizia. 2019. "Drawing as a Mode of Translation." *American Anthropologist* online. Accessed Jan 25, 2023. www.americananthropologist.org/ethnographic-storytelling/bonanno-drawing-as-a-mode-of-translation

Causey, Andrew. 2016. *Drawn to See: Drawing as an Ethnographic Method.* Toronto: University of Toronto Press.

Graphic Medicine. www.graphicmedicine.org

Grimshaw, Anna. 2001. *The Ethnographer's Eye: Ways of Seeing in Anthropology.* Cambridge: Cambridge University Press.

Hamdy, Sherine, Coleman Nye, Sarula Bao, Caroline Brewer, and Marc Parenteau. 2017. *Lissa: A Story about Medial Promise, Friendship, and Revolution.* Toronto: University of Toronto Press.

Magaña, Maurice Rafael. 2022. "Multimodal Archives of Transborder Belonging: Murals, Social Media, and Racialized Geographies in Los Angeles." *American Anthropologist* 124: 703–20. https://doi.org/10.1111/aman.13772

McCloud, Scott. 1994. *Understanding Comics.* New York: Harper Collins.

Pink, Sarah. 2021. *Doing Visual Ethnography.* London: SAGE.

Taussig, Michael. 2011. *I Swear I Saw This: Drawings in Fieldwork Notebooks, Namely My Own.* Chicago: University of Chicago Press.

Using a Three-Step Coding Process to Co-Compose Song Lyrics from Qualitative Interviews

A Lesson for Intermediate-Level Researchers

Kael Reid

Creative Ethnographic Toolkit: Songwriting, coding, interviewing.

Creative approaches to analyzing qualitative interview data can provide compelling topics, stories, and lyrics for songs. This prompt teaches you how to analyze qualitative interviews and co-compose songs with a research participant, using a three-step process that involves macro, narrative, and **verbatim coding** (Figure 10.6).

The three-step coding process is part of an arts-based research method developed by the author called collaborative ethnographic songwriting, which allows researchers to collaborate directly with research participants to narrate an aspect of their lived experience in song. This exercise is about pinpointing an experience (or collection of experiences), expanding on that experience in lyric, and then layering that experience with music. Collaborative ethnographic songwriting is an embodied creative experience: it involves connecting with people in story and song and feeling the resonance of a research participant's story inside us through the collaborative process of helping them translate their experience into music. As researchers, composing lyrics and music with a participant can allow us to feel the resonance of their lived experiences inside us. This prompt guides student researchers through this shared process of creation and is geared towards those who have some experience with conducting semi-structured, qualitative interviews and writing songs or poetry.

Prompt

Develop a set of 8–10 interview questions on a topic you are interested in exploring. Conduct your interview with someone who is willing to be a research participant in your study, collaborate with you on composing a song, and has a shared interest in this topic. Obtain your participant's **informed consent** at the beginning of the interview. You may wish to audio record them stating that they consent to participating. With their permission, audio record the interview. Then, transcribe the interview. With your participant, read over the transcript in its entirety. Ask your participant if there is anything they would like to change, add to, or delete from in the transcript. Make those changes. This is an important ethical step in ensuring

DOI: 10.4324/9781003365228-39

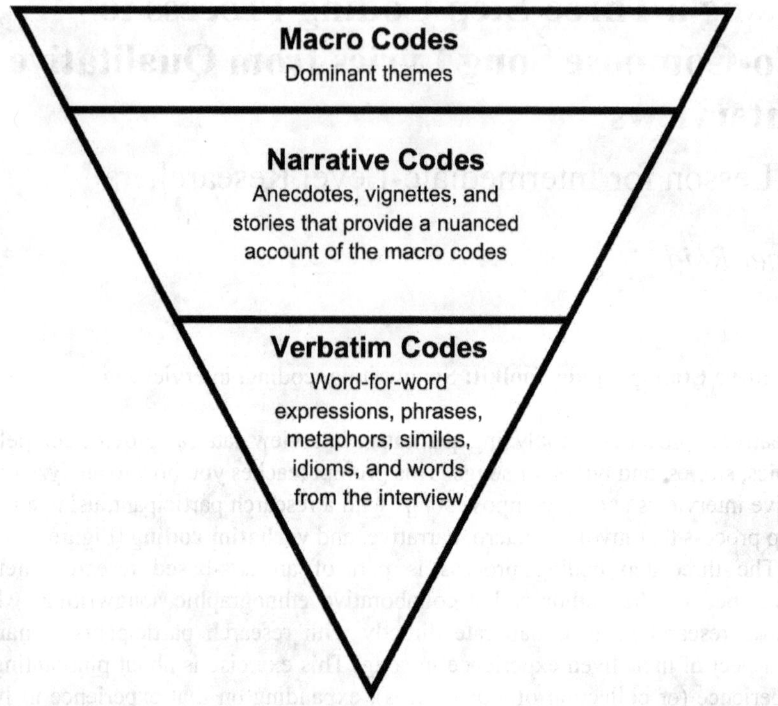

Figure 10.6 The three-step coding process.

your participant has control over what they spoke about in the interview, and ultimately, the song you will compose with them.

Researchers define coding in different ways. For the purposes of this chapter, I define the "coding" of qualitative data as a method for extracting, labeling, and grouping data into themes to understand the relationships between them and their significance related to the research topic.

To understand the process of three-step coding, let's work with an example that draws from a research project I worked on as a research assistant. The project was called "LGBTQ Families Speak Out,"[1] which investigated the experiences of 2SLGBTQI+[2] families and students in the public schooling system in Ontario, Canada, through semi-structured video interviews.[3]

The theater script was written in collaboration with the interview participants and was based on a diverse group of people's experiences rather than individual experiences. So, instead of collaborating with research participants to compose these songs, I used a similar but slightly different songwriting method where I composed the songs for this project directly from the script for the play *and* the interviews.[4] But, this example still illustrates how the steps I outline below will guide you in composing a song with your participant.

Part 1

Macro coding

This is the first level of analysis you will do to analyze your interview transcript. A **macro code** allows you to recognize and choose a dominant theme from the interview to guide your songwriting. Read over the interview transcript again with your participant. Then, discern the tone and feel of the interview. Document the dominant themes, big ideas or concepts, and recurring patterns in the interview. You may recognize several macro codes within the interview but choose one macro code only to guide your songwriting.

Working with our example about the experience of 2SLGBTQI+ families and students in public schools, some dominant themes (macro codes) that surfaced in the interviews and, subsequently, the theatre script were: belonging, coming out, relationships, exclusion experiences, or activism. Let's choose "coming out" as our macro code.

Narrative coding

Survey the transcript again with your participant, and color-code it for specific anecdotes, vignettes, or stories that focus on your participant's particular lived experiences that relate to the topic you are exploring. **Narrative codes** are detailed, nuanced accounts of lived experiences that fall under your dominant theme (macro code). Choose a label to represent each color code.

Thinking back to the schooling experiences of 2SLGBTQI+ families and the macro code of "coming out," you might have a narrative code label of "homophobia and transphobia." Your narrative codes[5] will be any anecdotes, vignettes, or stories that your participant may share related to experiences they've had with homophobia or transphobia. While searching for narrative codes in the interview transcript, pay attention to moments where the participant is particularly expressive, whether through words, emotion, tone of voice, facial expression, or body language. These emphatic moments often signal that what your participant is sharing holds personal importance to them. You and your participant may wish to include mention of these anecdotes or stories in the lyrics you compose. Make sure to discuss any questions, thoughts, or assumptions you have with your participant to ensure that you are gleaning an accurate understanding of what they have told you in the interview. Your song may draw on data from more than one narrative code that fits under the dominant theme of "coming out."

Thinking with our example about the schooling experiences of 2SLGBTQI+ families, other narrative codes that surfaced in the data was that after coming out, some student participants experienced acceptance by a loved one, found a community of 2SLGBTQI+ students, and experienced allyship from heterosexual and cisgender school staff.

Verbatim coding[6]

Re-read your transcript a third time with your participant and pinpoint key word-for-word expressions, phrases, metaphors, similes, idioms, and words that stand out as thought-provoking, compelling, resonant, or evocative. These bits of verbatim data will be connected to the macro and narrative data you highlighted. **Verbatim codes** assist you in embedding words or phrases into your song as actual lyrics that are directly spoken in the interview by your participant. Highlight verbatim data by color-coding, underlining, or noting them in the margin of the transcript. Thinking along with our macro code of "exclusion experiences" and a small selection of anecdotes, vignettes, or stories that are related to homophobia and transphobia, make sure to pick verbatim expressions, phrases, metaphors, similes, idioms, and words that your participant spoke during the interview when sharing these exclusion experiences. Similar to narrative codes, your song may draw on data from several verbatim codes.

Here is an example of a verbatim code that I used in the song "Pushing the Envelope" composed for the project about the schooling experiences of 2SLGBTQI+ families. During one interview, a lesbian participant talked about how her family felt excluded in various ways from her child's public school, whether it was through lack of queer representation in school curriculum, having to fill out school forms that referred to parents as "mother and father," or needing to speak to her child's teacher in advance of Father's Day activities at school to let the teacher know that there was no father in their household. This participant talked about the different ways she and her family made their presence known in the school and larger society by saying, "we weave ourselves into the fabric of the world." This verbatim phrase from this interview was included in the theater script *and* in the song, "Pushing the Envelope."[7]

Part 2

Set up a songwriting sheet with the template provided, which uses a standard pop song framework (see Table 10.1). Alternatively, you may choose to set up a songwriting sheet using another common North American song structure.[8] Here would be a good place to discuss with your participant the genre of music that suits the telling of their story. Or, perhaps your participant resonates with a particular genre

Table 10.1 Songwriting sheet template (standard pop song framework).

Macro Code (dominant theme from interview; theme of song): (insert macro code here)	
Data	*Song Lyrics*
Narrative data (add narrative codes here)	Verse 1 (narrative code:) Chorus (macro code:) Verse 2 (narrative code:)
Verbatim data (list verbatim codes here)	Chorus (macro code:) Bridge (narrative code:) Chorus (macro code:)

from which they would like to draw. You may consider combining one or more of these genres, rap/hip hop, folk protest/singer-songwriter, rock 'n' roll, country, punk, bluegrass, pop. These genres are influenced by different social and cultural groups, yet they are all standard, Westernized musical genres. If your participant prefers a genre beyond these styles, discuss how you might compose within that genre.

Next, decide on a theme for your song. Choose one macro code (dominant theme) that surfaced in your interview on which you and your participant would like to focus your song. Write that macro code at the top of the sheet.

Under the heading, "Data," type out narrative and verbatim data on the left side of your songwriting sheet. Include any personal connections of your own to your participant's experiences. Your personal connections to your participant's story may or may not be used in the song so make sure to discuss this with your participant before adding them to the songwriting sheet.

Next, keeping the theme of the song in mind (macro code), discuss the narrative data you and your participant choose to correspond with the macro code for the song. These narrative data will be used to compose each section of the song, that is, the verses, chorus, and bridge. On your transcript, make note of these anecdotes, vignettes, or stories you narrowed down. Here, you may prompt your participant by asking, "What anecdote, vignette, or story do you want to start with related to (macro code)?" "Which narratives do you want to lift from the transcript and expand on?" "What do you want people to know about your experience?"

To help you thematically arrange select narrative data on the songwriting sheet, add *labels* that represent specific narrative data beside the subheadings, "Verse," "Chorus," and "Bridge." Let's return to the previous example of research with 2SLGBTQI+ participants. Recall from the study about the experiences of 2SLGBTQI+ families in public schools that our macro code example is "coming out" to a range of people (e.g. peers, teachers, school administrators). If the macro code (dominant theme) of your song is "coming out," the label for Verse 1 might include "homophobic and transphobic experiences." This label represents narrative data related to this topic that you coded in your transcript. Write the label, "homophobic and transphobic experiences" beside "Verse 1." You may choose different narrative data for each verse, as long as they correspond to your macro code. Using our example, the narrative code for Verse 2 could be, "acceptance by a loved one." Write this label beside "Verse 2." Then, add a label beside "Chorus" (Macro Code) and "Bridge" (Narrative Code) (see Table 10.2).

In the prose above and/or table below it would be helpful to let the reader know this is actual data from a study, perhaps reference that study and illustrate from a specific study what readers might do in their own specific studies with other macro considerations (climate change, bilingual education, catholic pilgrimage traditions, etc.).

Next, choose one narrative code for each verse (remember a narrative code is an anecdote, vignette, or story) and migrate that entire code over to the right side of the document under "Song Lyrics." Ask your participant to expand on this narrative data if you think more detail is needed.

Because the chorus should be closely linked to the macro code that guides your song, ask your participant to think about a *take-home message* for the chorus that

Table 10.2 Macro code (dominant theme from the interview and theme of the song): *coming out.*

Data	*Song Lyrics*
Narrative data (anecdotes, vignettes, and stories that provide detailed, nuanced accounts of macro codes)	Verse 1 (narrative code: *homophobic and transphobic experience*)
Examples could include:	
1) homophobic and transphobic experiences 2) acceptance by a loved one 3) finding a community of 2SLGBTQI+ students	Chorus (macro code: *coming out*)
4) experiencing allyship from heterosexual and cisgender school staff	Verse 2 (narrative code: *acceptance by a loved one*)
Verbatim data (phrases, metaphors, similes, idioms, and words from the transcription)	Chorus (macro code: *coming out*)
Examples could include:	
1) we weave ourselves into the fabric of this world	Bridge (narrative code: *finding a community of 2SLGBTQI+ students*)
2) their words pierced my skin 3) my daughter wanted to fade into the background 4) the path beneath my feet 5) we dance between wanting to be seen and wanting to blend in 6) rain on my face like tears I couldn't cry	Chorus (macro code: *coming out*)
Researcher's personal connections/related ideas or experiences	
Examples could include:	
1) an anecdote about a similar experience 2) a question about allyship 3) a reflection about how schools could be more inclusive	

relates to your macro code. Type out their response in the "Chorus" section on the songwriting sheet. Ensure it is grounded in their lived experience and doesn't sound "preachy" or didactic.

Then, work on the bridge.[9] Even though the bridge of a song typically reflects a lyrical and/or musical shift in the song, it should still be linked to the macro code of the song. Revisiting our example of the song about 2SLGBTQI+ experiences and "coming out," the narrative code used in the bridge might be related to an "experience of acceptance." This is different from the themes of the verses (homophobic and transphobic experiences; love and partnership). Yet it still relates to the macro code of "coming out." Using the label you chose for the bridge, migrate a narrative code of your choosing from the left side of the songwriting sheet over to the right side under the "Bridge" section.

Next, turn to your verbatim data. When choosing data that are verbatim, keep in mind that they must be connected to the song theme (macro data). Insert relevant verbatim data at select moments throughout the song. Try to include 2–5 pieces of verbatim data.

Finally, play with your narrative data to shape them into lyrics. Because you will likely have a lot of material, whittle down each section of the song by condensing ideas, shortening or removing extraneous or less compelling phrases, and trimming off unnecessary words. Include at least two references to the seven bodily senses: sight, sound, taste, touch, smell, body, and motion. Add explicit or implied details about "who," "what," "when," and "where" to help frame the narrative of your song. As you and your participant compose lyrics, more experienced songwriters and musicians may want to experiment with chord progressions and vocal melodies, keeping in mind the musical genre you are working within.

Why This Assignment

In collaborative ethnographic songwriting, the researcher and participant can be understood as ethnographers who, working together creatively, draw from the participant's lived observations of their own experiences to craft a song. Using lyrical composition, voice, music, and rhythm to interpret interview material and tell someone's story adds an affective and sometimes spiritual dimension to interview material. Through a supportive, step-by-step process, this method provides a creative opportunity for people to express themselves and share stories that they might not have the opportunity to fully tell in a way that feels focused and emotionally detailed.

How to Extend

Pattison's (2011) chapter on "Object Writing" and his chapter (2009) entitled "Object Writing: The Art of the Diver" are very useful reads. These chapters explain how to draw on the seven bodily senses when composing lyrics and how to write about "who," "what," "when," and "where" in your song. To help you write using the powerful tools of metaphor and simile, check out Pattison's (2009) chapter "Making Metaphors."

What to Listen To / Read

I conducted a collaborative ethnographic songwriting project with an 8-year-old newcomer girl (Reid 2022). This project was part of a larger research project that investigated how engagement with community music and arts programming supported the settlement processes of newcomer and refugee young people and fostered their wellbeing. Based on the dominant theme of friendship and belonging that surfaced in my macro analysis on the interview I conducted with her, she and I wrote and recorded a song together called, "Hermione and Me," which is a story about my young collaborator's fantasy friendship with Hermione Granger from the *Harry Potter* novel series. I also wrote and recorded a song with a friend of mine about her experience with young adult breast cancer, for which we also created a music video. This process is also documented in an article we wrote together (Hauge and Reid 2019).

Notes

1 The principal investigator of this project was Dr. Tara Goldstein and the project took place at the University of Toronto, Canada. To provide context for the songs, see also the play *This is Our Family* (Goldstein et al. 2021) (*Out at School* in previous publications), the accompanying book chapter "Queering Classrooms and Schools" (Reid and Goldstein 2021), and Dr. Goldstein's project website www.lgbtqfamiliesspeakout.ca.

2 2SLGBTQI+ stands for Two Spirit–lesbian–gay–bisexual–transgender–queer–intersex. The + is an *umbrella marker* indicating that there are infinite ways in which people express themselves and infinite labels with which to do so. From these interviews, the research team developed a 90-minute, multimedia theater production called *Out at School*, for which I composed and recorded three songs: *Pushing the Envelope*, *Let Love be the Way*, and *Risk Hope*.

3 Kael, Reid. "Kael Reid." LGBTQ Families Speak Out and Out at School. Word Press. 2023. https://kaelreid.com/lgbtq-families-speak-out-and-out-at-school/.

4 See also Kael Reid, "Risk Hope: Using Songwriting Methods to Compose Music for Research-informed Multimedia Theatre," LGBTQ Music Study Group (blog), September 22, 2022 www.lgbtqmusicstudygroup.com/post/risk-hope-by-kael-reid-phd.

5 URL: https://kaelreid.com/lgbtq-families-speak-out-and-out-at-school/

6 Verbatim is a Latin word that literally means "word for word." To do verbatim coding, you put the transcript under a microscope and look for small but relevant "bits" of data (phrases, metaphors, similes, idioms, and words) that were spoken by the participant. Then, you highlight those short excerpts, word for word.

7 To read more about common song structures in North America, here is a helpful link: www.masterclass.com/articles/songwriting-101-learn-common-song-structures.

8 *Pushing the Envelope* by Kael Reid (2017) (excerpt from lyrics):

Verse 3:
We weave ourselves into the fabric of this world
Disrupting constructions of "boy" and "girl" and "boy-meets-girl"
Changing language and policy
Celebrating families, loves ones, and identities
If we raise our voices strong, we shall overcome
Chorus: One day we won't need to be Pushing the envelope
We won't be represented by
Permission slips home
It won't be trendy
To advertise our families
And we won't be legitimized
By posters on a wall

9 A bridge is an interruption in or an interesting diversion from the verse–chorus–verse–chorus pattern of a song. It often helps release the tension built up during the chorus or can be used to build more tension. As Alex Lavoie (2023) says a bridge "is used to create a path to wherever the song ultimately ends up." For more on how to write a bridge in a song and some examples of interesting bridges, see https://blog.landr.com/bridge-music/. URL: www.youtube.com/watch?v=YhvVzIsv1wM

References

Goldstein, Tara, Pam Baer, and Jenny Salisbury. 2021. "This is Our Family: A Verbatim Theatre Script." In *Our Children are Your Students: LGBTQ Families Speak Out*, edited by Tara Goldstein, 41–103. Gorham: Myers Education Press.

Hauge, Chelsey, and Kate Reid. 2019. "A Production of Survival: Cancer Politics and Feminist Media Literacies." *Studies in Social Justice* 13 (1): 118.

Lavoie, Alex. 2023. "Bridge in Music: How to Tie Your Song Together." *Landr Blog*, August 3. https://blog.landr.com/bridge-music/

Pattison, Pat. 2009. *Writing Better Lyrics: The Essential Guide to Powerful Songwriting*. USA: Writer's Digest Books.

Pattison, Pat. 2011. *Songwriting Without Borders*. Des Moines, Iowa: Writer's Digest Books.

Reid, Kael. 2017. "Pushing the Envelope." Recorded 2017. Kael Reid, single, 2017, mp3. https://kaelreid.com/lgbtq-families-speak-out-and-out-at-school/

Reid, Kael. 2018. "Let Love be the Way." Recorded 2018. Kael Reid, single, 2018, mp3. https://kaelreid.com/lgbtq-families-speak-out-and-out-at-school/

Reid, Kael. 2019. "Risk Hope." Recorded 2019. Kael Reid, single, 2019, mp3. https://kaelreid.com/lgbtq-families-speak-out-and-out-at-school/

Reid, Kael. 2022. "The Children's Creative Voices Project: Using Collaborative Ethnographic Songwriting to Express Musical Agency and Imagine New Worlds." *The Recorder: Ontario Music Educators' Association Journal* LXIV (3): 10.

Reid, Kael. 2023. "Kael Reid." *Arts-based Research.* Word Press. https://kaelreid.com/research/

Reid, Kate and Tara Goldstein. 2021. "Queering Classrooms and Schools." In *Our Children are Your Students: LGBTQ Families Speak Out*, edited by Tara Goldstein, 105–46. Gorham: Myers Education Press.

For Those Who Would Wear the Whale Mask

Using Mask-Making to Perform and Transform the Ethnographic Monologue

Sally Campbell Pirie

Creative Ethnographic Toolkit: Arts-based research, composite characters, comics.

Figure 10.7

DOI: 10.4324/9781003365228-40

"THERE ARE PEOPLE IN THIS WORLD WHO CAN WEAR WHALE MASKS AND PEOPLE WHO CANNOT, AND THE WISE KNOW TO WHICH GROUP THEY BELONG"
Tom Robbins Jitterbug Perfume
This quote refers to a character in Robbins' novel who, as a perfumier, wears a whale mask to show respect for the noble creature's ambergris.
When we write about people in ethnographies, we might try on the
Whale Mask
too, to help us
write with more honor,
empathy and understanding—
and also to be more conscious
of our own roles and relationships.
In my arts based research
seminar, we MAKE literal
masks to help us make
all this abstract
stuff more concrete — and also to enrich the creative, performative way in which we use monologue to make better understanding.

Figure 10.8

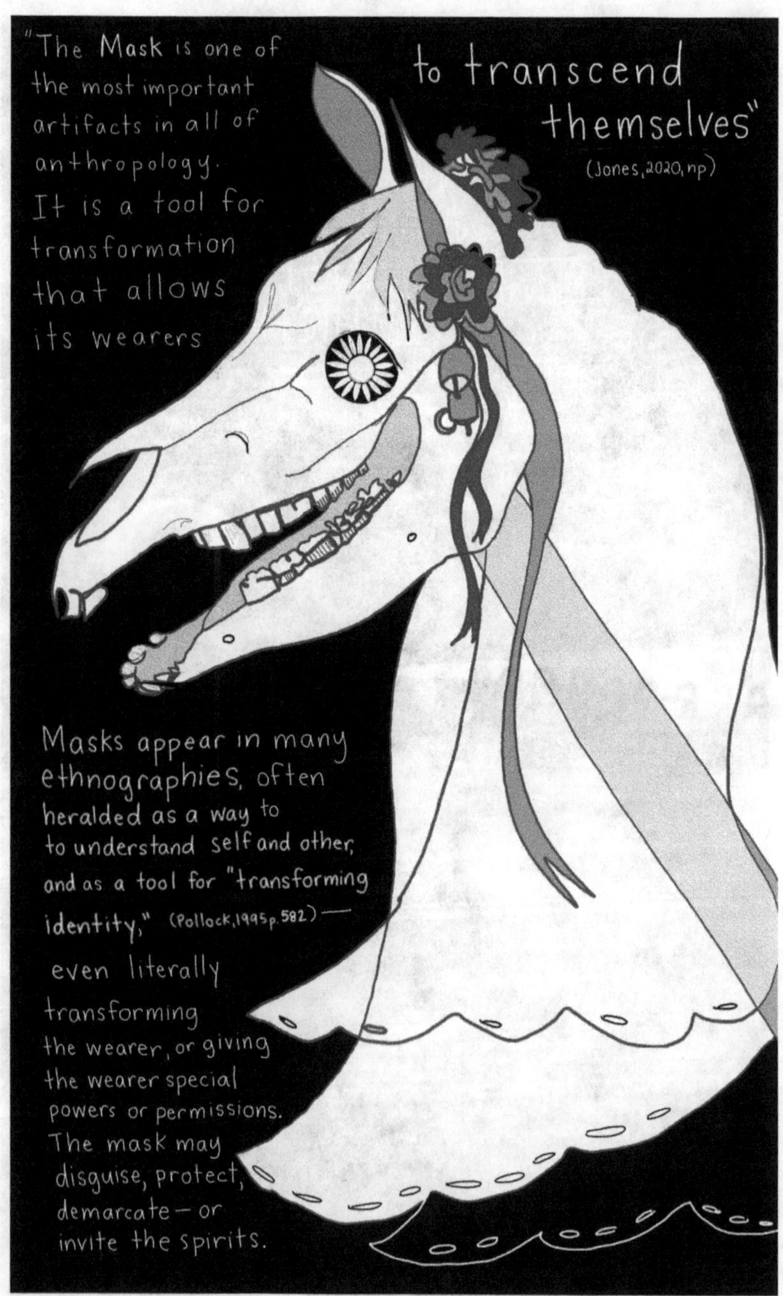
"The Mask is one of the most important artifacts in all of anthropology. It is a tool for transformation that allows its wearers
to transcend themselves"
(Jones, 2020, np)
Masks appear in many ethnographies, often heralded as a way to to understand self and other, and as a tool for "transforming identity," (Pollock, 1995 p. 582) — even literally transforming the wearer, or giving the wearer special powers or permissions. The mask may disguise, protect, demarcate — or invite the spirits.

Figure 10.9

Literally TRY IT ON
What you need:
1. Your data-specifically involving the people you want to write about.
2. Stuff-this can be material from your field site, or from the recyling bin, or where ever. I like to use only found materials.
(See Urist Green "The Holley Principle" 2020, p 233)
Some inspo for stuff:
eyes! eyes! eyes!
plastic
animals
cardboard
picnic cutlery
string stuff
paper plates
Panty Hose (stuffed?)
tissue paper
tin foil
paper cups
fake flowers
tiny foam balls or pompoms.
Fabric
Jar lids
Buttons
3. A mask base
You can find these at any craft store and yes they are creepy.
4. A hot glue gun.
BE CAREFUL!

Figure 10.10

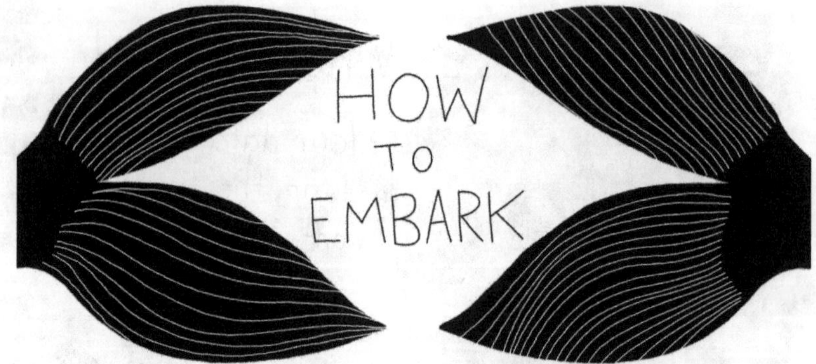

1. Read the relevant data. Feel what's there.
2. Begin to imagine a character based on the people. Write a rough monologue from the point of view of that composite character
3. Still feeling, use your materials to make a mask that will obscure YOU and honor THEM as you perform the monologue.
4. Videorecord the masked monologue. Memo about how it felt and how your data feel NOW. Watch it many times.
5. Rewrite your monologue using those memos and feelings.
6. What did this experience do to you? To others?

Figure 10.11

When you
return to
writing
after the
mask-making
and wearing, you
may find the
people you
describe have been
breathed to life, and
your understandings
equally more vibrant.

Figure 10.12

Why This Assignment

I teach a seminar in arts-based research. As I am a visual artist and comics-based ethnographer (see Pirie 2021a; 2021b) I always find that when I work to visually represent research participants as either anonymized individual or composite characters, I am able to access deeper and more nuanced understandings of them and their experiences. Comic artists call such artistic and intellectual acrobatics—effectively working ethnographic data into a comic—the process of "restorying" (Weaver-Hightower, 2017). After I "restory" data in this way, I usually have not only a clearer idea of the story I ultimately want to write and draw but also new analytic insights around the dataset as a whole. And while this kind of drawing is a method with many uses, I had difficulty translating a comics-based process into a creative turn for the performative arts in my seminar.

It is not unsurprising that, as a visual artist, my anchor point in performance came through making a visual art work—in this case, the mask itself. However, as Della Pollock (1995) notes, masks "are not simply pictures of the spirits, animals or other beings they represent (when, indeed, they do represent); masks are also and simultaneously icons and indexes of identity, and it is this conjunction of semiotic functions and fields that give the mask its particular form in any society and its particular fascination for anthropologists" (p. 594).

As noted in this piece, masks figure prominently in anthropological study in many complex contexts both literal and figurative (e.g., Boas 1911; Goffman 1959). Gill (1976) wrote about Hopi participants donning the Kachina mask and in doing so "giv[ing] life and action to the mask …he becomes the Kachina, yet continues to be himself (p. 55). Urban and Hendricks (1983) also observed that the mask can be many things in reference to the wearer: representative, indexical, emotive, or a disguise, such that "masks are not merely pictures of other beings, but are more fundamentally considered to be ways in which the identity of those beings is attributed to or predicated of the mask-wearer as well" (Pollock 1995, p. 583). Actors in Greek dramas used masks to enable one actor to take on multiple roles and for multiple actors to take on the same role in unison, and then—as now—masks force actors into greater physicality in whatever roles they take up. And, the mask is a public facing experience. As Jones (2020) observed, even the functionality of the cloth mask during COVID was also one of transformation and understanding across and between self and other. He writes "the use of a cloth mask situates the individual wearer as an actor in a broader social drama . . a creative expressive way of subsuming one's identity within a social movement - - and one's voice within a collective cry for justice" (np). Masks as both everyday and ritual objects can help render the abstract concrete. This is potentially powerful when it comes to understanding people and meaning.

As I note in this piece, masks can be taken off and on to symbolize a different way of being, even as they conceal, protect or transform the wearer. I use as an example: my favorite mask from my own cultural tradition as an example: the terrifying Mari Lywd. The Mari gives the wearer semi-supernatural powers as well as comic, unruly license to roam, jeer, and provoke. She is profoundly visually and socially arresting, not unlike a good monologue: the aria of contemporary theatre. And, she conceals while she acts. "The mask works," writes Pollock (1995), "by concealing the signs of identity which conventionally display the actor, and by presenting new values that …represent the transformed person, or an entirely new identity" (p. 581). It is with the mask, then, that we bring together a key human artifact with the transformative, vulnerable task of arts-based data analysis and performance. It is most apt, then, that masks are employed here as vehicles to imagine, generously construct, take on, and try out the skin of another, yet with the boundaries so very concretely and firmly intact. The mask can come off and become a separate object again. The researcher and writer retains their role.

If you choose to use this assignment, I wish to draw your attention to two small but important points.

First, the mask is a physical, hand-crafted object crafted object requiring some time and attention. I would encourage mask makers to focus on and enjoy the process of assembly as just that—a process. It is one that has meditative qualities to it, choosing materials, attaching them, waiting for glue and gesso to dry, can be a time to slow and think. The periods of thinking are often overlooked in the oh-so-fast work and pressured work of the academic catapult. Making an object forces a slowdown. Similarly, the end product is not as important as the process of its construction, the materials one might choose, and the balancing act of assembly. These seemingly mechanical processes also speak to what might prick up our ears (Pirie 2021b) and reveal a new theme or generative avenue for analysis. Art takes time. Let this assembly work draw from that richness, even though hot glue dries comparatively quickly.

Also in this vein, encourage students to experiment with materials. It is possible that the end product will not be perfect (and pieces might fall off) but the process should be open-ended and discovery-oriented. I have made masks where I chose unusual materials—in one case, crumpled up field notes that I dipped in papier-mâché and bent into rosettes and horns around a creature's mouth—that didn't always "take"—but the process worked as a kind of physical restorying.

Second, I have written the comic form of this assignment to "work" for either a single or **composite character**, but it is important to note that I believe your results will be better and more luminous working with composite. As described by Jarzabkowski, Bednarek, and Le (2014), composites "merge the characters and events from multiple ethnographic observations into a single composite narrative" (p. 281). So, using a composite approach means that the researcher is not telling a verbatim participant story, but rather gathering threads of commonality to generate a character that is work of creative non-fiction. So, the characters in this exercise should be composites rather than literal imitations of people in your field site. While making a mask and acting out the mannerisms, speech, and feeling of a key informant is certainly possible from an analytic viewpoint, composite characters are more useful here for practical, as well as ethical, reasons. For one, creating a composite is an analytic restorying process that is certain to deepen understanding. Also, the composite is also useful if you have participants that constitute an easily identifiable population for which a mere pseudonym will not suffice. This is frequently the case with my work with transgender people in small communities and as such I do create composite vignettes out of information from several participants (see Pirie 2021c).

Finally, those who hope to wear the whale mask must do so from a place of thanks, generous construction, and emic understanding. This is not parody. This is honor.

How to Extend

I use the monologue here as a performance toward more nuanced analytical feeling-and-subsequently-thinking. However there is no reason that students could not write and direct short scenes that are emblematic of important moments in the field, with more than one mask and more than one character. There is a rich tradition of performance in arts-based research, with several resources listed below.

What to Read

The best advice I have for you is that you read widely—as widely as you can. Read fiction, read poetry, read weird essays about ants and sharks and ritual wailings that have no genre. And choose academic works that speak to both your area of expertise and also beyond. Browse wildly.

References

Boas, Franz. 1911. The Mind of Primitive Man: A Course of Lectures Delivered before the Lowell Institute, Boston, Mass., and the National University of Mexico, 1910–1911. Macmillan.

Gill, Sam D. 1976. "The Shadow of a Vision Yonder." In *Seeing with the Native Eye: Essays on Native American Religion*, edited by Walter Holden Capps, assisted by Ernst F. Tonsing. New York: Harper & Row.

Goffman, Erving. 1959. *The Presentation of Self in Everyday Life*. Garden City, NY: Anchor.

Jarzabkowski, Paula, Robert Bednarek, and Juliette K. Lê. 2014. "Producing Persuasive Findings: Demystifying Ethnographic Textwork in Strategy and Organization Research." *Strategic Organization* 12 (4): 274–87. https://doi.org/10.1177/1476127014554575

Jones, Graham. 2020. "A Collective Cry for Justice." Massachusetts Institute of Technology School for Humanities Arts and Social Sciences (SHASS) News, July 2. https://shass.mit.edu/news/news-2020-pandemic-masks-anthropology-graham-jones

Pirie [as Galman], Sally C. 2021a. "Yes and." American Anthropologist. www.americananthropologist.org/online-content/insights-forms-of-engagement. www.americananthropologist.org/insights/galman

Pirie [as Galman], Sally C. 2021b. "Follow the Headlights: On Comics-Based Data Analysis." In *Analyzing and Interpreting Qualitative Data: After the Interview*, edited by Charles F. Vanover, Paul A. Mihas, and Johnny Saldaña. London: SAGE.

Pirie [as Galman], Sally C. 2021c. "Wedges: Stories as Simple Machines." *Health Promotion Practice*. https://doi.org/10.1177/15248399211045974

Pollock, Della. 1995. "Masks and the Semiotics of Identity." *Journal of the Royal Anthropological Institute* 1 (3): 581–97. https://doi.org/10.2307/3034576

Urban, Gregg and Janet W. Hendricks. 1983. "Signal Functions of Masking in Amerindian Brazil," *Semiotica* 47: 181–216.

Weaver-Hightower, Marcus B. 2017. "Losing Thomas & Ella: A Father's Story (A Research Comic)." *Journal of Medical Humanities* 38: 215–30.

11 Writing it Up

Multimodality, Genre, and How to Translate Creative Activity for an Academic Audience

Recording an Ethnographic Soundscape

Jay Hammond

Creative Ethnographic Toolkit: Audio production, musical composition, deep listening, soundscape recording.

Field recording as a creative and methodological tool has been central to the work of anthropologists since the discipline's inception (Feld and Brenneis 2004). This assignment introduces you to the idea of a "**Sounded Anthropology**" (Samuels et al. 2010; Martin 2019) through a step-by-step exercise, informed by the Deep Listening practice of composer Pauline Oliveros (2005). Particularly, you will come to understand the idea of "schizophonia" taken up by anthropologists of sound (Feld 1996; Bitter et al. 2021) through an embodied and intuitive practice of listening, journaling, recording and listening back to your recordings. Schizophonia as a concept shows us that sound recordings—i.e., the separation of a sound from its source—don't always communicate the "truth" of a cultural context in the ways that we might predict. Composers and anthropologists also use the term "schizophonia" in order to discuss the social, cultural and political implications of these changes between live and recorded sound. Like writing, audio recording is a generative tool for representation that takes skill, practice and craft. This assignment is an introductory step towards thinking with and developing field recording not only as a method for field research, but as a way of communicating findings and telling stories.

Prompt

In this 10 minute in-class exercise, you will record an ethnographic soundscape. An ethnographic soundscape is a piece of audio meant to convey feelings and information about the nature of a geographic place. Do not worry if you are not an experienced audio engineer. There is no equipment necessary other than a smartphone with audio recording capabilities. Recording audio is a skill not at all unrelated to the skill of taking field notes. It is, in fact, just another way of re-presenting data, just like ethnographic writing.

Find a comfortable spot to be still, either in a classroom setting, in a hallway, or in an outdoor space. For Part 1, you will be still. If you are in a quiet classroom setting, the listening experience may seem dull at first, as if there is not much to listen for. Sit with that discomfort, and continue to listen to the small, quiet details of the classroom space. If you are sitting outdoors or in a noisier space, do your best

DOI: 10.4324/9781003365228-42

to sit still, and to take in as many sounds as possible without focusing on any one sound in particular. For Part 2 you will be free to move about the space, or to be still.

Part 1: Listening (5 minutes)

Take 5 minutes to sit quietly and listen. As you listen, pay attention to what the composer Pauline Oliveros calls "**focal**" and "**global**" **attention** (Oliveros 2005). Focal attention means that you are listening to one sound in your environment, such as a bird call, or a person speaking. Global attention means that you are taking in the entire soundscape of your environment all at the same time. Can you focus your attention on one sound, while also paying attention to the soundscape as a whole? This is a skill that takes daily practice, one that Oliveros calls "Deep Listening."

Part 2: Recording (5 minutes)

After 5 minutes of listening, take another 5 minutes to record. Using your smartphone or a field recorder and microphone(s), record continuously for 5 minutes. Feel free to move about the space or sit still. As the recorder is running, consider how best to capture the sounds that interested you as you were listening. These could be sounds that strike you on an aesthetic level, sounds that feel particularly communicative of a cultural phenomenon that interests you, or—best-case scenario—sounds that do both of these things at the same time. Listen to an ethnographic soundscape about human encounters with fungi here: https://ernstkarel.bandcamp.com/album/mycological-2015 and listen to an album of piano music that uses field recordings of cicadas here: https://benseretan.bandcamp.com/album/cicada-waves. You may find that the sounds made by your classmates change the sonic environment. Welcome that change, while continuing to seek out the sounds to which you were drawn during Part 1. For homework, listen back to your recording with the following questions in mind:

- What changed between listening to your environment in real time and listening back to your recordings?
- Do you hear things in the recording you didn't hear live, or vice versa?
- Could you have recorded things differently?
- How do those changes between live and recorded sound inform what you are trying to communicate about your environment and/or cultural context through sound?

How to Extend

It is possible to extend this 10 minute in-class exercise into a 20 minute in-class exercise. Extending the prompt will provide the full spectrum of the process of creating an ethnographic soundscape, while the un-extended prompt will provide a bite-sized introduction to that process.

Part 1: Journaling (5 minutes)

After 5 minutes of listening, take another 5 minutes to jot down a list of the sounds that you hear. When you begin, you might begin with phrases that provide an object name and an action. For example, you may write "a car drives by," or "a person is talking." Accept these impulses and write them down, while also considering other ways to represent sound through language. For example, is the car driving slowly or quickly? On a paved road or on gravel? Is the person speaking in a low tone or loudly? How do these details change the words you choose to represent the sound? Can you use onomatopoeia?

Part 2: Listening Back (5 minutes)

After the 5 minutes of recording, take the final 5 minutes to listen back to the soundscape that you have recorded. As you listen back, use the same journaling and deep listening techniques that you used when listening to the non-mediated environment at the beginning of this exercise. What changed between listening to your environment in real time and listening back to your recordings? Those implications often include unintended consequences that can be harmful to social, cultural and political ways of life. Sometimes, however, such differences can have an exciting and generative artistic application. Composers use the term "acousmatic" (Schaeffer 2004) in order to discuss such applications. How do those changes between live and recorded sound inform what you are trying to communicate about your environment and/or cultural context through sound? Could you have recorded things differently? Do you hear things in the recording you didn't hear before or vice versa?

What to Listen To and Read

There are many "tricks of the trade" within audio production. If you are entirely new to audio production and would like to learn more, I suggest that you start with the "recording" chapter and supplementary materials of Karen C. Collins book *Studying Sound* (Collins 2020).

Anthropologists and Composers approach the genre of ethnographic soundscape in different but related ways. For an excellent example of an ethnographic soundscape from an anthropologist, listen to and read the notes for *Notes on Spaces of Consciousness* (Karel 2016). For an excellent example of an ethnographic soundscape from a composer, listen to "Into the Labyrinth" from the Album "*Into India*" (Westerkamp 2002). Both pieces seek to represent Indian culture through sound, and each has its own unique methodologies and outcomes.

As you become more familiar with recording and/or audio editing techniques, sound can become a powerful way to communicate the findings and/or theoretical resonance of your work. For an example of work that combines the audio production fluency of composition with anthropological insight, listen to "The Voices of the Rainforest" (Various Artists 1991) and also read "Doing Anthropology in Sound" in *American Ethnologist* (Feld and Brenneis 2004).

References

Bitter, Joella, Cade Bourne, Megan J. Gette, Jay Hammond, Harrison Montgomery, and Michelle Helene Mackenzie. 2021. "Notes on 'Ordinary Schizophonia: Field Recordings as Multimodal Experiment'." *Visual and New Media Review, Fieldsights*. September 14, 2021.https://culanth.org/fieldsights/notes-on-ordinary-schizophonia-field-recordings-as-multimodal-experiment

Collins, Karen. 2020. *Studying Sound: A Theory and Practice of Sound Design*. Cambridge: The MIT Press. www.studyingsound.org

Feld, Steve and Donald Brenneis. 2004. "Doing Anthropology in Sound." *American Ethnologist* 31 (4): 461–74.

Feld, Steven. 1996. "Pygmy POP. A Genealogy of Schizophonic Mimesis." *Yearbook for Traditional Music*, 28: 1–35. DOI: https://doi.org/10.2307/767805

Karel, Ernst. 2016. "Notes on 'Space of Consciousness (Chidambaram, Early Morning).'" *Anthrovision. Vaneasa Online Journal* 4 (2). https://journals.openedition.org/anthrovision/2383

Martin, Allie. 2019. "Hearing Change in the Chocolate City: Soundwalking as Black Feminist Method." *Sounding Out!* (blog). August 5, 2019. https://soundstudiesblog.com/2019/08/05/hearing-change-in-the-chocolate-city-soundwalking-as-black-feminist-method/

Oliveros, Pauline. 2005. *Deep Listening: A Composer's Sound Practice*. New York, NY: iUniverse.

Samuels, David W., Louise Meintjes, Ana Maria Ochoa, and Thomas Porcello. 2010. "Soundscapes: Toward a Sounded Anthropology." *Annual Review of Anthropology* 39: 329–45.

Schaeffer, Pierre. 2004. "Acousmatics." *Audio Culture: Readings in Modern Music*, 76–81.

Various Artists. 1991. *Voices of the Rainforest*. Smithsonian Folkways. https://folkways.si.edu/voices-of-the-rainforest/world/music/album/smithsonian

Westerkamp, Hildegard. 2002. *Into India: A Composer's Journey*. Earsay Productions. https://earsaymusic.bandcamp.com/track/into-the-labyrinth

Write to Discover What You Truly Want to Say

Nicoletta Demetriou

Creative Ethnographic Toolkit: Memoir, fiction.

Very often ethnographers find it difficult to be clear about what it is we want to do in the field—which line of inquiry to follow, which questions to ask, where to go, who to meet and interview and how. Similarly, we may also find it hard to organize our thoughts on paper, once we're back from the field. By giving ourselves the freedom to write without stopping to check, or without actively thinking and organizing our thoughts, anthropologists tap into our unconscious mind to figure out what *truly* is most important to us and our work.

This is an exercise anyone can do, in preparation for fieldwork and/or for writing up the results of their research. It's a very "low-tech" exercise; all you'll need is a notebook (or a few loose pieces of paper), a pen or pencil to write with, one or two colored pens or pencils to underline with, and a highlighter. The time commitment is limited to 10 minutes, but there's a catch: you'll need to repeat it for 5 days in a row. On day 5, you should try to set about half an hour aside, in order to complete all the different parts of the exercise. No prior experience is necessary, and everyone—beginner, intermediate, advanced student or established scholar—can benefit from it.

Prompt

Take a notebook or a large piece of paper and a pen/pencil. It is very important to do this exercise by hand.[1] Set your timer for 10 minutes and, without thinking or preparing much, start writing freely, beginning with "I want to explore." Write for 10 minutes without stopping to check your spelling, your grammar or punctuation, whether or not you've stayed within the margins, etc.—in short, do not stop to check *anything*. If you get stuck, go back to your prompt: "I want to explore." It's vital to keep your hand moving, so as not to block any fresh, uncensored, perhaps even hidden thoughts. At the end of the 10 minutes, put your notebook (or piece of paper) aside, and resist the temptation to read through.

The following day, do the same; if you want, this time you can change the prompt slightly to "I want to investigate," or "I want to research," or "I want to

DOI: 10.4324/9781003365228-43

write about"—you choose. The important thing is to, once again, keep writing for 10 minutes straight without stopping. Repeat this exercise for at least 3 days.

On the fourth day, make a mind-map. Set your alarm for 10 minutes, so that you don't keep checking your watch. If you feel you don't need it simply write, resisting any urge to check the time or surf the web. Write your prompt in the center of the piece of paper ("I want to explore," "I want to write about," etc.), and then let the "tentacles" of the map take you wherever they want. Let yourself be as curious as you want. *Do not censor your curiosity.* You should have fun while doing this exercise, and feel as playful as a child (see Figure 11.1).

On the fifth day, go back to your notebook (or pieces of paper), with a colored pen/pencil or a highlighter. This part of the exercise might take you longer than 10 minutes, but shouldn't take more than half an hour. Underline or highlight anything—from all five days of writing—that strikes you as "true," as being close to your heart and your truest desires. Is there anything in your notes that sounds like something you want to work on/write about? Is there anything you would like to devote more time to investigate or explore? Go back and circle any repetitions you find in the free-writes. Then check your mind-map, and see if any of those truthful ideas or repetitions appear there as well. If so, underline, highlight or circle them too. Then take a fresh piece of paper and make a list of all the things that seem to interest or excite your creative imagination—what you have already underlined, highlighted or circled. After you have done this, try to complete the sentences below. It's important to limit yourself to one sentence per prompt; the briefness here is meant to help you crystallize what it is you want to research/write about.

- "My research/fieldwork is about…"
- "My main research questions/fields of inquiry are…"

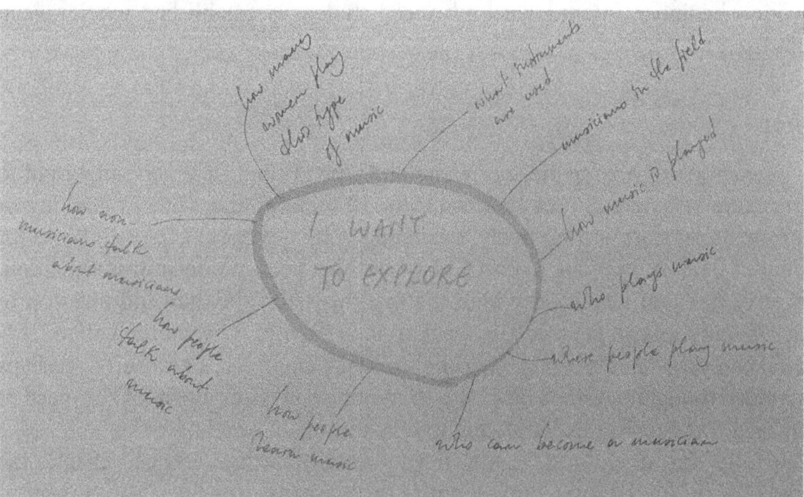

Figure 11.1 An example of a hand-drawn mind map.

- "I would like to investigate these by…" List different methods you would like to investigate the questions of greatest interest to you; for example:
  "I would like to investigate this by

  (a) interviewing musicians in the field;
  (b) playing music with them;
  (c) visiting sound archives;
  (d) studying with a local master musician."

- "I feel confident about…"
- "I'm concerned about…"
- "…makes me worried/scared/insecure."
- "My current plan is…"

Why This Assignment

The repetition of the first part of the exercise (free-write) helps us to see more clearly what our mind is mostly concerned with—our repetitive, sometimes even obsessive, thoughts. By figuring out what these are, we have a better chance of doing something about them: either following them as fields of research/inquiry or if they don't serve us, letting them go. The mind-map allows us to be playful with our thoughts; and the list allows us to put some initial structure into them. The two types of organizational tools are supposed to help both linear and non-linear thinkers—not only by doing what comes naturally to them (list and mind map, respectively), but, mostly, by doing what does *not* come naturally to them. Doing something that may initially appear as counter-intuitive takes us out of our comfort zone and gently pushes us to look at our work differently. Finally, the short sentences to be completed (see bullet points above) aim to help us be clear and concise with what we want to do. The sentences on what we fear most and what we're concerned about are meant to objectify our gravest worries; very often, when we see them written down, they no longer appear so scary. Other times, writing them down can allow us to strategize on how to address them more skillfully.

The final completed sentence ("My current plan is…") is meant to form a sort of personal commitment for the imminent future of the student/scholar/writer. Write this plan on a piece of paper, a sticky note, or something bigger and bolder like cardboard using colored markers, and pin it/stick it on a wall, a mirror, or your desk—in short, somewhere you can see it every day, and remind yourself of the commitment you've made to yourself.

How to Extend

Discuss the process of doing the exercise with two or three of your classmates. Aim to have at least 5 minutes each to talk about your exercise. Ask your classmates how the process felt for them, whether they found it useful, and whether any of the final "findings" on their list surprised them. As you go through this process, ask as many questions and be as rigorous as you want about *how* you conducted your own research (methodology, research questions, structure, fieldwork plans, etc.), but try to be as respectful as possible of each other's ideas and research content—particularly if that content is in any way personal and/or self-reflective. After you've discussed what the exercise was like for each one of you, take a few more minutes to go round the table and read your shorter sentences out loud to one another ("My research/fieldwork is about…," etc.). See how it feels for you to read them out loud to a group of peers, and see if your classmates' questions or reactions help you to rethink or finetune any of your findings.

What to Read

Natalie Goldberg's (2006/1986) *Writing Down the Bones* gives great ideas of how to use writing itself to explore what it is you want to write about. Goldberg is a world-renowned writing teacher, and a true advocate of the wonders of free-writing and of writing practice. The whole book is worth reading; if you must choose, then read "Beginner's mind, pen and paper," "First thoughts," and "Writing as a practice." Cathy Rentzenbrink's (2022) *Write it All Down* is a fantastic guide on how to write memoir, and can prove useful to any ethnographer wanting to give a self-reflexive bent to their work. Elizabeth Gilbert's (2015) *Big Magic* is a gentle reminder of how to keep your curiosity alive and how to create—and *keep* creating—"beyond fear." You can dip in and out of any of these books as and when you feel that you need a friendly voice to help you to decide what it is you truly want to research and write about—*and* to help you keep going.

Many writers and writing coaches talk about free-writing and how it could be done to yield the best possible results. Check out the following (in chronological order):

- *Becoming a Writer* by Dorothea Brande (1934/1981). Brande talks about "effortless writing" (her term for "freewriting"), on pp. 71–73 of her book.
- *Writing Without Teachers* by Peter Elbow (1973/1988) popularized freewriting (or, as he spells it, "free-writing"), especially as a pedagogical practice. Have a look at his first chapter "Freewriting Exercises."
- *The Artist's Way* by Julia Cameron (1992) is another classic that has remained in print since it was first published. Cameron talks about freewriting and what she calls "the **morning pages**" in the chapter entitled "The basic tools."

Note

1 Here are three articles (in reverse chronological order) on the benefits of writing by hand and the freedom it can make us feel:

https://www.nytimes.com/2022/01/21/insider/the-case-for-writing-longhand-its-about-trying-to-create-that-little-space-of-freedom.html
https://www.psychologytoday.com/us/blog/the-athletes-way/202107/why-does-writing-hand-promote-better-and-faster-learning
https://www.nytimes.com/2014/06/03/science/whats-lost-as-handwriting-fades.html?_r=0

References

Brande, Dorothea. 1981 [1934]. *Becoming a Writer*. New York: Jeremy P. Tarcher/Putnam.

Cameron, Julia. 1992. *The Artist's Way*. New York: Jeremy P. Tarcher.

Elbow, Peter. 1988 [1973]. *Writing Without Teachers*. New York: Oxford University Press.

Gilbert, Elizabeth. 2015. *Big Magic: Creative Living Beyond Fear*. London and New York: Bloomsbury.

Goldberg, Natalie. 2006 [1986]. *Writing Down the Bones: Freeing the Writer Within*. Boston and London: Shambhala.

Rentzenbrink, Cathy. 2022. *Write it All Down: How to Put Your Life on the Page*. London: Bluebird.

Creating an Ethnographic Exhibit

Kwame Phillips and Debra Vidali

Creative Ethnographic Toolkit: Installation, exhibit, museum display, display creation, audience engagement, public anthropology.

What would it look like to convey your ethnographic research through an exhibit? Ethnographic displays and installations appear in museums, art galleries, and conferences. Increasingly, new forms of ethnographic exhibition defy conventional styles of museum display that are static, enclosed in glass cases, and devoid of commentary about the conditions of collection and display (see von Oswald and Tinius 2020). Ethnographic exhibits push the boundaries of how research can be translated for exhibition and they invite direct engagement of visitors in knowledge production and discovery.

For example, Cantarella and Hegel (2012) drew upon Alexandra Pelosi's documentary on homelessness in Southern California to create an installation representing a motel room inhabited by a fictional family. Visitors to the "motel room" could move through it to discover actors and objects communicating the perspectives of people featured in the documentary. A bedside alarm clock played a recording of a child's story. T-shirts in a laundry basket had printed words representing interviewees' commentary about laundry routines. Cans of food were relabeled with people's comments about their financial calculations. (Also see Cantarella, Hegel, and Marcus 2019.)

Elizabeth Chin created "Wakanda University," an encounter space at an anthropology conference that provided "an ethno-future space beyond whiteness that challenges anthropology from the ground up" (Ethnographic Terminalia 2019). Conference attendees could experiment with "**Becky** Be Gone Spray" and dress in lab coats crafted from West African fabrics. These elements functioned as material inversions and counter-narratives to forms of white power. The spray functioned to detoxify environments from White surveillance and racial dominance, referencing a pest repellent name and a colloquial term for white women, "Becky" (Williams 2020). The colorful lab coats were a visceral critique of the purported neutrality of conventionally used color, white.

DOI: 10.4324/9781003365228-44

Figure 11.2 The "*Kabusha* Radio Remix" installation and a visitor in Le Cube, Paris (photo by Kwame Phillips, 2016).

The "*Kabusha* Radio Remix" installation that we created (Vidali and Phillips 2014-2018) uses a single desk as a display surface to communicate about the ethnographic realities of Zambian radio broadcasting during the late 20th century (Figure 11.2). The exhibit bring the worlds of radio producer and radio listener into one location. We chose to foreground the material textures of radio production and home listening environments, through audio cassette tapes, typed program scripts, and household items such as wall calendars and family photos (Phillips and Vidali 2017; Vidali and Phillips 2020). Objects from a popular Zambian talk show host's office are on the left side of the desk. While items from a typical listener's home are on the right. In the center, a boombox plays a remixed version of the famous Bemba language program, *Kabusha Takolelwe Bowa* ("The Person Who Inquires First, Is Not Poisoned by a Mushroom") with an English language transcript available to viewers. Our audio remix emulates the question and answer format of the original show, by splicing *new* recordings of new letter writers' questions with *old* recordings of radio host David Yumba providing answers. See: https://scholarblogs.emory.edu/bemba/kabusha-radio-remix/

For other examples of creative installations see: Kate Hennessy's "Making Culture Lab," Craig Campbell's "Bureau for Experimental Ethnography," and Cannupa Hanska Luger's "Future Ancestral Technologies."

Prompt

For those interested in creating their own ethnographic exhibition, this prompt is designed in three parts: (1) reflecting; (2) designing; (3) realizing and analysis.

Part 1: Reflecting

Select a body of research material that you have used to explore the subject of your ethnography. This might be your fieldnotes, recordings, a set of letters your grandmother wrote to you, a collection of household objects. For those who have not yet conducted fieldwork you may experiment with this practice using a group of your favorite stuffed animals, or some other kind of collection or archive close to a subject you wish to examine ethnographically. You'll need at least 8–10 objects or pages of fieldnotes in your collection. Now take a step back to reflect, using these questions:

1. What is your ethnographic research material (your "*archive*" or collection) and what is it made out of? (e.g., fieldnotes, recordings, documents, paper, household objects, wood, metal, cloth, plastic, etc.)
2. What voices, sensations, and objects stand out? Are there dominant voices? Subdued voices? Ambient sounds? What colors and textures are there? If your fieldwork is outside, you might think about sunlight or wind qualities. If indoors, you might think about spaces that people inhabit and create. Do spaces feel expansive or closed in? Cluttered or harmonious?
3. What are the main insights from your research?
4. What is your positionality as a researcher?
5. Do you think other researchers would have similar findings as you? Why/why not?
6. Do you think people in your research would highlight the same things as you? Why/why not?
7. What do you think people in your research want others to know?

Part 2: Designing

Imagine creating a display or installation to communicate about your research. Write notes on the following:

1. How might you design a physical installation that draws on your reflections in prompt? Would you create a display on a table? An interactive room? Or something else?
2. What would be in the exhibit?
3. What ethnographic realities, human experiences, and ways of being-in-the-world would your installation convey? What power dynamics or structural relations would it convey?
4. Make a list of 3–5 ethnographic insights that you would like to communicate.[1]
5. How are these ethnographic insights connected to the physical items in the installation?

6. Create a list of 3–5 things that you would want visitors to do, learn, and/or be curious about as they engage with your exhibit.
7. How are visitors guided to interact with the exhibit?
8. Where would this installation be located?
9. Draw a rough sketch of the exhibit space.

How to Extend

Part 3: Realization and Analysis

For more advanced students, consider creating the installation you have designed in Parts 1 and 2 and sharing in a public space. To do this, you might:

1. Make your installation (in full, partial, or modified form). Design an installation that follows from Parts 1 and 2, and that provides a multimodal, translated experience of your research.
2. Alternatively (or additionally), write a 500 word reflection that discusses:
   - What practical limitations are there for creating your installation/exhibit? What resource limitations are there?
   - How would your installation engage issues of positionality and power, **accountability** to ethical and equitable practice, and accountability to the people who are represented?
   - Imagine that the people in your research are the primary audiences for your work. How would this change the work itself or how it is presented?
   - How would your installation engage creative issues of multimodality, knowledge production, and public scholarship?
   - What is gained by this approach to ethnographic knowledge production?

Why This Assignment

At the heart of this exercise is a process of reflection. Creativity is important, but as significant is understanding what this creativity is based on, what it draws from, what it says about you as a scholar. There is not a "*one size fits all*" form of knowledge production. As you propose an installation/exhibit that expands upon your research material and data, you are asked to be reflexive about issues of positionality, accountability, and materiality. You are also invited to think about how your proposed installation brings forth new forms of value and calls into question more conventional forms of ethnographic curation and display.

Note

1 Ethnographic insights might include reflections on the way your mural relates to lived experience, for example, structural inequalities across the lines of race, ableism or gender identity as these exist in the United States or many other countries.

References

Campbell, Craig. 2023. Bureau for Experimental Ethnography. Accessed September 7, 2023. https://bureauxethnography.dwrl.utexas.edu/

Cantarella, Luke and Christine Hegel. 2012. "214 Sq. Ft." Accessed January 30, 2023. http://productiveencounters.com/wp/214-sq-ft/

Cantarella, Luke, Christine Hegel, and George E. Marcus. 2019. *Ethnography by Design: Scenographic Experiments in Fieldwork.* London: Routledge.

Coghlan, David and Mary Brydon-Miller. 2014. "Positionality." *The Sage Encyclopedia of Action Research.* Los Angeles, London, New Delhi, Singapore, Washington DC: Sage.

Ethnographic Terminalia. 2019. "Wakanda University." Accessed September 7, 2023. https://ethnographicterminalia.org/wakanda-university

Gillespie, Tarleton, Pablo J. Boczkowski, and Kirsten A. Foot, eds. 2014. *Media Technologies: Essays on Communication, Materiality, and Society*. Boston, MA: The MIT Press.

Given, Lisa M., ed. 2008. "Accountability." In *The Sage Encyclopedia of Qualitative Research Methods,* 3–4. Los Angeles, London, New Delhi, Singapore, Washington DC: Sage.

Hennessy, Kate. 2023. "Making Culture Lab." Accessed September 7, 2023. http://hennessy.iat.sfu.ca/mcl/

Luger, Cannupa Hanska. 2023. "Future Ancestral Technologies." Accessed September 7, 2023. www.cannupahanska.com/fat

Misawa, Mitsunori. 2010. "Queer Race Pedagogy for Educators in Higher Education: Dealing with Power Dynamics and Positionality of LGBTQ Students of Color." *International Journal of Critical Pedagogy* 3(1): 26–35.

Phillips, Kwame and Debra Vidali. 2017. "Collisions of Memory, Voice, Sound, and Physicality though a Multi-sensorial Radio Remix Installation." *Seismograf,* special issue "Sound Art Matters." http://seismograf.org/fokus/sound-art-matters/collisions-of-memory-voice-sound-and-physicality-though-a-multi-sensorial-radio-remix

Vidali, Debra and Kwame Phillips. 2014–2018. *Kabusha Radio Remix: Your Questions Answered by Pioneering Zambian Talk Show Host David Yumba (1923-1990).* Installed at Hierarchy Gallery (Washington, D.C., 2014); Le Cube (Paris, 2016); Goldsmiths, University of London (London, 2017); and The British Museum (London, 2018).

Vidali, Debra and Kwame Phillips. 2020. "Ethnographic Installation and "the Archive:" Haunted Relations and Relocations." *Visual Anthropology Review* 36 (1): 64–89.

Vidali, Debra and Kwame Phillips. 2020. Ethnographic Installation and "the Archive:" Haunted Relations and Relocations, Supplement with teaching applications and creative activities. www.visualanthropologyreview.org/var361-suppl-vidali-phillips

von Oswald, Margareta and Jonas Tinius, eds. 2020. *Across Anthropology: Troubling Colonial Legacies, Museums, and the Curatorial.* Leuven: Leuven University Press.

Williams, Apryl. 2020. "Black Memes Matter: #LivingWhileBlack With Becky and Karen." *Social Media + Society* 6 (4). https://doi.org/10.1177/2056305120981047

After the Field Site

Writing About the Unexplained

Cristina Moretti

Creative Ethnographic Toolkit: Prose poetry, fieldnotes, creative non-fiction, reflexivity, attending to different perspectives, connecting events and commentaries to social contexts.

Ethnographers often encounter circumstances or commentaries during their fieldwork that are unexpected, uncanny, or remain unexplained long after their research. This prompt offers you, as a student or more experienced anthropologist, a format for allowing a jarring incident from your research to become an echoing line in a piece of poetic prose. By centering your enduring sense of surprise and attending to your experience without "flattening" it, the process of writing as well as the polished piece, can allow new questions to emerge about your fieldwork relationships and social contexts.

Prompt

This exercise will take approximately 1 hour; anticipate writing between 300 and 600 words.

Step 1

Think about an event, conversation, or occurrence in your fieldwork that surprised you, or that you are still grappling with because it remains unexplained. It could be an unexpected coincidence, a jarring story or encounter, a mysterious event, or even a moment that felt akin to "magic." Set a timer for 5–10 minutes and do a free-write about that moment, without stopping to reflect and without deleting, editing, or re-reading your words.

While you write, evoke what was jarring and why. What did it feel like at the time? What was uncanny about it? Was there a particular word, sound, or image that was puzzling and now anchors this experience? What elements of magic and/or unexplained circumstances animated or troubled this moment or encounter? Include phrases from conversations you had with people, words you heard, ideas you remember.

DOI: 10.4324/9781003365228-45

Step 2

At the end of your free-write, read your writing aloud to someone else (for example, a classmate). Choose a sentence or phrase from your writing that best conveys the taste of surprise and the echo of the unexplained. It can consist of your own ideas and words (a thought you had during your fieldwork, a statement about what happened, an observation that still lingers) or it could be a comment by another person that you included in your free-write.

Step 3

Starting from this sentence or these words, write 1–2 pages in the format below. Use poetic prose or poetry (don't worry, it does not need to rhyme).

Use your chosen phrase as an opening line.
Follow it with one paragraph of prose or 5–10 lines of poetry describing what happened and why it was surprising. If you used a specific word in the field, feel free to use it here too. Work with the specific terms that emerged in your free-write: which expressions did you or your interlocutors use at that moment?

Choose evocative language, engaging as many of your senses as you can (taste, touch, sight, smell, sound). You can write in full sentences, or in fragments. Include enough details to make it vivid to yourself and your readers. Include only what is necessary,[1] so that your prose does not become heavy with words and explanations.

Repeat here your chosen phrase – hear it become an echo through time. Now describe the wider contexts. Places, people, scents, and sounds. Power relations, and histories lived. What must we know about where, what, who, and how? Write about the connections and disconnections that this episode made visible.

Repeat here your chosen phrase – it will start to feel familiar and resounding. What does this ethnographic moment feel like now? Write two possible explanations in the form of unanswerable questions. Write about the ways doubt and memory linger.

Repeat your chosen phrase as an ending line.

Tips for Writing Poetic Prose

Shorten your sentences. Part with all that is unnecessary. Give attention to word choice. Why this word and not another? Does each noun, verb, or adjective grasp what you sensed, thought, or wondered? Which images, characters, and gestures are brought to life? Listen to the sound of your writing—flow, rhythm, pauses, or emphasis are you creating?

Tips for Writing about the Complexity of Social Worlds

Is your voice the one of an all-knowing narrator? When possible, choose to write inside from specific standpoints: what does this moment look and feel like to an embodied, moving person in the field?

Try describing the same event from three points of view, using "I," "you," and "they/she/he." How are the differences and similarities between these perspectives connected to sociocultural narratives and processes, and to unequal social positions?

Help your readers see "cultural life as systems of lived contradiction" (McGranahan 2020, 6): write about paradoxes, the coming together of connections and disconnections, and the ways meaning can shift unexpectedly.

If you are working with different languages, include in your writing untranslatable words or expressions: how do they gesture towards incommensurability? How does the understanding conveyed by one language exceed what can be said in the other?

Example

In this example, I write about a fieldwork conversation that I still find puzzling after more than two decades. As a graduate student, in 1996, I researched a grassroot coalition in Ecuador promoting women's rights in low-income neighborhoods of Quito. When recounting her life as a political organizer, and how this shaped her role in the coalition, one of the group leaders described the mental experience of having already visited South American towns before ever having actually arrived—something that felt like "magic" to me, the listener. Her memory, she said, encompassed the very colonization of South America, as well as its alternative history, what "would have been." In her narration, the latter was not an imagined or possible past, but rather a history that she remembered. As a student doing fieldwork for the first time, the jarring coming together of temporalities and the uncanny, intimate quality of her knowing hundreds of villages left me wondering how to approach and write about this fieldwork moment.[2]

> *I walked to every town in Latin America, she says.*
>
> It is sunny in her courtyard, where we sit together for her to tell stories, for me to listen. A day in Quito, Ecuador. My interlocutor – an activist, theatre producer, and elder – recounts and performs her life story for me. So much to teach to a young student from far away.
>
> *I walked to every town in Latin America, she says,*
>
> on foot. It took years.
>
> As I listen to her words, time stands still. My surprise a quiet spin within.
>
> She continues: I remember everything. Every square in each village. I visited them all. Wherever I go, I know where everything is, because I go to places in

my mind before getting there. My memory spans hundreds of years. I remember what this continent would have been without colonization.

I walked to every town in Latin America, she says.

Liquid sunlight pools around us. What is this memory that walks in a future untethered? I am left with the weight of that story, its reach across time and generations, the known and the imagined. And I wonder: Is this the only way for her to explain to me the effort it takes to organize a woman's movement?

I walked to every town in Latin America, she says (Moretti 1997).

Why This Assignment

Ethnographers often encounter situations, stories, or events in their fieldwork that are deeply surprising or uncanny and that remain unexplained long after their research. They also encounter circumstances in the field that can be upsetting, even traumatic. Michael Taussig's opening of his book on ethnography and drawing is an example of such a moment. He recounts seeing a woman and a man in Medellin, Colombia, lying on the ground in a tunnel in the narrow gap between the wall and highway traffic. The woman was "sewing" the man as well as herself, "into a white nylon bag, the sort of bag peasants use to hold potatoes or corn" (Taussig 2011, 1). This scene, and his drawing of it, kept coming back to Taussig's mind—and yet "he still couldn't believe what [he] had seen" (ibid.). The "mix of calm and desperation" (Taussig 2011, 2) in the woman's effort of creating a shelter, and the striking precarity of their "cocoon" (Taussig 2011, 5) became a point of departure for Taussig to discuss the violent history of the town and the impacts on the inhabitants. This exercise will help you to write about a puzzling occurrence in your fieldwork by letting in your writing in the form of a repeating line. Rendering this enduring moment into an echo allows it to raise questions about your fieldwork contexts, relationships, and social world, without flattening your experience or "explaining it away."

More generally speaking, ethnographic fieldwork asks researchers to immerse themselves in situations, perspectives, and social worlds that are often unfamiliar or that question the ways of thinking and reference points of the researcher. Davidson carried out research with widows in Jola villages in Guinea-Bissau, but found out that the very word for widow did not exist in the Ejamat Jola language (2020, 43–44), calling into question her very inquiry. Finkelstein describes being "confused and disoriented" (2020, 4) when finding herself in the textile mills of Mumbai, a supposedly nonexistent place because, as she had been told, this Indian city had been deindustrialized. The dominant narratives about the textile factories no longer being in operation were a striking contrast to her daily conversations with the workers next to their buzzing machines. Significantly, both Davidson and Finkelstein found that these ethnographic puzzles helped them analyze what was important in their respective field sites.

When confronted with puzzling fieldwork circumstances or stories, it is often difficult to find a way of conveying why this matters. Academic writing can become a burden as encounters, experiences, or conversations in the field challenge a linear, descriptive academic language and explanation. Writing, however, can also become a creative and critical method to grapple with these complexities, by mirroring and following closely the questions and interruptions brought by fieldwork encounters.

How to Extend

Transform your written piece into a dialogue that could be performed as a spoken word commentary. To do so, work with a classmate or a fellow student and practice reading aloud alternating lines or sections of your writing. You can then perform your dialogue in a graduate seminar, a class, or a writing group. Hearing about a research encounter or event through two voices will help your audience to attend in new ways to the complexities of fieldwork relationships.

What to Read

In her ethnography of textile factories in Mumbai, India, Finkelstein writes about the puzzling comment of one of the workers: "My legs ache from twenty years of standing" (Finkelstein 2020, 57). These words continued to return to her memory and to perplex her during and after her research. Repeating her interlocutors' phrase throughout her chapter (Finkelstein 2020, 57–62) helped Finkelstein to anchor her fieldwork observations and analysis. Appadurai (2019) explores the concept of repetition through films and déjà vu.

Notes

1 In order to determine what is truly necessary, you might ask yourself: does this sentence serve the story I am telling? Is it essential to the story? If not, these sentences should be cut.
2 I discuss this encounter in more detail in my M.A. thesis: "Narrative, experience and the political," SFU, 1997.

References

Appadurai, Arjun. 2019. "The Ready-Made Pleasures of Déjà Vu: Repeat Viewing of Bollywood Films." *Cambridge Journal of Postcolonial Literary Inquiry* 6 (1): 140–52. https://doi.org/10.1017/pli.2018.38

Davidson, Joanna. 2020. "The Problem of Widows." *American Ethnologist* 47 (1): 43–57. https://doi.org/10.1111/amet.12869

Finkelstein, Maura. 2020. *The Archive of Loss*. Durham: Duke University Press.

McGranahan, Carole (eds.). 2020. *Writing Anthropology*. Durham: Duke University Press.

Moretti, Cristina. 1997. *Narrative, Experience and the Political: The Intersections of Lives and Activism in an Ecuadorian Women's Organization*. Simon Fraser University. M.A. thesis (Department of Sociology and Anthropology).

Taussig, Michael. 2011. *I Swear I Saw This*. Chicago: University of Chicago Press.

12 Creative Ethnographic Fieldstarters

Digging Deep into the Essentials of Ethnographic Writing

Ruth Behar

Creative Ethnographic Toolkit: Storytelling, place writing, vulnerable observation, fieldnotes, close listening, vulnerability, anthropology that breaks your heart.

Over the years, I've taught different versions of my graduate seminar Ethnographic Writing. Many of my former students now teach their own version of this course to their students, so it's had an afterlife beyond my classroom.

The course attracts a wide range of students, from anthropology, history, sociology, education, art, music, architecture, African American Studies, Latina/Latino Studies, South Asian Studies, and from creative writing, both fiction writers and poets. As a result, I've had to find ways of teaching it so that it's compelling for anthropologists while introducing non-anthropologists to the genre of ethnographic writing. This has led me to digging deep into the essentials of ethnographic writing to show that it's not simply a form of writing conforming to the needs of a single academic discipline, but a capacious narrative that allows us to think about journeys, encounters, and relationships through the lens of vulnerability.

To this day, many anthropologists approach their research from a distance. This means silencing the story of your entanglement with a specific set of people in a specific place at a specific moment in time, as well as how knowledge gets produced in this messy, haunting, unrepeatable process. By concealing your feelings of vulnerability as an observer and how the social world you're observing connects with your life, you can supposedly be *unobtrusive*, *neutral*, and *more objective*. But that stance asks you to deny any emotional connections to those who open their lives to you as an observer. In my book *The Vulnerable Observer: Anthropology That Breaks Your Heart* (2022 [1996]), I give voice to the alienation I've felt as I've tried to remain detached as an ethnographic researcher and writer. Instead, I propose that we write anthropology that breaks our hearts and that we write as "I" to address what it means to observe others and write about them. Who am "I" to have the right to do that? I've come to realize that what is going on in my own life at a moment of observation has consequences for what I can and cannot see and what I can and cannot understand. This knowledge needs to be worked through in the writing, because it is in the retrospective act of writing that you process the multidimensional and sensorial experience of doing anthropological research and forming

DOI: 10.4324/9781003365228-47

deep attachments to the people and places you return to over and over in real and imaginary journeys. What we're enacting here is our shared mortality. For me, that has always been at the core of the concept of vulnerability.

After introducing the concept of vulnerability, we read and discuss examples of ethnographic writing in the first half of the course. At the same time, I assign three short writing assignments to students so that they can *read like writers*. Then, in the second half of the course, students take turns to share their writing in a workshop format, when we all read and discuss the work and offer oral and written comments. I provide guidelines on how to be helpful and compassionate in offering comments and criticism. By the end of the semester, everyone has gotten to know each other's writing very well and there's a wonderful sense of joyful teamwork, which I reinforce by assigning each person with a writing buddy twice during the semester, with whom to discuss their writing one-on-one beyond the classroom.

The following three short writing prompts provide a baseline from which to build longer ethnographic pieces. The three essentials of ethnographic writing that they reflect on are being an observer, being a storyteller and a story listener, and being in places. Anthropology has a long and complex history of observing the lives, hopes, and dreams of others and how the self who is observing brings a particular background and set of expectations and assumptions to the experience. Ethnographic encounters are unique and finite; no two observers are exactly alike and the individuals and communities we work with are ever-changing. There is vulnerability in this process, both for the observer and the observed, who each are mutually observing each other (see also Jacobsen, this volume, "Writing Someone Else's Life Story"). So, the act of being an observer who is also going to tell the story of the encounter has a certain *magic* to it, as well as a certain beauty and a profound sense of loss, because it is ephemeral. All of that experience, at once so fleeting and so intensely lived, must somehow be captured in our writing. The first prompt attempts to bring us, as writers, into that space so we can reflect deeply on who we each are as observers.

Prompt 1: Being an Observer

Premise

The narrative, or literary, turn in anthropology opened up possibilities for autoethnography and created a new awareness of ethnography as a form of literary writing. Ethnographers began to dare to say "I" and experiment with different ways of being present in their texts. They started to call into question the practice of fieldwork and even the writing of fieldnotes. Feminist ethnographers started to turn to the personal voice to think about the fashioning of their own identities through the categories of race, sexuality, ethnicity, nationality, and social class. It became an urgent matter to bring emotional poetics into the crafting of ethnography and think about the anguish of being an observer.

Assignment

Write an autoethnographic piece about an insider–outsider predicament that you have experienced. Ultimately, try to reach an answer to the following question: What kind of an observer are you?

There are many different ways to respond to this prompt. You could write about a tender relationship with a grandmother who no one else in the family seems to think is interesting. You could write about being a perpetual observer and wishing it were possible to let go of that identity. You could write about how introverted you are and how difficult it is to reach out to people in your role as an anthropologist. No matter where a student of mine has gone with this assignment, it has set the stage for the writing they have done in the course. Almost all of my students have written something in this opening exercise that has inevitably formed part of their final writing project.

Prompt 2: Being a Storylistener and a Storyteller

Premise

Ethnographic writing has sometimes been described as a form of ventriloquism, as an effort to speak in the voice of the *other*. There are many ways to quote people in ethnography. They range from the classical method of choosing a few spoken remarks and framing them with analytical text to producing extensive life story or oral history texts that give all of the space on the page to the voice of others. Either way, the role of the ethnographer is to talk to people at length and carry out interviews, either informally or formally. From those interviews (as well as observations), ethnographies are produced that can seem *peopled* or *unpeopled*, depending on how skillfully the ethnographer has translated the voice of the other onto the page.

For this second writing assignment, we aim to move beyond reflections of the self who is doing the observing to the person or persons being observed. We address the question of how, as writers, we bring the voices and presence of those we wish to write about to the page in ways that do justice to their complex multidimensionality as human beings. In this exercise, you are asked to carry out an interview and then craft a monologue that allows the reader to hear and feel what was said. I also suggest writing a transcript of the interview and adding a postscript to discuss how you edited and shaped the writing. Too often, we don't stop to consider our process as writers or what steps we took to arrive at the final version. This exercise allows us to gain a deeper understanding of the layers of decision-making that go into the act of writing. Huge trust makes the passing of a story from storyteller to storylistener possible, while huge optimism allows a storylistener to then become a storyteller; both bring us to the realization that our hearts often break and open wide in the course of the work we do with others.

Assignment

Find a person who is willing to be interviewed. You can choose a family member, a friend or acquaintance, or a person you are meeting for the first time. Carry out the interview using a digital recorder or your phone, if this is feasible. For the interview itself, you can start with a simple question, such as "Tell me about an important moment or changing point in your life." You can also start with something smaller and more immediate, like "Tell me about your day." Whether or not you record, take notes on the conversation. When you have completed the interview, write a first-person narrative in the other person's voice. Decide how to insert yourself into the piece or not to insert yourself at all. Plan to share your notes and transcript. Add a postscript in which you discuss how you shaped and edited the narrative and perhaps why you deleted certain questions and extraneous remarks to create a compelling first-person voice. Also discuss how this exercise broke your heart and what that means.

Here, too, as can be imagined, my students have responded in a variety of ways. Some have interviewed those they felt they should be close to, like a mother or father or even a wife, husband, or romantic partner, but who they have never asked formally to talk about their life stories. They have always been surprised by what they learn and how much they learn. Some have had interviews they've carried back from the field but haven't known what to do with, so they listened to the recordings and re-encountered the people they met with the distance to really hear what they were being told and why. Some have decided to interview total strangers that they might otherwise have viewed as invisible, like an immigrant dishwasher they met in a restaurant or a neighbor they only crossed paths with in the park when they were both walking their dogs. This exercise reminds us that everyone has a story to tell and that the better we become at storylistening, the better we will become at ethnographic writing.

Prompt 3: Being in Places

Premise

Capturing the relationship between a community and a place has long been at the heart of ethnographic writing. In classic ethnographies, it is the ethnographer who travels elsewhere to bring back the stories of people rooted in distant places. This paradigm has shifted with the complex changes brought about by immigration, increased transnational travel, and globalization. Yet place, and the conjuring of place, continue to be a key part of ethnographic writing. But what exactly do places mean today, both to ethnographers and the people they write about?

For this third writing prompt, we address the meaning of places, sites, locations, and destinations that ethnographers view as crucial to their mission as writers. In the days of colonialism, anthropologists displaced themselves and traveled far and wide to exotic locales, spending extended periods of time being voluntary exiles immersed in the cultural otherness of somewhere that wasn't home but became almost-home over the course of their fieldwork. Today, such notions of travel now feel very antiquated, for sure, but we are still trying to figure out what constitutes a field site in our time. At this moment, perhaps every place is home or no place is home. Ethnographers now choose to carry out fieldwork in places that nurtured them or places their families abandoned and they returned to as part of a diaspora, or they choose to do virtual fieldwork projects involving online communities. All of these notions of place can be embraced when responding to the third prompt.

Assignment

Spend some time immersed in a field site (i.e., a place or setting that feels familiar and foreign to you) and write a vignette that captures the complex intersections of that place where diverse groups of people, commodities, memories, acts of forgetting, geographies, desires, dreams, disappointments, and disillusionments come together. Or if you prefer, you can focus on your own memories of a place or the historical memory of a place.

It is always fascinating to see how my students respond to this prompt. I find it inspires lyricism. One student quoted Toni Morrison's poem "Home," starting with the haunting lines "This house is strange./Its shadows lie./Say, tell me, why does its lock fit my key?" This led to a deep engagement with a home that had been in the family for generations, but not without estrangement for many of its members. Another student, also writing about home, explored a grandmother's move to her daughter's house and the sorrow of the only relic from her apartment being the recliner she spent all her time in, dozing in and out of sleep, living between the long past of her memories and the short present left to her in old age. Another student remembered fieldwork in Romania, surrounded by the ruins of communism, and how people sought out trees in the countryside that weren't tarnished with this history.

Walking the Road of the Story

After completing these three writing prompts in my course, I ask each student to present a written **proposal** of what they want to write about in more depth over the second half of the semester. While I believe writing is a mysterious process that can't be predicted before actually going on the journey of walking the road of the story word by word, it still is good to have an idea of the topic, people, place, and purpose of the project, as well as potential stumbling blocks. The three prompts you have just completed have built the foundation for you to write a brief research proposal. With this blueprint, it becomes possible to build the house in which the story will reside.

Prompt 4: Writing a Proposal

Assignment

Write a proposal for your final project to be shared with peers. Describe your field site or setting, the participants, the research you have done or need to do to carry out your project, and how you will be positioned within the project and the text you plan to write. Discuss any ethical issues and writing problems you expect to encounter. Describe which genre (autoethnography, sensorial ethnography, ethnographic poetry, ethnographic fiction, chronicle, photo-essay, etc.) or mix of genres you plan to use. Consider the dramatic potential of the story you plan to tell. Think about how you will bring productive tension into the work by being aware of things such as turning points, showdowns, hardships, life reversals, rituals gone wrong, arguments, and conflicts (not only between individuals but also, more broadly, between, say, local and global forces). You may wish to follow Kirin Narayan's suggestion to "Write a scene that shows you explaining your project to the people you'll be writing about; to a respected authority figure; or in conversation with yourself" (Narayan 2012: 100). For this proposal, you should have a separate heading for each category listed above, including "field site," "ethical issues," and "genre." Include an **annotated bibliography** of the available literature on your subject.

If you get stuck along the way in your ethnographic writing journey, you can always come back to the three fundamental prompts: who am I as an observer; who are the people speaking to me and why; what does it mean to be in one place and not another. Even when traveling without a map, which is how I always travel, I promise my students that they won't be lost.

References

Behar, Ruth. 2022 [1996]. *The Vulnerable Observer: Anthropology That Breaks Your Heart* (25th anniversary edition with new afterword). Boston: Beacon Press.

Narayan, Kirin. 2012. *Alive in the Writing: Crafting Ethnography in the Company of Chekhov*. Chicago: University of Chicago Press.

Trauma and Turning around the Ethnographic Gaze

Renato Rosaldo

Creative Ethnographic Toolkit: Poetry, antropoesía, thick description, writing from multiple perspectives.

Poetic exploration resembles ethnographic inquiry in that insights emerge from specifics more than from generalizations. In neither case do concrete particulars illustrate an already formulated theory. In antropoesía, my term (in Spanish) for verse informed by ethnographic sensibility, I strive for accuracy and engage in forms of inquiry in which I am surprised by the unexpected. Antropoesía is a process of discovery more than a confirmation of the already known. If you know precisely where a poem is going before beginning to write it, there is no point in going further. The same can be said of thick description (Geertz 1973) in ethnography, where theory is to be discovered in the details. The details inspire theory rather than illustrate already formulated theory.

In this prompt, I encourage you to take a moment in your life during fieldwork and spin it out from different angles, beginning with yourself and then opening up to the perspectives of others. In this way, you are able to ultimately view yourself and your world from multiple angles beyond your own and write from both the center and the margins of the experience, playing with differing points of view in the process.

Why This Assignment

The subject of my collection of poetry (Rosaldo 2014) is a particular event: the death of my then-wife Michelle Zimbalist Rosaldo while we did fieldwork with our two young sons in the Philippines. This event shattered my life, but also a number of other lives in the village of Mungayang and the nearby towns of Lagawe and Kiangan. This collection, from which I provide excerpts below, attempts to capture the eruption caused by this event and its reverberations through the medium of poetry. In writing these poems, I found that my memory and my field journal supplemented each other. At times, I remembered incidents that I had neglected to record in my journal; at other times, I failed to recall names, places, or incidents that I had written about.

DOI: 10.4324/9781003365228-48

In antropoesía, description is central. One poet who articulates this perspective is the late New York writer Harvey Shapiro, who spoke of himself as being "very loosely" an Objectivist.[1] Being an Objectivist, for him, "is a belief in the healing power that resides in the eye's ability to see the world… . It's the belief that words don't point to words but that words point to real things in the world. It's the opposite of the Language Poets"[2] (Williams 2001: 4).[3] In my view, his distinction more usefully underscores the tension that is inherent in all poetry, which transpires from striving to find the music or *magic* of language and seeking to explore the world through nature, politics, society, or psyche. In my verse, I attend to language but I do not try to replicate a person's speech as if I were a recording device. Nor do I believe that representation is transparent or that we can automatically map meaning onto words. Instead, I seek to unveil details that characterize a person or revealing phrases of everyday speech that transcend by being luminous, ominous, or, perhaps, uncanny.

Poetry has proven compelling for me because it allows me to dwell in powerful experiences and perceptions. It enables me to render these feelings intelligible, vivid, and present. In lyrical moments, I seek the larger significance in telling details. However, my task is not to give clarity to feelings that are, in fact, unclear. In the initial moment of shock, which I depict in the collected poems, my feelings were as ill-defined as they were overwhelming. My verse does not try to transform the ill-defined into the well-defined. My task, as an antropoeta, is to render intelligible what is complex and bring home to the reader the uneven and contradictory shape of that moment. In the prompt below, making things that are complex, uneven, and contradictory seem intelligible is your job as well.

A note on voice and voicing: In *The Day of Shelly's Death* (2014), I often speak for other people in their first-person voices. This approach has its risks, particularly in terms of projection (the imposition of your perceptions onto those of others). Yet these social relations, however accidental or fleeting they might have been, were vivid and significant. I learned from them. In addition, my collection of poems shines the spotlight on the kinds of people who are placed off-stage in most ethnographies: a tricycle taxi driver; a soldier; priests and nuns whose hospitality I depended upon entirely. I entrusted myself and my sons to their care. I owe them an incalculable debt.

What to Read

Poets speak, perhaps with irony, of the poetry of mere description. Consider Fairchild's "The Machinist, Teaching His Daughter to Play the Piano:" "The brown wrist and hand with its raw knuckles and blue nails / packed with dirt and oil, pause in mid-air, / the fingers arched delicately" (1991: 217). Or consider "Sunday in the Empty Nest" by Sharon Olds: "Slowly it strikes me how quiet it is./ It's deserted at our house. There's no one here, / no one needing anything of us/ and no one will need anything of us/ for months" (2002: 53). Or consider Juan Felipe Herrera's "19 Pokrovskaya Street:" "My father lights the kerosene lamp, his beard bitten, hand/

wet from the river, where he kneels to pray in the mornings,/ he sits and pulls out his razor, rummages through a gunnysack" (2008: 300).

These poems create deep feelings through the accumulation of concrete particulars rather than by beginning (as so many fine lyric poets do) with a named subjective state and elaborating through image and metaphor. Specificity matters. Like ethnographers, antropoetas look and look and listen and listen until they see or hear what they did not apprehend at first. This form of inquiry resembles field research in that it involves observation, asking questions, attending with patience and care, and knowing that meaning is there, waiting to be found, even if the observer–poet does not yet know what it is.

The first poem I wrote about Shelly's death was "The Omen of Mungayang" (Rosaldo 2014: 53), which I initially drafted in the summer of 2000. It concerns the moment I learned of Shelly's accident and ran to her body.

> Minutes later, Conchita
> steps into the hut and rasps, *She fell*
> *into the river.* I run, reach Shelly's body, drop
> to her side. A fly buzzes in, then out of her mouth.

The fly entering her mouth is a poetic image of finality. Brute. Traumatic. But above all, it is the recollection of a harrowing experience and a moment of devastating loss, as well as a personal realization of mortality. In the poem, my sons further instruct me about mortality in ways I do not expect: "I put Sam on my shoulders, tell him his mom is dead./ He wants to know when he will get a new one." (…)

In *The Day of Shelly's Death,* my poems explore the subjectivities of people I encountered on that day of trauma. We all were affected, though differently, by Shelly's death. In writing about the people I encountered (people who, for the most part, I barely knew or had never met), I learned how deeply my feelings resonated within and were shaped by a field of accidental social relations. The people in this field into which I was thrown had various attitudes toward me: attentive, caring, aggressive, inappropriate, and mixed. The fact that there were so many people toward the caring end of this spectrum is more than I could have dared hope. I am still grateful.

The prose poem "In a White Cubicle" explores something of the range of these relations, beginning with the inappropriate.

> At the clinic in Lagawe strangers form a
> crowd and stare at me. One man with a cheery
> smile asks, *How did it happen?* The room
> fades to very white.
> Help comes to me by grace, without my asking:
> A woman from the pharmacy asks for the
> American. I nod. She hands me diapers,
> sodas, snacks, and mosquito nets.

A local mayor proves brutal in his not unjustified reprimand:
  The Mayor of Lagawe shouts, *How could*
    you allow your wife to walk the trail alone?
    Why don't you embalm the body here in
    Lagawe?
And caring help comes uncalled when I desperately need it:
  Father George says, *Never mind the Mayor,*
    he's drunk, then drives me and the boys to the
    convent in a VW bug."

Through particular poems I explore the qualities and impact of individuals in my field of accidental relations. I also probe into my feelings as refracted through the perceptions of these others, including ethnographic observations of the self as I might have been perceived by others. From one poem to the next, I change focus, subject matter, mood, and tone.

For example, in "The Tricycle Taxi Driver," the driver is waiting for me. He has heard of Shelly's death and knows I'll walk down the road where he is parked. The poem begins and ends with his saying: "Please accept my gift." He takes pride in his work: "In Lagawe I own the only/ tricycle taxi, orange, yellow, red,/ fresh paint, curving lines." Not unlike the soldier, the tricycle taxi driver observes my state of exhaustion and devastation.

The American man shoulders
his five-year-old son,
his walk heavy, shirt soaked,
face streaked with dirt,
his tears behind red eyes,

I offer to pay for the ride, but the driver says again that he wants no pay: "Please accept my gift." In fact, it was not until I wrote the poem that I received the blessing of the tricycle taxi driver's gift. I am deeply grateful.

Prompt

Using the different perspectives offered in *The Day of Shelly's Death* as a starting point, write a poem about a moment of extreme grief, hardship, or loss from multiple perspectives. If you've already done fieldwork, this could be a moment from the field. If you haven't yet done fieldwork, then this could be about another type of grief that you choose to share. You could consider starting with your fieldnotes, if you have them, or jottings from a journal, if you keep one. Start with yourself and your own experience of the event and move out from there. Who else was involved in this moment of loss? What were their perspectives of the situation and how did they view you? Your poem can be written in prose or using a specific metric structure. It can be a single, longer poem or multiple small ones. Choose the structure that best reflects what you want and are trying to express in your writing.

In this prompt, I want you to look and look and listen and listen until you see or hear what you did not apprehend at first. What accumulation of concrete particulars could you add to your poem(s) in order to render the felt experience of the accidental field of social relations you are trying to describe? Finally, who was offstage in the event you describe and how could you render them fully visible? How were others, both human and non-human, observing you in this moment? For full credit, your poem should include at least four different perspectives and one of these should be your own.

What Else to Read

Anthropologists who are also poets usually trace our genealogies to the eminent ancestors Edward Sapir and Ruth Benedict. Benedict published her poetry under the name Anne Singleton (see this volume, Introduction). (For samples of their poetry and their correspondence about poetry, see Margaret Mead's *An Anthropologist at Work: Writings of Ruth Benedict* (1959)). Other notable predecessors include Paul Friedrich and Dell Hymes. More recently, a number of anthropologists have written verse and about verse in other cultures. Among them are Jerome Rothenberg, Dennis Tedlock, Lila Abu-Lughod, and Ivan Brady. To bring this incomplete list more up to date, I would like to add Ruth Behar, Melisa Cahnmann-Taylor, Valentine Daniel, Michael Jackson, Adrie Kusserow, Kent Maynard, and Nomi Stone. Many of these poets have been involved with *The Society for Humanistic Anthropology*, which sponsors panels, readings, and workshops for these and other poets, as well as noted ethnographic writers of memoir and fiction, at the annual meetings of the American Anthropological Association.

Notes

1 Objectivists were a loosely affiliated group of American poets who were writing in the 1930s and 40s.

2 Language poetry refers to an avant garde poetry movement that began in the late 1960s by poets such as Ron Silliman and Susan Howe as a response to narrative and confessional movements, such as by Anne Sexton and Robert Lowell. Language poetry draws the reader's attention to the look and sound of a word as meaning itself.

3 Shapiro distinguishes these two poles—words that point to words versus words that point to the world—in order to differentiate two schools of poetry: the Objectivists as opposed to the Language Poets.

References

Abu-Lughod, Lila. 2016 [1986]. *Veiled Sentiments Honor and Poetry in a Veiled Society*. 30th Anniversary Edition. Berkeley: University of California Press.

Behar, Ruth. 2007. *An Island Called Home: Returning to Jewish Cuba*. New Brunswick, NJ: Rutgers University Press.

Benedict, Ruth [see Anne Singleton]

Brady, Ivan. 2003. *The Time at Darwin's Reef: Poetic Explorations in Anthropology and History*. Lanham: Alta Mira Press.

Cahnmann-Taylor, Melisa. 2016. *Imperfect Tense*. San Pedro: Whitepoint Press.

Daniel, Valentine. 1996. *Charred Lullabies: Chapters in an Anthrography of Violence*. Princeton: Princeton UP.

Fairchild, Bertram Harry Fairchild, Jr. 1991. "The Machinist, Teaching His Daughter to Play the Piano" (poem). *TriQuarterly* 81: 217.

Friedrich, Paul. 2006. *From Root to Flower: Selected Poems*. Chicago: Virtual Artist's Collective.

Geertz, Clifford. 1973. *The Interpretation of Cultures*. Vol. 5019. New York: Basic Books.

Herrera, Juan Felipe. 2008. "19 Pokrovskaya Street." In *Half of the World in LIght: New and Selected Poems*. Tucson: The University of Arizona Press.

Hymes, Dell. 2003. *Now I Know Only So Far: Essays in Ethnopoetics*. Lincoln: University of Nebraska Press.

Jackson, Michael. 2013. *Midwinter at Walden Pond*. Bloomington, IN: AuthorHouse,

Kusserow, Adrie. 2024. *The Trauma Mantras: A Memoir in Prose Poetry* Durham: Duke University Press

Maynard, Kent. 2002. *Sunk Like God Behind the House*. Kent: Kent State UP.

Mead, Margaret 1959. *An Anthropologist at Work: Writings of Ruth Benedict*. New York: Avon Books.

Olds, Sharon. 2002. "Sunday in the Empty Nest." *The Unswept Room*. New York: Alfred A. Knopf, 53.

Rosaldo, Renato. 2014. *The Day of Shelly's Death*. Durham, NC: Duke University Press.

Rothenberg, Jerome. 1999. *A Paradise of Poets*. New York: New Directions.

Sapir, Edward. 1949. *Selected Writings on Language, Culture, and Personality*. Ed. David Mandelbaum. Berkeley: University of California Press.

Singleton, Anne [pseud. of Ruth Benedict]. "Intimacies." In *Poetry: A Magazine of Verse, 1928*.

Stone, Nomi. 2008. *Stranger's Notebook*. Evanston: TriQuarterly Books.

Tedlock, Dennis, trans. and ed. 1996. *Popol Vuh: The Mayan Book of the Dawn of Life*. New York: Simon and Schuster.

Williams, Michael. 2001. "Problems of knowledge: A critical introduction to epistemology." Oxford: Oxford University Press.

13 Looking Back and Moving Forward

Ethnographic Songwriting, Deep Hanging Out, and Keeping Our Practice Alive

Intention, Showing Up, and Feeding Our Inner Scholartist

Kristina Jacobsen

Creative Ethnographic Toolkit: Finding a research project, social theory as praxis, ethnographic songwriting, artistic practice, methods and forms of sharing data.

I was living in Chicago when I finally gave myself permission to start writing songs. It was 2005, and, burnt out from my PhD program in Ethnomusicology at an Ivy League university, I was taking a year off while suffering from a bad case of "academic perfectionism" (NCFDD 2023), or what I sometimes refer to when speaking to my graduate students as analysis paralysis.[1] During my year off, I also recognized a visceral need to rejuvenate and reconnect with the things that made me feel alive. I began volunteering at the Old Town School of Folk Music, which is a community music school that believes that making art is a human right. I also started teaching classical flute lessons on the side to make ends meet. I saw a songwriting class being advertised on the class roster and signed up. I remember a heightened sense of both nervousness and adventure as I entered the classroom on that first night and met our teacher, the songwriter Steve Dawson. Our very first song prompt was to write a song from a picture, which is a prompt that readers encountered earlier in this book (Chapter 6) in expanded form. Having grown up in a family of folk singers, I already loved to sing and harmonize, but I felt stymied by the mechanics of songwriting and questioned whether I had anything valid or important to say in a song. I also felt limited by my musical accompaniment chops on the guitar and embarrassed by my inability to play a steady rhythm or know the different styles I could use to accompany myself. After learning to be an *expert* in graduate school, returning to a beginner's mind as a songwriter felt unnerving, audacious, and scary.

I had also long wanted to join a country band. I love the expressive vocal style, the tight harmonies, the *cry* in country singer's voices, and the ways in which country songs tell stories I can follow and relate to. I had been introduced to country music as a teen through an AM radio station dial when I worked on the Navajo Nation as a seasonal Park Ranger and was starting studying the Navajo language, but I felt that my classical training as a flutist and being from western Massachusetts, where few people in my community listened to country, somehow prevented me from crossing over from the elite music of Sunday morning to the honky tonks of Saturday night. As I began my PhD program, I was introduced

DOI: 10.4324/9781003365228-50

to the recordings of singer, songwriter, and country singer Merle Haggard by my advisor, who was a deep lover of Merle's music. But listening to and analyzing country music from the space of an Ivy League university in a city was one thing; learning how to sing it authentically and write songs in that style felt like something completely different.

So, with a leap of faith and a prayer, I also joined the honky tonk ensemble at the Old Town School and began singing in earnest (the first song I sang lead on was a sassy Kitty Wells response song to Hank Thompson's *The Wild Side of Life*, called *It Wasn't God Who Made Honky Tonk Angels*). I bought a vintage lapsteel guitar on Ebay and named her Pearl after the early country singer Minnie Pearl. I also found a teacher, Steve Doyle, to take lessons with on the lapsteel guitar.[2] After a few months, I was hooked. Then, I began writing songs and playing country music in tandem with each other and they became synergistic, creating something greater than the sum of its parts.

My year at the Old Town School allowed me to play with being a songwriter and being a country artist, in an exploratory, low-stakes way, surrounded by hundreds of other people who loved these genres of music and were playing music and writing songs primarily for fun and as a hobby. It was also during my year in Chicago when, working on my first academic research article based on my earlier master's thesis research, also in Ethnomusicology (ASU 2003), I had a realization that fundamentally shifted the way I now understand what research is and the work it does for us in the world: the themes that were surfacing in my original songs in our beautiful, light-filled living room on Hermitage Avenue were the same themes I was addressing in the research article I was writing in my office down the hallway. What I had so neatly compartmentalized into two different physical spaces in my house were actually interconnected. So, at the same time I was writing the song *Inez* (*Three Roses* 2015), which is a song about a Diné woman (now mentor) and the impacts of US settler colonialism on her everyday life, I was also writing an article about placemaking, settler colonialism, and belonging on the Navajo Nation in Diné country music (Jacobsen 2009, *Ethnomusicology*). In other words, the song and the article were two sides of the same coin rather than two bifurcated sides of a split self. Through this experience, I began to realize that academic writing and songwriting are different genres, or modes of expression, to address the same themes from different angles and thus, work through questions of both personal and social scientific import. I began to understand that these two worlds, rather than one being my *work* and the other being a *hobby*, were both a part of my work, but work in a broader and more holistic sense as vocation, centering the questions that propel us as human beings and, often, as anthropologists and artists as well. In other words, to borrow Marshall McCluhan's phrase, the medium, in many ways, *is* the message (McLuhan 1964).

Without this year of regenerative artmaking, I don't think I would have continued graduate school. My year off, this gap year of what the writer Julia Cameron refers to as artistic recovery, between graduate programs gave me the boost of energy, sense of joy, self-confidence, and creative playfulness that I needed to sustain myself in completing the arduous (and often lengthy!) process of completing a

PhD program. But my year of learning the lapsteel and the basics of country songwriting is also what prepared me to audition with country bands for my dissertation fieldwork.

Fast forward 4 years to 2009, and this artistic exploration is what led to my doctoral dissertation in anthropology, for which I sang and played lapsteel with Navajo and Diné country and Western bands on the Navajo Nation in Arizona and New Mexico (Jacobsen 2012; 2017). In this research, which centered around playing music as a form of musical participant observation, I wanted to understand how questions of Diné (Navajo) identity and cultural politics were reflected and created through the performance of country music in a place where country music was ubiquitous (there are over 50 active country bands on the Navajo Nation) and passionately loved, and has been since the early 1930s (Jacobsen 2009; 2017; see also Romero 2019). Why was country music so meaningful to this group of primarily Diné men? This 2½ years of fieldwork, singing and playing in **bordertown** bars with the band Native Country (Jacobsen in Bishop and Watson 2023), began another form of musical and ethnographic training and a new musical community of practice that schooled me in another, culturally specific form of hard country music that allowed me to finally start calling myself a country artist, however complex that moniker is in our current political and sonic moment[3] (see Bishop and Watson 2023 for further discussion; see also Nussbaum 2023). For example, in this scene, *torch songs*, or slow ballads such as Patsy Cline's *Crazy*, weren't really included in the setlist; they were too slow and this was dance (and two-step) music (Jacobsen 2017)! And so, it was through playing with Diné bands and seeing, feeling, and understanding how much country meant to them and how they've been able to make it completely their own (even as a genre of music that is often perceived by outsiders as southern and White) that allowed me to make country music my own.

In this brief conclusion, I reflect on my own life as a touring singer–songwriter, song retreat leader, and bandleader and the ways it relates to, and is inspired by, my own anthropological practice. While I focus on songwriting here, my hope is that whatever your chosen artform, you find pieces that relate to your own ethnographic–artistic practice.

Finding a Place to Play

So, where do you start as an aspiring or practicing anthropologist, scholar, or qualitative researcher who wants to dig into artistic practice? And what if you are suffering, as I did and sometimes still do, from analysis paralysis?

I would first start with noticing which artforms you are drawn to, listen to, and pay attention to on a regular basis. Pay attention to your attention. Also notice who you are currently following on social media. Dig into the biographies of the people you are paying attention to: who have they worked with and how did they receive their training as an artist? Also, why do you love their work as much as you do? Then, as soon as possible, I would find a community of practice and a low-stakes environment where you can *play* in/with your chosen artform. Start making/doing whatever artform that is as soon as possible. Play isn't frivolous; play is deeply regenerative and essential to our wellbeing (Clark 2016; Marsh 2017). If you don't already have a budding practice, start watering those seeds. And, if you do have a practice, whether musical, visual, writing, or something else, start carving out a little bit more time to take it seriously, allowing the seeds to grow into a plantling. This could be a small group class or private lessons if those are accessible to you (many folks are now working with teachers virtually at a fraction of the cost).

In my first years of songwriting, this looked like the class I took at the Old Town School and signing up for a week-long songwriting workshop once a year, where I would cowrite a song with a new person (often very an experienced songwriter) each day. Through writing with someone else, I was able to witness and experience their own thought process, which, in turn, taught me a lot about the craft of songwriting. Your songs may be rough in the beginning: that's OK! *Thinking* about making art is very different from actually making it and one cannot substitute the other (Rubin 2023). In order to go deeply into any artform, we must also get our hands dirty, make it, and dance with it, too. *Armchair art* isn't an option.

I also find it helpful to remember that it is not frivolous to make art. When the inner critic arises, gently ask it to go and sit in the corner while you create stuff. You can say: "Thank you, critic. Now go and sit in the corner for the time being. I got this."[4] Beginner's mind or don't know mind is an "attitude of openness, eagerness, and lack of preconceptions when approaching a person or a situation" or form of art (Suzuki 2006: 3), which is essential to watering these seeds (see also Kabat Zinn and Hanh 2009). Remember that making art is a human right and an essential, anthropological part of being human, not just something for *artists*. You're developing a new skillset, and while your prowess may be in early elementary school or junior high, it may have been left behind, or atrophied, in your pursuit of other skillsets and accolades!

At this early, awakening-your-artist stage, I highly recommend using some kind of workbook or prompted guide to support you as you awaken your artist. A book I find particularly helpful is Julia Cameron's *The Artist's Way* (1998; 2006), which is both a book and a workbook. There are many, many groups that follow this book, both online and in person, and it's a great way to find support as you embark on your artistic journey, whatever the genre. It's a 12-week program to artistic recovery and features daily writing prompts, morning pages, and weekly artist dates. While dated in some respects, the prompts are timeless and invite us to tell the inner critic to go and sit in the corner while we let our artist play, which is something we do not allow ourselves to do as scholars.

Many times, the excuse we make is a lack of time. This is a legitimate concern, but don't let it stymy you! Just 15 minutes a day can work wonders, especially if it's how we *begin* our day. This is what writers call *showing up to the page* and what mindfulness practitioners call *showing up to the cushion*. And this is where routine, or what I like to think of as ritual, comes in. This must be non-negotiable and cannot be replaced by an emergency email to a student, professor, partner, friend, or colleague. Another option is to find someone who is offering daily or weekly writing prompts that you like, adding them to your feed and using them for whatever artform you are wishing to channel and explore. Suleika Jouad's

Isolation Journals (Jouad 2023) prompts are one of many examples of prompts that are often nuanced and ethnographically informed. Pat Pattison's daily, 10-minute object writing (Pattison 2023) prompts are another short, fun way to write when you have limited time in your schedule.

On my teaching days, I get up 30 minutes early so that I can have a short, 20-minute, power-packed guitar practice session and 10 minutes of object writing. I may get through only 3–4 songs, but I enter the classroom that day knowing that I made some art, for myself, first thing. My voice is warmed up from singing and I generally feel more fully present and alive as a result of this quick session. I also cultivate my ethnographic writing chops on a weekly basis. I feel that most of us can spare 15 minutes! Thus, it's not about epic, intensive, long artmaking sessions everyday: they aren't realistic and set us up for failure, but also aren't necessary! It's about doing the thing and paying ourselves first before we venture into the world where we will be offering things to other people for most of the day. In the afternoon, when I'm done teaching, I love to go to my local coffee shop and do ethnographic freewriting, noticing and taking in the smells, taste, touch, feel, and sights around me and of the fellow humans in my midst. I will often time these for 5–10 minutes so that I dive in deeply, describing everything I notice. Then, I'll take a brief pause to relax, drink my coffee, and simply be in the space. Or, when I have a bit more time at the weekend, I'll do 30 minutes of morning pages (Cameron 1998; 2006; also see Demetriou, this volume, Chapter 11) to start my day or I'll do 10 minutes of object writing directly after teaching as a way to decompress from the workday and shift gears *into* writing or creative practice and loosen the tight space of my analytic brain. In these ways, I am waking up, and then staying present with, my ethnographer and my artist hand-in-hand, from the beginning to the end of each day.

Risks of Combining Art with Anthropology

There are also risks to holding the shared identity of an artist and a scholar. One of these risks is that it allows *both* identities, anthropologist and songwriter, to be called into question at times. Years ago, I applied for a major National Science Foundation (NSF) grant to support a project on ethnography and songwriting in the western Mediterranean. This was a project for which I had already completed extensive ethnographic fieldwork and produced peer-reviewed research publications, and for which I would later receive a Fulbright and a Wenner-Gren[5] grant, resulting in many new publications and artistic projects (Jacobsen 2019, 2021, 2023, 2024). The project explicitly foregrounded the interface of rigorous ethnography, social theory, and artmaking. When I received the reviews, I felt hurt and perplexed when one reviewer, who did not see the merit of the project, decided to critique it not by discussing the research project (i.e., the methods, theories employed, or proposed findings) but by critiquing my music! At the time, I was devastated. I considered quitting songwriting and returning to more traditional anthropological research, at least for the purposes of grant writing. By submitting samples of both my scholarship and my art for this prestigious grant, I had opened myself up to critique of not only my anthropology but also something much more vulnerable: my art.

In hindsight, I now understand this moment differently. I understand, from Julia Cameron, that the meanest critics are often those who aren't in touch with their own artistic practice and that non-constructive critique can come from our own deepest vulnerabilities and inadequacies, as well as the artistic envy of others. If we don't allow ourselves to make art, then how dare someone else? Envy and jealousy are certainly emotions I, too, have experienced in my journey as an artist, and they can be incredibly destructive, both for ourselves and those we critique. At the same time, aesthetics (i.e., taste) is very personal, and it's OK for us to write music that doesn't appeal to someone else and it's OK for them to not like it. This is very different, however, from deciding on the merit of someone else's work *as an artist.* Our job as artist–anthropologists, as I see it, is to simply keep making art, get better, and continue developing as an artist in our chosen medium.

While much of this stigma has diminished, exemplified by the beautiful work of the contributors to *The Creative Ethnographer's Notebook,* both in this book and far beyond, what remains is the perception that art and anthropology are separate domains that have very little to say or offer to each other (for critiques of this view, see Schneider and Wright 2021; Marcus and Myers 1995). So, too, remains the perception that serious anthropology must be saturated with social theory that is filled with jargon and virtually inaccessible to many readers, including those with PhDs (Ortner 2006; Riles 2008). Thus, the esotericism of anthropology can sometimes be perceived as a sign of its value or contribution to the field. This is a perception that arts-based anthropology actively seeks to dispel, with the goal of making anthropology feel active, alive, and relevant to our lives and lived experiences.

Keeping Artistic Practice Alive and Growing a Thick Skin

What keeps my artistic practice alive now is travel, mindfulness, and the integration of songwriting and ethnography in the places I live, love, and travel to for extended periods of time. But these are also the things that keep my ethnographic practice alive. And, increasingly, these two identities have become fused. Rather than being suspicious of this fusion, I am learning, slowly, to embrace it and integrate these identities into a fuller and more complete sense of myself as a scholartist, world traveler, and ethnographer. This means bringing my anthropologist identity onto the stage when I perform and bringing my songwriter identity into the classroom, faculty meetings, and my anthropology talks. In this sense, my approach to things like promotion and tenure has also been a *both/and*, rather than emphasizing one field over the other.

As I write this conclusion, I am preparing to voyage to South Africa with my Merle Haggard-inspired, feminist honky tonk band The Merlettes on our first international tour. In Cape Town and Johannesburg, SA, we will perform shows, teach workshops to emerging artists, and collaborate with a South African bassist on her own original song in the Tswana language. We will perform at a major music festival, for which I am also now the Cultural Anthropology Consultant, which is a position that began when I attended the same festival with a Diné jazz trio last year (Jacobsen 2022). After this, I'll travel to northern Spain, where I'll lead a group of songwriters on the historic pilgrimage route, the *Camino de Santiago*, in a workshop focused on daily songwriting, creative practice, and waking up our artistic self through mindful walking. These events feel particularly joyful as I get to bring my fullest self, the anthropologist *and* the artist, to artistic and cultural conversations in international contexts. It feels like my ethnographic and artistic skillsets are each being pushed and, in turn, also pushing one another.

But growing also means intentionally surrounding myself with other songwriters and anthropologists who push my limits, critique my songs and ethnographic writing, and are free to be honest about what's not working in my songs. I attend monthly songwriting critiques and song circles, go on yearly retreats where we write a song a day for 6 days and receive feedback each night, and participate in weekend self-retreats for myself and other songwriters in my region to write and share our music, for which I am a peer and an artist rather than a teacher of songwriting. For every day I am teaching and/or facilitating the artistic process of others, I am *filling the well* with a day of writing, creative rest, and retreat for myself. In critique settings, it can also really help to come up with a list of specific questions you are having about your song in order to provide some structure for the person offering you a critique! This is essential not only for improving my craft, which is a lifelong endeavor, but for reminding me that songwriting matters to other people, which in turn reminds me of why it's important and meaningful to me. Without this continual exchange and reciprocity of ideas, my songwriting could start to calcify and feel stale.

Keeping practice alive means being willing to rewrite. A lot. Both songs and scholarly ethnographic prose. Over days, months, and years, with pen to paper or with guitar in hand, singing the lines over and over again until they feel right in my body and in my mouth as I sing them. And not settling for the inspired first draft alone. The first draft, in so many forms of writing, is often the most energizing and exciting for the artist, especially if you are gifted with a burst of artistic energy and intuition, sometimes also called *inspiration* (to breathe in, from the Italian "inspirare"), when a song or ethnographic vignette flows easily from the pen. But a first draft is also just that: a template. It's the jotting down of something young that still needs to be fully loved, formed, and made into its most complete self (Rubin 2023). In songwriting, this means making sure that every single line of the song is maximally significant and that there are no *throwaway* lines. "Shitty first drafts" (Lamott 1995) are essential for getting to the better second and third drafts. *Every line counts.* This means avoiding the predictable rhymes and expected clichés and drilling even deeper into the well of my own lived experience so that it is my data that feed my song, not someone else's idea, perception, or description that I am then trying to make my own. As the playwright Oscar Wilde said (perhaps apocryphally): "be yourself; everybody else is already taken."[6]

When and Who to Share Your Songs with: The Concentric Circle Model

While you want to develop a thick skin for receiving and digesting constructive criticism, you also want to be intentional and discerning in who you share your art and/or ethnographic writing with and in what order. This is an essential form of artistic and creative self-care.[7]

A wise teacher once suggested I think of sharing art in terms of three concentric circles. There is the *inner* circle, comprising the chosen few (two or three people) who you trust unconditionally and who will be tender-hearted and supportive when they listen to your songs. They may offer some gentle feedback, but their primary role is to listen attentively, offer their authentic emotional response, and serve as the initial first aid response team. This is Circle One. Circle Two is a bit broader and may include some trusted members of your artist community (in my case, other songwriters) but is still relatively small (between 5 and 10 people). This group is located between your core support group and anonymous members of the public, who may come to a show or a reading, for example.[8] When sharing your songs with Circle Two, you can ask some specific questions to guide the feedback that you are offered or share things that you are struggling with in your songs, for example: Does the story make sense? Does the song need another verse or a bridge? Do the chords serve the song or do I need different chords and harmonic language to tell the story?

Finally, Circle Three (10–15 people) contains your tougher critics whose opinions you still value and who you believe will make your songs better. This could include other professionals in your field, mentors, artists you admire but don't know well, or people that have a knack for a certain approach or skillset in songwriting (for example, I like to share my work with lyricists or people who know how to write fantastic bridges). You only want to share your songs with Circle Three once you've already established for yourself, *in* yourself and in your bones, that the songs are of value, are *good enough*, and feel true and authentic to what you are trying to communicate through the songs. Not all songs get to Circle Three, and that is OK. Knowing these things will allow you to have a thicker skin when receiving harder critiques but also to be tenacious and keep working on your songs because you will feel invested and believe that they are songs worth revising.

Final Creativity Prompt

1. Take a moment and then draw three concentric circles on a piece of paper and color each one in a different color of your choice. Spend a few minutes sifting through your social and artistic circles and think about who is in *your* three circles. Add the names of these people to each circle.

   Which 2–3 people belong in your Circle One?
   Who else would you then share a song with to create your Circle Two and Circle Three?

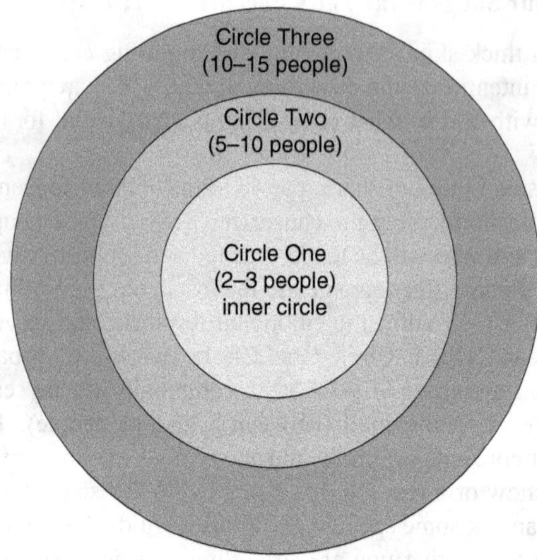

Figure 13.1 The three concentric circles model.

Put this drawing up on your wall: somewhere you'll see it every day. Use these circles as a guideline and try not to self-sabotage, i.e., share something that is still in the birthing process with your harshest critic!

2. Now, share one of your song with at least one person from Circles One, Two, and Three.
3. After you've done this, briefly journal about this journey of sharing your art with at least one member from Circles One, Two, and Three. What did that feel like? Did you feel seen or heard? If not, why not? Do you need to adjust your circles and who is in each one?

Why This Assignment

Discerning who is in your different circles is important. Sharing a song too early with a harsh critic is a sure-fire way to kill that song while it is still in the birthing process, relegating it to our "grief bag" of songs (Perkins 2009) that are never played again. For example, I had a songwriting student who would automatically share any new song *baby* with their older brother. They were just so excited to share it! The older brother, in turn, was a talented guitarist and musician who was no longer making music. Each time his younger sibling would share a new song, he would offer a searing critique and the student would be devastated. They would come to the next class with no new song and for some weeks, they would no longer want to write a new song or even make music! They were treating their brother as a member of Circle One, when in reality he belonged to a concentric circle much, much further out.

Ethics of Artmaking in Ethnographic Contexts

What are the ethics of our artmaking? While ethics have been exhaustively discussed in the context of fieldwork in anthropology, this has been addressed less often in ethnographic artmaking. Part of these ethics, I think, is drawing attention to our own positionality as both artists and researchers, and seeking to level the playing field with other artists, when and where possible. For example, in order to draw attention to the process and not just the product, I prefer to do collaborative artmaking/cowriting, where all credit is shared 50/50 between me and the other artist. This is the method I used when writing the song *i.will.cross.* with my colleague and poet Ather Zia (this volume, Chapter 9), i.e., asking permission to use her poem before I even picked up my guitar and then sending drafts of the recording over for feedback as the song developed. I also was able to do collaborative songwriting for an EP of cowritten songs with the singer–songwriter Meredith Wilder (*Elemental* 2018), as well as with songwriters, poets, language activists, and musicians on the Italian island of Sardinia for the album *House on Swallow Street* (2021), which was released by the Italian label Talk About Records. The latter project was supported by a US Fulbright grant, which is earmarked for both artists and scholars to research about and make art in Italy's south.

Other times, however, we may be less intentional about setting out to make art. Sometimes a song comes and it flows, and we are simply the conduit. I do not ever say no to a song if it comes to me. I take it as a gift and, when the inner critic arises (it almost always does!), I gently tell my critic to go and sit in the corner. Other times, we may write a song but aren't necessarily meant to perform it (Simos 2017). It is meant for someone else to perform. Later in the rewriting stage, I'll drill down into a song's believability or, if I'm writing a biographical song, its accuracy and cultural and historical specificity. But, in general, I believe in letting ourselves write when inspiration comes. We are the vessel and receiving a song is a gift. It is bigger than us. And the song/poem/piece of writing or art *can always get better*.

Identifying Grants and Carving Out Time to Create

As a former Fulbrighter and my College Fulbright representative on campus, I am a huge believer in the power of grants, like the Fulbright,[9] to carve out time and space to play, create, and go deeply into another culture. Grantwriting and applying to artist residencies to buy yourself time as an artist and scholar can be worth their weight in gold! The Fulbright Foundation offers grants for artists, working professionals, and scholars (Fulbright Student and Fulbright Scholar) to create their dream projects overseas and is open to anyone with a bachelor's degree or above. These grants are an incredible way to create space and time (and something that Melisa and I have both happily been supported by in our own artmaking) to really live within a project. Grants range from 3 months to 1 year in length. I have friends that have studied opera in Italy, composed symphonies in Austria, studied a style of fiddle-playing in France, and learned politically non-dominant languages in Mexico through a Fulbright grant. Other anthropology grants, such as the Wenner-Gren and yes, sometimes the National Science Foundation as well, will support arts-integrated anthropology projects and are another powerful way to support research and fieldwork, or deep hanging out (Geertz 1973; Jacobsen 2024 forthcoming), particularly at the PhD and post-PhD levels. Another example is a songwriter friend of mine who was working at Whole Foods. She won a month-long artist residency to live in a casita in the mountains of Taos (northern New Mexico), where she had access to a state-of-the-art recording studio and was surrounded by other artists. She recorded a stunning EP of songs while she was there.

Getting Unstuck and the Benefit of Art-Adjacent Spaces

As a songwriter, I also love to participate in creative writing groups for writers who know nothing about songwriting. I find it inspiring and refreshing, and I feel much less pressure to write something *good* than if I were around a group of songwriters. I also love it when writers and poets attend my songwriting workshops! Seeking out art-adjacent spaces, i.e., places where we can make art that is related to but different from our main form of artistic practice, can open up new energy and possibilities and ultimately, reinvigorate our primary form of art. The songwriter Joni Mitchell, who is also a painter, refers to this as "crop rotation" (Mitchell in Ghomeshi 2013). If you are feeling stuck in your artmaking or ethnographic writing, is there an art-adjacent space you can explore? One art-adjacent space I've had a lot of fun exploring is writing OpEds (opinion pieces) for local newspapers in the southwest (see Jacobsen 2020). I learned how to do this through the OpEd Project's Write to Change the World program, which mentors writers and academics in how to write for a broader public. This genre of writing is another form of applied anthropology and one OpEd, which was published in the *Sante Fé New Mexican*, ultimately led to a song I also wrote that was inspired by the same topic of vibrant aging in Sardinia, called *Franzisca*.

Getting Your Art Out There and Measuring Success

How do you know if your art is good enough to share in a public forum? When should you consider recording an album or publishing some of your writing? This is a tricky one, and I think the quickest answer is time depth. How long have you been creating your art for? Have you had time to receive feedback and critiques from other artists whose work you respect? Are you regularly performing your songs (some people use the metric of 1000 shows)? Do you have 4–6 songs that consistently receive really strong responses when you perform them? Have other artists who you respect suggested that you consider recording or publishing? For most of us, recording or publishing won't make us a star, but it can be a powerful way to circulate and share our art around the world and network and build community with other artists who we could invite to collaborate with us.

If you do decide to record, be diligent about the specifics! Always list all cowriters on the song credits. Be sure that they are registered to receive song royalties and that their names appear correctly on all digital media platforms. Also, make sure that your cowriter knows you are recording the song and that they are OK with it! You may also wish to have a conversation with them about the possibility of recording two different versions of the song: one by you and one by them. I did this with my cowritten song *Three Roses* (Jacobsen and Dillenberg 2015) and it was amazing to hear and see how differently the song came out!

Lastly, be clear in yourself what *success* looks like, or else this can become another stumbling block. I encourage you to journal about this and come up with a short list of yardsticks for yourself about *why* you are sharing your art in the public sphere. Again, be intentional! For me, success as a songwriter and ethnographer isn't about being famous or even well-known. It's about being and feeling seen and heard as a human being by a small group of people (often 20–30), with whom I feel I am really able to share my songs as part of the fabric of my life experience. These shows could be on the Navajo Nation or in Sardinia, Cyprus, or Scandinavia. These are my most rewarding moments, both as an ethnographer and s singer–songwriter.

Concluding Thoughts

In the end, I am a huge believer in the power of art and the power of ethnography. Songwriting is accessible storytelling that can change hearts and minds to change the chemistry of a room. It's why I've written this book with Melisa. It's why finding the nexus of how and where art and ethnography meet has been so productive for me, artistically and as a researcher. It's also why I founded culturally immersive songwriting retreats for songwriters, ethnographers, and intrepid mindful travelers and facilitate them each year in my various field sites around the world. These include workshops on the Navajo Nation, in Sardinia, and along the *Camino de Santiago* in northern Spain.

But I'm also a believer in holding space for you, as creative ethnographers, to come alive in your own, unique synergies of research and artistic practice. What unique blend of art and ethnographic practice will you create? What textures will it have? What sounds, smells, and feelings will it evoke? Forza!

And so, dear creative ethnographers, I'll love and leave you with a song. In this one, cowritten with the artist and pilgrim John Parish, I explicitly use a term from social theory: Marshall McLuhan's "the medium is the message." This is an attempt to make social theory more accessible for anthropology students, both in and through a song. It's a song about process, lingering, and staying present for our own creative and ethnographic journeys, whatever they may look, sound, or feel like.

The Medium is the Message
Kristina Jacobsen and John Parish, copyright 2019
~with thanks to Marshall McLuhan (1964)~

Yes I could text you and it would get there faster
Message delivered, said and done
But would you see my hand on this note
smudge of coffee spilled as I wrote
Or how my cursive gets more slanted
When I'm excited about what I want to tell you

So I'd rather write you a letter
Sometimes the medium is the message

Yes driving in my truck is more efficient
And less hassle, all around
But I'd miss the smell of tamales from El Modelo
And the scent of sage on Rio Grande
And the raw humanity on 2nd street
Reminds me of who I mean to be

So I'd rather ride my scooter
The medium is the message

Sometimes slowing down is just the thing we need
to return to our truer, kinder selves
And no, it's not efficient at all
But neither is a marvelous dance!

The Buddhists say, "haul water and chop wood"
Pilgrims say, "Solvitur ambulando"
And after the ecstasy there's still laundry
To hang in my backyard
So let's walk with discomfort 'stead of running from this pain that's the joy of living
Yeah stay with the process sometimes it's all we can do
The medium *is* the message
The medium *is* the message

Notes

1 I define this as arriving at a point where we are frozen in both our creative and academic work. I am not referring to physiological paralysis; rather, it is the feeling that after spending so much time *thinking* about anthropology, actually *doing* something in the field, such as fieldwork, feels impossible to get right. It is a feeling of *damned if you do and damned if you don't.*

2 The lapsteel is also referred to as the Hawaiian guitar and was the precursor to the pedal steel guitar. You play it with a slide bar in your left hand (I use a ¾" concave bullet bar) and with picks on the thumb and middle and index fingers of your right hand.
3 My forward-thinking anthropology advisors strongly supported my musical endeavors. They understood (better than I did, I think) that in order for me to thrive in graduate school, I would need to keep my artistic side alive. I am forever grateful for their foresight and the generous path they showed me in sharing the intertwining of art, politics, and personal practice in their own lives.
4 This approach was inspired by a similar phrase offered to me in a workshop with Nashville-based songwriter Mary Gauthier.
5 The Wenner-Gren Foundation for Anthropological Research.
6 The date of this Wilde quote is ambiguous, but it is often cited as being published in the *Hudson Review* in 1967 (style.mla.org).
7 While I discuss this method using examples from songwriting, it applies equally well to any form of art or writing, including ethnographic writing.
8 A related approach is also offered in Tara Schuster's book *Buy Yourself the F*cking Lilies: And other Rituals to Fix Your LIfe from Someone Who's Been There* (2020). See the chapter "Hype Men, Road Warriors, and Those you Must Avoid: Know Your Team" (p. 75).
9 Fulbright grants are for students, scholars, and artists from the US or abroad to carry out projects in a host country that enhances mutual understanding and facilitates cultural exchange between the US and the host country. To learn more, look for the Fulbright Student (students) and Fulbright Scholar (scholars) programs.

References

"Artistic Growth | Creativity During COVID | Reflecting on the Pandemic | Creative Meditation." n.d. *The Isolation Journals*. www.theisolationjournals.com

Bishop, Paula and Jada Watson, eds. 2023. *Whose Country Music? Genre, Identity, and Belonging in 21st Century Country Music Culture.* Cambridge: Cambridge University Press.

Cameron, Julia. 1998. "*The Artist's Way.*" Harmondsworth, England: Penguin Press.

Cameron, Julia. 2006. *The Artist's Way Workbook.* Harmondsworth, England: Penguin Press.

Clark, Cindy. 2016. *Play and Wellbeing.* New York: Routledge.

Dawson, Steve. 2023. https://stevedawsonmusic.com

Dillenberg. 2016. *Three Roses.* https://open.spotify.com/track/7rDqRbnohWEl9y9jYgGYQ8.

Doyle, Steve. 2023. www.oldtownschool.org/teachers/Steve-Doyle/

Geertz, Clifford. 1973. *The Interpretation Of Cultures*. New York: Basic Books.

Ghomeshi, Jian. 2013. "Oh sure, I blazed a lot of trails." Interview with Joni Mitchell. https://jonimitchell.com/library/view.cfm?id=2751

Jacobsen, Kristina M. 2003. "Native Bands of Diné Bikeyah: Navajo Country and Contexts." M.A. Thesis, Arizona State University.

Jacobsen, Kristina Michelle. 2012. "Navajo voices: Country music and the politics of language and belonging." PhD dissertation citation, Department of Cultural Anthropology, Duke University. UMI Proquest.

Jacobsen, Kristina. "House on Swallow Street." *Talk About Records*. Santu Lussurgiu, Sardinia. https://talkaboutrec.bandcamp.com/album/house-on-swallow-street

Jacobsen, Kristina. 2009. "Rita(hhh): Placemaking and Country Music on the Navajo Nation." *Ethnomusicology* 53 (3): 449–477.

Jacobsen, Kristina. 2015. "Inez." *Three Roses,* Three Roses Music. www.youtube.com/watch?v=-h0c3-X_mHc

Jacobsen, Kristina. 2015. *ThreeRoses.* https://soundcloud.com/kristinajacobsenmusic/09threeroses

Jacobsen, Kristina. 2017. *The Sound of Navajo Country: Music, Language and Diné Belonging.* Chapel Hill: University of North Carolina Press.

Jacobsen, Kristina. 2019. *Medium Is The Message.* https://soundcloud.com/kristinajacobsenmusic/medium-is-the-message

Jacobsen, Kristina. 2020. "A Society That Honors Elders Is More Caring | My View | Santafenewmexican.Com." www.santafenewmexican.com/opinion/my_view/a-society-that-honors-elders-is-more-caring/article_382ce026-45a8-11eb-9b1a-8328d0de8816.html

Jacobsen, Kristina. 2022. "How a Song Bridged Diné and Ndebele Worlds: An anthropologist recounts a magical moment of songwriting collaboration between Diné (Navajo) and Ndebele artists gathered for the WOMAD Festival in South Africa." *Sapiens.org.* www.sapiens.org/language/womad-festival-south-africa/. 11/30

Jacobsen, Kristina. 2022. "How a Song Bridged Diné and Ndebele Worlds." *Sapiens.* November 30, 2022. www.sapiens.org/language/womad-festival-south-africa/

Jacobsen, Kristina. 2022. *I.Will.Cross.* https://soundcloud.com/kristinajacobsenmusic/iwillcross

Jacobsen, Kristina. 2023. "Playing at the Border: Matter Out of Place and Bordertown Racism in Navajo Country Western Music," in *Whose Country Music? Genre, Identity, and Belonging in 21st Century Country Music Culture,* Jada Watson and Paula J. Bishop, eds. Cambridge: Cambridge University Press, 193–209.

Jacobsen, Kristina. 2024. *Sing Me Back Home: Ethnographic Songwriting and Language Reclamation in Sardinia, Italy.* Toronto: University of Toronto Press. Under contract.

Jacobsen, Kristina. n.d. "Navajo Nation Songwriting Retreat – Kristina Jacobsen, SingerSongwriter: Place-Based Songwriting." https://kristinajacobsen.weebly.com/navajonationsongwriting.html

Jacobsen, Kristina. n.d. "Songs of Santiago: Contemplative Songwriting Retreat in Northern Spain – Kristina Jacobsen, Singer Songwriter: Place-Based Songwriting." https://kristinajacobsen.weebly.com/songs-of-santiago-contemplative-songwriting-retreat-in-northern-spain.html

Jacobsen, Kristina. n.d. "Songs of Sardegna – Kristina Jacobsen, SingerSongwriter: Place-Based Songwriting." https://kristinajacobsen.weebly.com/songsofsardegna.html

Jacobsen, Kristina and Meredith Wilder. "Elemental." https://kristinajacobsenmeredithwilder.bandcamp.com/album/elemental

Jouad, Suleika. 2023. "The Isolation Journals." www.theisolationjournals.com

Kabat-Zinn, Jon and Thich Nhat Hanh. 2009. *Full Catastrophe Living: Using the Wisdom of Your Body and Mind to Face Stress, Pain, and Illness*. El Dorado, AR: Delta.

Lamott, Anne. 1995. *Bird by Bird: Some Instructions on Writing and Life*. Anchor Books.

Marcus, George E. and Fred R. Myers, eds. 1995. *The Traffic in Culture: Refiguring Art and Anthropology*. Oakland, CA: University of California Press.

Marsh, Kathryn. 2017. "Creating Bridges: Music, Play and Well-being in the Lives of Refugee and Immigrant Children and Young People." *Music Education Research* 19 (1): 60–73.

McLuhan, Marshall. 1964. "Media Hot and Cold." *Understanding Media: The Extensions of Man*: 22–32. Boston: MIT Press.

"Meredith Wilder." n.d. "Meredith Wilder." https://meredithwilder.bandcamp.com

"Merlettes." n.d. www.facebook.com/TheMerlettes.

Native Country Band. 2017 from Jacobsen, Kristina. "Songs, Interviews and Field Recordings for the Book, "The Sound of Navajo Country" https://on.soundcloud.com/WUVg9

Nussbaum, Emily. 2023. "Country Music's Culture Wars and the Remaking of Nashville." *The New Yorker.* July 17.

"Objectwriting.Com – Sense Based Creative Writing for Songwriters." https://objectwriting.com/

Old Town School of Folk Music. 2023. "Old Town School History." www.oldtownschool.org/history/

Ortner, Sherry B. 2006. *Anthropology and Social Theory: Culture, Power, and the Acting Subject.* Durham, NC: Duke University Press. https://doi.org/10.1215/9780822388456

"Overcoming Academic Perfectionism." 2023. National Center for Faculty Development and Diversity. Webinar. www.facultydiversity.org

Pattison, Pat. n.d. "Daily, Seven Minute 'Object Writing'." www.objectwriting.com

Perkins, Brett. 2009. Listening Room Retreats. Ben Lomond, California.

Riles, Annelise. 2008. "Cultural Conflicts." *Law and Contemporary Problems* 71 (3): 273–308. https://scholarship.law.duke.edu/lcp/vol71/iss3/13

Romero, Simon. 2019. "Navajo Country Music Shatters 'Cowboys and Indians' Stereotypes." *New York Times.* November 19. www.nytimes.com/2019/11/30/us/navajo-country-music.html

Rubin, Rick. 2023. *The Creative Act: A way of Being*. Harmondsworth, England: Penguin.

Schneider, Arnd and Christopher Wright. 2021. "Between art and anthropology: *Contemporary ethnographic practice*." *Between Art and Anthropology*: 1–21. Oxford: Berg Publishers.

Schuster, Tara. 2019. *Buy Yourself the F*cking Lilies.* New York: The Dial Press.

Simos, Mark. 2017. "The Performing Songwriter's Dilemma: Principles and Practices." In *The Singer-Songwriter Handbook*, edited by Justin and Katherine Williams, 7–16. New York, London: Bloomsbury.

Suzuki, Shunryu. 2006. "Zen Mind, Beginner's Mind." London: Shambala Press.

"The OpEd Project." n.d. The OpEd Project. www.theopedproject.org

"US Fulbright Program – Fulbright U.S. Student Program." n.d. https://us.fulbrightonline.org/fulbright-us-student-program

"US Scholar Awards – Fellowships Abroad for Scholars & Professionals | Fulbright Scholars." n.d. https://fulbrightscholars.org/us-scholar-awards

When Poetry Became Ethnography and Other Flying Pig Tales

An Ode to Dell Hymes, as well as Creative Ethnographic Mentors Past, Present, and Future[1]

Melisa Cahnmann-Taylor

Creative Ethnographic Toolkit: Ethnopoetics, the history and foundations of scholartistry, literature review, stating a problem, fieldwork.

When I found a small slip of paper at the American Anthropological Association (AAA) Chicago conference hotel in 1999 announcing an evening open mic session for poetry and other creative renderings of data, I made sure to attend. As I breezed down the carpeted corridor past scholars removing name badges as they prepared to enter the room, I was filled with hope. An **ensemble** of scholartists awaited me. I could hardly keep still in the cushioned metal chair. I recall a woman who read from a play she'd written based on her fieldwork with Salvadoran refugees in California, which moved me to tears. I also resonated with another scholar's poems that wrestled with her outsider status in an Indigenous community.[2] On that long-ago evening as a new PhD student in Educational Anthropology, I shared my own creative ethnographic work, "Driving through North Philly" (Cahnmann 1999; 2016: 39–40), which was a poem that had recently been published by the city paper where I did my fieldwork (reprinted at the end of this chapter). I felt then, as I feel now, that in many ways, the poem captured the essence of my experiences in bilingual Philadelphia schools more than the scholarly paper I'd presented through the Council for Anthropology and Education earlier that day. The truth was that as a new graduate student, I often felt stuck in an imitative mode when writing in scholarly prose, adopting whole sentence structures and multisyllabic words from other language scholars and often feeling unsure of what I was trying to say and how. In contrast, when I processed what I was recording in fieldnotes through poetry, I relaxed into plain language, personal rhythms, and, most importantly, *surprise*, which Hirshfield (2007) defines using the Latin roots "sor" (beyond) and "presa" (grasp). While research required me to plan ahead (e.g., theoretical foundations, research questions, literature reviews, approaches to data collection and analysis, etc.), art asked me to consider that which was beyond grasp. In writing ethnographic poems, I had permission to be surprised by emergent understandings and, as Emily Dickinson famously wrote, to "Tell all the Truth but tell it slant."[3]

When the open mic readings concluded, the event moderator announced that this session was part of the annual business meeting for the Society for Humanistic Anthropology (SHA), which was an organization that awarded ethnographies for

DOI: 10.4324/9781003365228-51

their creative writing style, as well as their scholarly content, and held an annual contest for ethnographic fiction and poetry. So refreshed by what I'd heard, I asked those present if anyone thought that it would be possible that those poems, stories, and plays may someday be the center of our ethnographic work, rather than peripheral representations.

I remember a much older man toward the front of the room who immediately stood up and stated that he was Dell Hymes. My heartbeat raced. *The* Dell Hymes?! The father of my doctoral program in Educational Linguistics at the University of Pennsylvania? The man who began the "ethnography of communication" (Hymes 1972)? Indeed. *The* Dell Hymes faced me and answered without hesitation: "No." The father of my field communicated with certainty that poems (as well as short stories and plays) would never serve as legitimate ethnography and that it was as impossible as "when pigs fly," as the Duchess in Lewis Carol's *Alice in Wonderland* is noted for saying. In more serious terms, Hymes asserted that we should remain prose ethnographers and settle for art on the side. In another context, my university leadership agreed, referring to my seminars on arts-based research and poetic inquiry as "boutique courses." In other words, quaint, pretty, unnecessary, and costly additions that science could do without. Both Hymes and these administrators spoke with authority and certainty. Hymes (1981, 1985) had long ago engaged in these conversations and things were not going to change. It was time to end the open mic entertainment at the anthropology meeting, keep our ham hocks on the ground, and go to bed.

To say I was at first disappointed is an understatement. Maybe my first mentor in creative ethnography was tired from the long conference day; maybe he was tired of this conversation; or maybe he was just playing devil's advocate, as good scholars are so wont to do. But as a new scholar bubbling with excitement, I was deflated and then puzzled: at the end of the meeting, Dell solicited poems for the annual ethnographic poetry contest, for which he was a judge. I later learned that Dell had started the field of ethnopoetics (Hymes 2003), studying Indigenous poetic forms. He was also a central figure in the literary (poetic) turn in ethnography, along with Paul Friedrich (2006), Stanley Diamond (1982), and Ivan Brady (1991), among others. Later still, when he was a featured colloquia speaker at the University of Pennsylvania, I was shocked when, having seen one of my poems, he asked me to submit to the annual contest in 2003 and, to my surprise, awarded me with a first prize in ethnographic poetry. I was honored, thrilled, and confused. I could understand why a university administrator looking at smaller enrollments in specialized College of Education seminars would be concerned about a poetry class, but Dell Hymes' insistence that art was marginal to social science puzzled me. Why would the same man who nurtured a place for poetry and ethnography to coexist and wrote poetic scholarship and poems himself not agree that poems constitute legitimate and central representations of ethnographic understanding?

Many years later, when Dell retired from his post as SHA poetry judge, I was invited to follow him as Chair. I proceeded to write arguments for the increased presence of the arts, particularly poetry, in all phases of empirical (e.g., Maynard and Cahnmann-Taylor 2010; Cahnmann-Taylor and Siegesmund 2008, 2018) and pedagogical processes (e.g., Cahnmann-Taylor and Preston 2008; Cahnmann, Bleyle, and Hwang 2016). Arguing against a father figure's admonitions, I commanded more poems, not fewer. However, as the novice ethnographic poems started to arrive from students and colleagues, I began to have my own reservations. Some of the hopeful ethnographic poets hurried verse lines with easy cliché and tired metaphors. Often, the poems' content seemed overly personal or the language failed to plait the poem with surprise and associative logic. Line breaks appeared haphazard or the music felt stilted or missing, as if the ethnographer merely broke a series of wordy sentences into what appeared to be poetic form. Some poems felt so centered on the writer's experience that it was difficult to see an ethnographic subject; conversely, other poems were overfull with academic jargon and obtuse abstraction. Having formally and informally studied poetic craft, I wanted ethnographic poems to be good (i.e., finely crafted, evocative, and full of fresh language and music) and some were. Some were very good (e.g., Kusserow 2002; Stone 2008). Some of the best poems with ethnographic sensibility seemed to come from poets who didn't identify as anthropologists, like Joy Harjo, Jane Hirshfield, Naomi Shihab Nye, and Tarfia Fazullah, who engaged implicitly in practices akin to ethnographic engagement. I worried that some of my early, creative ethnographic arguments might give license to mediocre poetry that would undermine the ethnopoetic project. I heard the sage wisdom of Ruth Behar (2008: 63), describing famous anthropologist Ruth Benedict's poetry as "cloying," advocating that anthropologists stick to genres they know well to enhance their artistic quality through the medium of poetic ethnography: "After all, we have a lot of poetic poets out there, but tell me, how many poetic anthropologists do you know?" She posed a rhetorical challenge to anthropologists to add more poetry to their prose rather than pursue sloppy or sappy verse without training in how to do it well. Behar herself seems to have moved away from her own advice, becoming an award-winning young adult (YA) fiction writer (Behar 2017; 2022). In other words, the creative ethnographic mentors who were my first role models also encouraged this work with some degree of hesitation and warning: if you conduct creative ethnography, your work may not be taken seriously as a social scientist, you may miss out on essential ethnographic focus and skill, and your creative work may not be any good. To these legitimate concerns, I want to add an encouraging note of advice. As artists and ethnographers, we *all* begin as novices. Afterall, every famous scholar and poet started somewhere! In addition, it is nourishing and generative to engage in beginner's mind throughout our lives and careers. My message to everyone, both those early on and those well established in your careers, is to be fearless in spite of the inevitable limitations, even failures, of our first and even later creative ethnographic efforts. To quiet the voices of critique, we must learn, practice, and grow. As we acquire both artistic and scholarly skills, creative ethnographers can learn to accept failure and errors as necessary to the creative process and for moving the field of creative ethnography forward.

In 2009, the year Dell Hymes passed away, I participated in a panel of ethnographic creative writers presenting poems and short stories at AAA during a regularly slotted session (no longer in a darkened conference room after hours).

The room was packed (many of the panelists appear in this book)[4] and Dell's guiding presence was palpable. The readings were given by a wide variety of established and more novice ethnographers; those who came to creative writing later in their anthropology careers and others who were growing up multimodal and writing (drawing or singing) ethnography in both creative and scholarly genres at once. I think Dell would have been proud to have been there and would have been as struck as I was by the presentations' high quality and impact.

Perhaps if Hymes, Behar, and other creative ethnographic mentors (among whom I count Renato Rosaldo, Fred Erickson, Ivan Brady, Shirley Bryce Heath, Christine Sleeter, Norm Denzin, Nancy Hornberger, David Swanger, and others) had initially responded to my graduate student queries with 100% enthusiasm, they may have licensed a dangerous early career move toward poetry and away from ethnographic fundamentals, including a focus on research method and theory. Had those scholars themselves focused solely on producing their own artwork, we might have missed out on the valuable poetic scholarship they've gifted to anthropology and other related fields, such as education, ethnomusicology, applied linguistics, and cultural studies. Since my own mentorship included plentiful opportunities to practice the artfulness of ethnography, my own advice is now often more focused on giving significant attention to practicing "the craft, practice, and possibility" (Cahnmann 2003) of making ethnographically informed art. I emphasize the importance of becoming an apprentice to artistic craft as much as an apprentice in how to craft an ethnographic study when creative ethnographers begin to experiment with new genres "at the edge of words" (Maynard and Cahnmann-Taylor 2010). Oftentimes, those with an interest in this direction bring de facto talent and apprenticeship into the conversation, whether having classical flute training like Kristina or a bachelor's degree in Fine Arts like Bernard Perley. Some artists, like poet Gary Snyder, have undergraduate degrees in anthropology and craft careers as artists with ethnographic sensibility. Others have pursued their own significant training in the arts during or beyond graduate degrees in the social sciences, either through attending shorter term workshops, summer training opportunities, and/or achieving formal masters in Fine Arts (MFA) degrees (like Nomi Stone and myself). Others come to creative ethnography in collaboration with those who have skills in the arts and/or with a willingness to study and train during early engagement.

There is no one pathway for creative ethnographers to acquire the skills needed to practice the art and science of this craft. However, there remains a problem: time. "Art is long and time is short." These words from Ben Franklin that were used to describe the challenges inherent in a liberal arts education are also true in ethnographic training. It is difficult, or impossible, to become fully trained in both the *art* and *science* of creative ethnography, separately. So, this book is designed for current social science scholars who wish to add exploration and practices in the arts to their researcher toolkit; artists who wish to add social science inquiry tools to their artmaking practices; and the next generation of scholartists who wish to consider merging both pursuits of art and science as one. I have co-authored and co-edited this book with Kristina, who shares a foundational understanding that it is along the continua between art and science where we find the most impactful work.

Numerous opportunities already exist in professional meetings and journals for "finding, taking, or wishing for permission to be current, public, and artistic anthropologists" (Cahnmann-Taylor 2013a). For example, AAA has been sponsoring *installations* (funded with $500 to $2000 awards)[5] that "break the mold of all other programming types" with dance performances, art installations, poetry slams, and other creative sessions where "imagination and creativity are your only limitations" (Installations 2023; Cahnmann-Taylor 2013b). "Ethnographic Terminalia" was one such installation that celebrated its 10th and final year of creative ethnographic work at the AAA meeting in Vancouver in 2019, where "Wakanda University" also appeared, as discussed by Phillips and Vidali (Chapter 11, this volume). In 2021, we titled our own funded performance installation in Baltimore "The Creative Ethnographer's Notebook" in anticipation of the book you are now reading! The long-ago open mic evening has continued and continues to exist at the annual AAA meetings (as long as there are SHA members who can run it!). In fact, Kristina and I first met at one of these open mic sessions in 2015, where I was stunned by her song *Inez* (Jacobsen, this volume, Chapter 6, p. 247; *Three Roses* 2015) and where the first ethnographic play I'd written was performed (Cahnmann-Taylor 2015). This was where we both began to dream of the book you are now reading. I have learned that art is indeed long in terms of the time it takes to dream projects into reality.

What else can we imagine for creative ethnographic futures? What new homes (departments, conferences, books, journals, awards, and stages) could we create? I believe that the next generation of scholars will inhabit, or more likely insist on, creative ethnographic centers. For example, at my home institution, an undergraduate student Surya Blasiole, who was dissatisfied with current degree options, proposed an all-new interdisciplinary major in creative ethnography; one that, in fall 2023, didn't yet exist. Surya wrote:

> *In addition to a major in music, I began my first year at UGA with an anthropology major. However, I switched to religion this year due to the environmental focus of the anthropology major at our university. My primary interest is in cultural anthropology, which I've only been able to study through the religion major (also not the right fit). I have been curious about the Interdisciplinary Studies major as an option to combine cultural anthropology classes from multiple departments. This would also hopefully allow me to cater to my more specific interest in anthropology as it relates to disciplines such as music, art, women's studies, philosophy, etc. In addition, I have studied Spanish so far in college and am working toward a goal of fluency. The Interdisciplinary Studies major requires that I build a thematically linked curriculum and have a committee of three faculty members that are willing to support this curriculum and my development through the major. I believe that your role would be to approve my curriculum, be available as a possible mentor for career or academic questions or concerns, and grade my final senior thesis. I am wondering if this is something you might consider?*

My answer: "Yes!"

This student and other bold dreamers like her are already shifting what *is* to what *could be*. What new degrees and departments could proliferate and expand? Such as the position Nomi Stone (Chapter 8, this volume) now holds at the University of Texas, Dallas, where "she teaches hybrid cross-disciplinary classes that straddle creative writing, literature, and anthropology" (website 2023). What new affordances could be made with Zoom and other virtual technology to bring more of us together? Such as the 2022 Practicing the Social conference.[6] This leads me to offer two final prompts for discussion and creative activity.

Discussion and Creativity Prompts

1. What has moved you to the core in the past week or month? What has sent you into belly-aching laughter or tears? How important and possible do you think it is for ethnographic work to evoke emotional or embodied responses? When and why could feeling and/or empathy be important to creative ethnography?
2. In what new spaces could creative ethnography thrive, making our inquiry projects more inclusive, ethical, aesthetic, and transgressive of disciplinary boundaries? Choosing prose, poetry, song, visual art, or film, work in a small group to showcase ideas for an imagined future for creative ethnography.

Why This Prompt in This Closing Chapter in This Book

For many of us, the answer to the first discussion prompt, "what has moved you?" is *art*: a painting, a soundtrack, a play, a comic, a television series, a poem. Still, too few of us can point to stand-alone ethnographies that have kept us engrossed cover to cover, as a novelist might. Many anthropologists hunger to bring the emotive and sentient aspects of our obsessions (e.g., the subjects we study) into our academic thinking and representations and some of us are determined to learn how, risking degrees of failure and uncertainty in order to do so. While a creative ethnographer's path is filled with risk, this is also true of any worthy intellectual and/or artistic pursuit. The surprise is when we can find new language, images, and movements that wake up our senses, as well as our intellects and emotions. In fact, as a matter of principle, graphic artist and anthropologist Sally Pirie (Pirie 2013) aims to produce all of her scholarship through drawings, modeling the vitality of using visual modalities to conceptualize research data, analysis, and representation. We need to find ways to raise the bar and ask what new thinking, learning, and feeling could be produced when we are unafraid and prepared to engage in artful science and scientific art.

This second discussion prompt invites readers to imagine what, who, and how creative ethnography will exist in the future. The expansive possibilities of virtual technology have made this the most exciting time to imagine the ease with which creative ethnographers could find each other and present our hybrid work with attention to excellence, access, ethics, and collaboration through the five fields of anthropology (archaeological, biological, linguistic, sociocultural, and applied), as well as other adjacent fields in the arts and social sciences.

How to Extend

When reading *The Creative Ethnographer's Notebook*, I see a reunion of old and new friends, many of whom have been mentoring themselves in how to sing, score, or fictionalize ethnographic understanding in isolation from each other. It is important for readers to know about the community of scholartists who are already engaging in creative ethnography. Go through the list of contributors and their biographies, accomplishments, and publications. Read some full-length works of creative ethnography or artistry with which each of them has engaged. Ask yourself whose work inspires you and how could it serve as a model for moving forward? Then ask yourself who and what are still missing? Is there any creative ethnographic work that appears to be more art than science or more science than art? Why or why doesn't this work using a *both/and* criterion? What constitutes creative ethnography at its best? When is creative autoethnographic work, i.e., work focused on self-study, enough and when do we wish there were more data from other participants? Having these kinds of critical questions can help to nourish the best work moving forward, but it is also important to honor our elders and be grateful to those who have come before (I humbly ask readers to honor previous generations for what we have gotten right and forgive us when our work may have missed a future mark!).

Closing Remarks

Looking back on the origins of this chapter, which was first published as an essay well over a decade ago in 2011 (Cahnmann 2011), I can see directions in creative ethnography that I never thought possible. In having so many fine models of creative ethnography, beginner and experienced social scientists alike may pursue the arts and sciences together from the get-go, breaking verse lines and rules and attuning to image and music. Creative ethnographers, like you, dear reader, will have to answer tough, as- yet unanswered questions about creative ethnography: How do we find time for it? How can it be more inclusive and accessible? How can we address the ethics of making art with and from other human and non-human stories? How do we know if we cross the line between artistic license and ethnographic fact? When and why does making art matter, especially in the context of the urgent crises of health, safety, and environment that abound? Just as I felt the initial rush of flight at my first face-to-face meeting with Dell Hymes in 1999, I fully expect to see pigs flying at future AAA meetings, as well as in anthropology journals and other academic and public contexts as more scholars soar through artful and scholarly renderings of what it means to live in human and non-human diversity. I also hope to see artists with greater attention to principles, theories, and research findings from anthropology's five fields: archaeology, biology, linguistics, socioculturalism, and applied practice. A creative ethnographer who has learned through both the arts and the social sciences will be attuned to the ambiguities, paradoxes, conflicts, and irresolution that are embodied in the phenomena under study.

I am in debt to mentors past, present, and future, including poets and pedagogues like Richard Hugo (1979/2017), who acknowledged the edges of our own bias by stating: "Every moment, I am, without wanting or trying to, telling you to write like me. But I hope you learn to write like you." I wish this for those reading this book, and I wish to encourage readers to awaken us with ethnographic possibility. I close with a republication of the poem I read at AAA in 1999, rendering a speech event from my dissertation about bilingual education in urban Philadelphia, called "Driving through North Philly" (2016, pp. 39–40).[7] This poem in its various and changing drafts foretold the creative ethnography that I would throw up into the air and "not wait for it to come down."

Driving through North Philly
(Cahnmann-Taylor, 2016, p. 39)

I see them. The shoes
on Eighth Street—there must be
thirty pair perched upside down.
An uneven silhouette of sneakers
slung over electric wire;

the lightness soaked out of them,
except for the eager
cleats, less familiar
with the whims
of weather. Here a boy

doesn't give up shoes
unless they give up on him;
a face bruised with September
and measured kicks
through corn chip bags crushed

in the side pockets of this city.
I think of other reasons for these pairs in flight:
maybe a test of gravity, feet got too big,
or a protest against restrictions
on tilted chairs, names gouged on desktops,

on-time, straight lines in the yard.
For weeks I wonder until I stop
to ask a kid from the neighborhood.
We study each other: a black boy,
backpack over left shoulder, pants

for two of him,
and me, a white woman, dressed
like a teacher with a notepad
and loopy earrings.
"Because it's fun, Miss" he says

as if the answer were scrawled
on the wall behind me
with oversized bubble letters.
and then, "So they remember you
when you're gone."

I think of the thirteen apartments
I've lived in over the last
nine years; how I've never left
anything behind. I look
at the newest pair, think

how impractical
to let colors
fade, perfectly good
and out of reach,
an empty walk on sky.

"I done it lots a 'times, Miss,"
he says with a grin.
How little I know about this joy,
what it's like to throw something
up in the air that's important, that weighs something

that takes you places–
and not wait for it to come down

Notes

1 A version of this writing appeared in *Anthropology and Humanism* (Cahnmann-Taylor 2011).

2 I regret that I've never been able to find these scholars since that evening; but in searching for them, I've met many other creative ethnographers, many of whom are represented in this book!

3 The full poem is located here: www.poetryfoundation.org/poems/56824/tell-all-the-truth-but-tell-it-slant-1263

4 Panelists on the 2009 "Coming Close—Literary Readings in Ethnography" at the AAA (Philadelphia) included Adrie Kusserow, Kent Maynard, Nomi Stone, Ruth Behar, Renato Rosaldo, Billie Jean Isbell, Paul Stoller, Kim Gutschow, Barbara and Dennis Tedlock, and Elizabeth Krause.

5 https://annualmeeting.americananthro.org/submissions/installations/

6 Practicing the Social: Entanglements of Art and Justice took place over Zoom due to the COVID-19 pandemic and in so doing, produced innovative scholarship in accessible and interpersonal ways. Conference organizers produced a short documentary film to share some of the essential takeaways from this artful academic experience: https://vimeo.com/823502689/a29d31b457?share=copy

7 A slightly different version of this poem was presented at the SHA awards, appeared in the *Philadelphia Inquirer*, and, much later, in my 2016 book. Many poets revise poems and have multiple, varied versions of a poem with the same title but different alterations. This version is the one that was presented in 1999.

References

Behar, Ruth. 2008. "Between Poetry and Anthropology: Searching for Languages of Home." In *Arts-Based Research in Education: Foundations for Practice*, edited by Melisa Cahnmann-Taylor and Richard Seigesmund, 55–72. London: Routledge.

Behar, Ruth. 2017. *Lucky Broken Girl*. London: Penguin.

Behar, Ruth. 2022. *Tía Fortuna's New Home: A Jewish Cuban Journey*. New York: Knopf Books for Young Readers.

Brady, Ivan. 1991. *Anthropological Poetics*. Savage, MA: Rowman and Littlefield.

Cahnmann, Melisa. 1999. "Driving through North Philly." *Community Voices section, Philadelphia Inquirer*, September 5: E–5.

Cahnmann, Melisa. 2003. "The Craft, Practice, and Possibility of Poetry in Educational Research." *Educational Researcher* 32 (3): 29–36.

Cahnmann-Taylor, Melisa. 2011. "When Poetry Became Ethnography and Other Flying Pig Tales." *Anthropology & Education Quarterly* 42 (4): 393–6.

Cahnmann-Taylor, Melisa. 2013a. "Finding, Taking, or Wishing for Permission to Be Current, Public, and Artistic Anthropologists of Education." Presenter and Chair at the Annual Meeting of American Anthropological Association (AAA), Chicago, IL.

Cahnmann-Taylor, Melisa. 2013b. "Going public with literary ethnography in the windy city: anthropologists and Chicago artists build new genres and a new future." Presenter and Organizer at the Annual Meeting of American Anthropological Association (AAA), Chicago, IL.

Cahnmann-Taylor, Melisa. 2015. "Tú y Usted, An Ethnodrama: Performing the familiar/strange phenomenon of American adult Spanish language study in Mexico." Invited Installation Presenter and Organizer at the Annual Meeting of American Anthropological Association (AAA), Denver, CO.

Cahnmann-Taylor, Melisa. 2016. *Imperfect Tense*. San Pedro, CA: Whitepoint Press.

Cahnmann-Taylor, Melisa, and Dorine Preston. 2008. "What Bilingual Poets Can Do: Re-Visioning English Education for (Bi)Literacy." *English in Education* 42 (3): 234–52.

Cahnmann-Taylor, Melisa, Bleyle, Susan, and Hwang, Yohan. 2016. "Teaching Poetry in TESOL Teacher Education: Heightened Attention to Language as Well as to Cultural and Political Critique through Poetry Writing." *TESOL Journal* 8 (1): 70–101.

Cahnmann-Taylor, Melisa, and Richard Siegesmund. 2008. *Arts-Based Research in Education: Foundations for Practice*. London: Routledge.
Cahnmann-Taylor, Melisa, and Richard Siegesmund. 2018. *Arts-Based Research in Education: Foundations for Practice* (2nd edition). London: Routledge.
Diamond, Stanley. 1982. *Totems*. Barrytown, NY: Open Book.
Friedrich, Paul. 2006. "Maximizing Ethnopoetics: Fine-Tuning Anthropological Experience." In *Language, Culture, and Society: Key Topics in Linguistic Anthropology*, edited by Christine Jourdan and Kevin Tuite, 207–28. Cambridge: Cambridge University Press.
Hirshfield, Jane. 2007. "Poetry and the Constellation of Surprise." *Writer's Chronicle* 40 (2): 28–35.
Hugo, Richard. 1979/2017. "The Triggering Town: Lectures and Essays on Poetry and Writing." New York, NY: WW Norton & Company. Retrieved July 2017 from http://ualr.edu/rmburns/RB/hugosubj.html
Hymes, Dell H. 1972. "Models of the Interaction of Language and Social Life." In *Directions in Sociolinguistics: The Ethnography of Communication*, edited by John Gumpertz and Dell Hymes, 35–71. Oxford: Blackwell.
Hymes, Dell H. 1981. "In Vain I Tried to Tell You:" Essays in Native American Ethnopoetics. University of Pennsylvania Press Anniversary Collection.
Hymes, Dell H. 1985. "Foreword." In *Reflections: The Anthropological Muse*, edited by J. Iaian Prattis, 11–13. Washington DC: American Anthropological Association.
Hymes, Dell H. 2003. *Now I Know Only So Far: Essays in Ethnopoetics*. Lincoln, NE: University of Nebraska Press.
Installations. 2023. American Anthropological Association website, downloaded May 31, 2024. https://annualmeeting.americananthro.org/submissions/installations/
Jacobsen, Kristina. 2015. "Inez." Three Roses, Three Roses Music. www.youtube.com/watch?v=-h0c3-X_mHc
Kusserow, Adrie. 2002. *Hunting Down the Monk*. Rochester, NY: Boa.
Maynard, Kent and Melisa Cahnmann-Taylor. 2010. "Anthropology at the Edge of Words: Where Poetry and Ethnography Meet." *Anthropology and Humanism* 35 (1): 2–19.
"Nomi Stone." 2023. UT Dallas Profiles. https://profiles.utdallas.edu/index.php/nomi.stone
Pirie [as Galman], Sally Campbell. 2013. *The Good, the Bad, and the Data: Shane the Lone Ethnographer's Basic Guide to Qualitative Data Analysis*. New York: Routledge.
Stone, Nomi. 2008. *Stranger's Notebook*. Evanston, IL: Northwestern University Press.

Glossary

Accountability Accountability refers to the obligations a researcher has to the various stakeholders in the research process, such as the research participants, the funding body, and the researcher's employing organization. In this context, it explicitly suggests standards of research practice against which research can be judged to determine appropriateness and ethical behavior.

Active Voice Active voice refers to writing that uses the "I" voice rather than the passive voice.

Adhan Adhan is the Islamic call to public prayer in a mosque, which is recited by a muezzin five times a day, traditionally from the minaret.

Animacy Animacy is the state of being alive. Many cultures define animacy as including more than plant and animal life.

Anishinaabe Anishinaabe or Anishinaabeg refers to a group of Indigenous sovereign nations that have historically resided and reside today in the Great Lakes region of both the United States and Canada.

Annotated Bibliography An annotated bibliography is a reference list focusing on a theme or topic, which includes a brief, 1–3 sentence summary of each reference.

Annotative Line An annotative line is a line that works against or in opposition to the syntax. Namely, the poet annotates or makes a comment on a sentence by severing it in an unusual place. This can often create a more jagged pacing or moment of rupture.

Anthropomorphism Anthropomorphism is when a writer attributes human qualities or forms of personification to anything non-human, including objects, concepts, and even animals or gods.

Anti-Miscegenation Anti-miscegenation refers to legislation that enforced racial segregation at the level of marriage and intimate relationships by criminalizing interracial marriage between Blacks and Whites in the United States. These laws were struck down in 1967, thanks to the Loving vs. Virginia court case.

Antropoesía/Antropoeta Antropoesía is verse informed by ethnographic sensibility and an antropoeta is a poet who writes such verse.

Art-Adjacent Art-adjacent refers to forms of art that are related to, but not the same as, the main art form under consideration.

Arts-Based Research Arts-based research refers to inquiry that includes the visual, performing, and/or literary arts in data collection, analysis, or representation.

Auto-Ethnography Auto-ethnography is the focus on studying one's own cultural experiences as a lens for analysis.

Assonance Assonance means words that have different consonant sounds but similar vowel sounds (e.g., crush and lunch).

Becky A Becky is a colloquial term for White women. It often functions as a pejorative for a White woman who is typically younger and is ignorant of her own prejudices and privilege.

Bildungsroman A bildungsroman is a narrative that focuses on the spiritual and educational growth of a character from youth to adulthood.

Bordertown Bordertowns are towns that border the Navajo Nation, which is a sovereign nation that spans portions of Arizona, New Mexico, and Utah. Bordertowns can also refer to towns that border other Native Nations and neighboring states and any other towns that sit along two national borders, such as those along the US–Mexico border.

Break Out Klee's notion of "break out" refers to an artist's capacity to open their being to the world in order to paint it truthfully.

Code A code is a neutral term that can be used to denote a language or a variety of a language.

Coding Coding is a method for extracting, labeling, and grouping data into themes to understand the relationships between them and their significance to a research topic.

Colloquial Colloquial language refers to language that uses familiar, everyday vernacular and is not overly formal.

Colonialism Colonialism is the process by which a stronger political entity exploits a weaker one to extract and/or expropriate their resources and subjugate their population, whether remotely or by occupation as settlers.

Composite Character A composite character is created from multiple encounters, events, and observations that are merged into one single character presentation in a text.

Consent Form A consent form documents that the informed consent process has taken place, whereby participants have a complete understanding of their involvement in research, including the risks and benefits of their participation. Adults may provide written, oral, or implied consent. Consent for children must be provided by their parent or guardian.

Consonance Consonance means words that have different vowel sounds but similar consonant sounds (e.g., crush and crash) or words that have different syllable counts but have an exact rhyme in the final syllable (e.g., capable and fable).

Couplet A couplet is a pair of lines in verse (aa) that often rhyme and have similar length and/or meter. Shakespeare's 14-line sonnets famously end in "heroic couplets" that are written in iambic pentameter.

Cowriting Cowriting is the act of collaboratively writing a song with someone else or in a group, for which all songwriters are credited.

Creative Ethnographer Creative ethnographers are those who practice and are trained in both ethnographic field methods and an art form that is integrated into their ethnography in some way.

Creative Sensory Ethnography Creative Sensory Ethnography uses embodied and creative activities, such as mindful observation of place, and creative practice to identify and represent sensory embodied experiences that have cultural and social significance.

Deep Hanging Out Deep hanging out is a colloquial way to refer to doing extended, long-term ethnographic fieldwork and is credited to the anthropologist Clifford Geertz.

Deep Listening Deep listening is a meditation and musical composition process developed by the composer Pauline Oliveros.

Digital Audio Workstation (DAW) A DAW is a digital audio workstation. The term also refers to the software applications used to record, edit, and produce audio.

Diné Diné is the ethnonym for "Navajo," meaning "the People."

Direct Translation Direct translation is the act of writing that appears in one code being interpreted into a different code by a translator. It may be the most common occurrence of more than one language appearing in a single text.

Dramatic Monologue A dramatic monologue, also known as a persona poem, is a poem that shares characteristics with theatre, in which a poet speaks through an assumed voice (of a human or non-human character) to a silent listener, who is usually not the reader.

End-Stopped Line An end-stopped line is a line that is self-enclosed by its own closing punctuation. These lines are good for declarative statements or question moments in poems.

Ensemble Ensemble is a term often used in theatre contexts, which refers to any group of people who carry out unique tasks and functions toward a collective goal.

Environmental Future Environmental futures are imaginings of possible futures in light of the environmental crises that the world is currently facing.

Ethnographer Ethnographers are anthropologists who conduct field research by observing and participating in a particular social context and listening closely to other people's stories and interpretations.

Ethnographic Fiction Ethnographic fiction refers to fictional stories that are created by researchers from their research material (e.g., interviews, participant observation field notes, archival sources, and oral histories).

Ethnographic Poetry Ethnographic poetry refers to poems, using line breaks and stanzas, created by researchers that reflect engagement with research material (e.g. language and observations from interviews, participant observation, fieldnotes, archival sources, and the researcher's own experiences).

Ethnographic Prose Poem An ethnographic prose poem is a piece of writing about ethnographic fieldwork, which is written in prose but has obvious poetic qualities, including intensity, compactness, prominent rhythms, and the use of figurative language, metaphor, simile and, vivid imagery.

Ethnographic Songwriting Ethnographic songwriting refers to songs that are informed by ethnographic fieldwork and are attuned to cultural specificity. These can be inspired by a specific place, cowritten with interlocutors in the field, or used and performed to elicit feedback to deepen understanding of specific cultural phenomena.

Ethnographic Vignette An ethnographic vignette is a short, evocative description of an experience, account, or episode that can stand alone as a mini-story within a broader ethnographic text.

Ethnography Ethnography is the in-depth study of a culture (either our own or another's) at a given moment in time, which is premised on intercultural inquiry and the ability to create empathy for communities, places, and persons we may not otherwise have come to know.

Ethnomusicology Ethnomusicology is the study of music in its cultural context.

Ethnopoetics Ethnopoetics is a method of analyzing linguistic structures in oral literature, which was coined by Jerome Rothenberg in 1968.

Études Short pieces, pieces that were written to provide practice material to help players (broadly conceived) hone a skill.

Exact Rhyme Exact rhymes are words that have the same number of syllables and exact rhymes (e.g., bat and cat or cable and fable).

Faction Faction refers to the wide range of valuable possibilities in writing, from carefully described observations to thoroughly invented make-believe.

Field Recording Field recordings refer to any audio recordings undertaken outside of a recording studio.

Fieldwork Fieldwork is the term used by anthropologists and many other qualitative researchers to refer to research that takes place among a designated community.

Focal Attention Focal attention means listening to one sound in a given environment, such as a bird call or a person speaking.

Generic Generic means more general and less specific, i.e., using language that is commonly used in everyday contexts.

Generic Metaphor A generic metaphor is one that has been used over and over and, therefore, may not evoke much emotion, insight, or resonation in a reader.

Genre Genres are the different styles of music, writing, and speech.

Ghazal A ghazal is a Persian poetic form written in couplets, which includes intricate use of repetition and rhyme. Each couplet ends on the same word or phrase (the radif) and is (often) preceded by the couplet's rhyming word (the qafia, which appears twice in the first couplet). The last couplet includes a proper name, often that of the poet. In the Persian tradition, each couplet is of the same meter and length and the subject matter includes both erotic longing and religious belief or mysticism.

Global Attention Global attention means taking in the entire soundscape of a given environment at the same time.

Grammatical Parallelism Grammatical parallelism is a form of repetition that exists when two or more phrases share the same or similar structures.

Happy accidents When poets address differences between conventional and vernacular language use, written or spoken, which may be attributed to a user's identity as non-native or non-normative.

Informed Consent When conducting research, obtaining informed consent from research participants is imperative. Informed consent means that participants are provided with all of the information about the processes of the research activity, including the possible risks and benefits, prior to proceeding.

Interlocutor Interlocutor is a word used to refer to a person in any given community with whom an ethnographer talks about their experiences and perspectives on a given subject.

Intimate Other An intimate other is someone with whom you have a close relationship but about whom you still have lots of questions or don't feel you know completely.

Institutional Review Board (IRB) Institutional review boards are established by any institutions that conduct or sponsor research. IRBs are committees that review and regulate research methods and the procedures of proposed and ongoing research, as well as protecting the rights and welfare of those involved.

Kashmiri Militant A Kashmiri militant is a non-state Kashmiri Muslim combatant who has taken up arms against the Indian government.

Knowledge Production Knowledge production refers to the practice of (and the ideology underpinning) research, as well as other educational and general academic activities related to producing new knowledge in order to create a source of reliable information on the world.

Line of Control The line of control is the ceasefire line that exists as a de facto border between Indian- and Pakistani-administered Kashmir.

Litmus Test In science, a litmus test is a procedure that tests for alkalinity or acidity using litmus paper. In songwriting, it refers to gauging a song's effectiveness in telling a story.

Macro Coding A dominant theme, big ideas or concept, and recurring pattern in an interview.

Magic Magic refers to any unexplained events or effects (images, sounds, appearances/disappearances, etc.), which often connect people, actions, objects, or stories across time and space.

Melodic Stress Melodic stress is where a melody feels stronger in relation to the beat.

Metaphor A metaphor directly compares two different things, i.e., it says that something is something else.

Mine the Gap Mining a gap means writing about what is left unsaid, what is prevented from being said due to cultural conventions of politeness and/or taboo, and what cannot or should not be spoken or written.

Morning Pages Morning pages refer to three pages of stream-of-consciousness writing that are written by hand every morning.

Morpheme The morpheme is the smallest unit of sound in a language that has meaning associated with it. It cannot be broken apart into other sounds.

Narrative coding Detailed, nuanced accounts of a research participant's lived experiences (including anecdotes, vignettes, or stories) that fall under dominant (see macro coding) themes.

New Materialism (Materiality) New materialism denotes scholarship that pays close attention to the material characteristics of objects and sometimes interprets these characteristics through the classic materialist lenses of capital and power relationships.

New Phenomenology New phenomenology is an approach that centers on first-person, embodied, sensory experiences of the world and uses these as a basis for understanding larger sets of relations.

OpEd [Opposite the Editorial Page] An OpEd is a short newspaper column that represents the informed and focused opinion of a writer on a current issue or event. It is a written prose piece that expresses the opinion of the author with no affiliation to the publication's editorial board.

Pantoum A pantoum is a Malaysian verse form comprised of quatrains, with the second and fourth lines of each quatrain repeated as the first and third lines of the next. The second and fourth lines of the final stanza repeat the first and third lines of the first stanza. It is a form that has been adapted by writers in English and other languages.

Parsing Line A parsing line is a line that fluidly follows the syntax of a poem, breaking at natural pause points for breath.

Participant Observation Participant observation is a key method in ethnographic fieldwork, in which the researcher is both an observer and an engaged participant in their chosen field site.

Participant Safety Participant safety refers to individuals feeling supported enough to relax and be themselves, and not worried about the threat of shaming, exclusion, or judgment in creative and collaborative work.

Photovoice Photovoice refers to a participatory research process that uses cameras to study participants so they can act as recorders of the phenomena under study.

Pitch The pitch of a note is how high or low it sounds.

Poetic Linguistic anthropologists consider the term "poetic" to mean language that draws attention to its form, i.e., how it is presented, rather than the message being conveyed.

Poetic Prose Poetic prose is prose that uses evocative, vivid, and poetic language to create rhythms, impressions, and/or feelings rather than just descriptions or explanations.

Portraiture Portraiture blends art and science to document the culture of institutions, the life stories of individuals, the stages of human development, and other essential relationships, processes, and concepts.

Positionality Positionality refers to the way in which a person is situated in terms of social location. Ways to discuss positionality as artists and researchers include via race, class, gender identity, religion, and national identity.

Proposal A proposal is a brief written overview of a project you want to undertake.

Rapport Rapport is the feeling of connection and trust between people.

Remixing and Reimagining In creative writing when authors work with inherited English language forms and writing conventions (e.g. the sonnet, villanelle, sestina, or five paragraph essay) and include variations such as the use of non-English languages and cultural references. Authors may also create and establish new formal conventions.

Rhyme Scheme A rhyme scheme refers to the pattern used for how the ends of lines (in a song or a poem) rhyme. Often, there is consistency or regularity from one verse to another.

Scholartist Scholartists are scholars who are artists or those for whom the arts are integral to their scholarship.

Score Film scores are typically original compositions made specifically for films, which are intended to underscore and accentuate the overall moods of scenes and emotional appeal.

Sestina A sestina is a French poetic form from the 13th century. Typically, a sestina is composed of six 6-line stanzas using a total of six different end words that are repeated six times. Those end words are then repeated again in the final 3-line stanza.

Simile A simile compares two different things using "like" or "as."

Slant Rhyme Slant rhymes are inexact but may have assonance or consonance.

Social Theory Social theory refers to social phenomena, including power relationships, gender identity, religion, race, and social change.

Sounded Anthropology Sounded anthropology refers to the movement among some anthropologists to communicate the findings of their work by producing audio in the form of ethnographic soundscapes.

Soundtrack A soundtrack is a form of diegetic music, that is, music that can be heard by the characters in a scene. Typically, soundtracks feature songs that were recorded independent from the film and were then included during scenes as part of the overall soundscape within which the characters exist.

Theory Theory refers to a set of ideas, usually found in peer-reviewed publications, that underpins the ways we "do" or think about anthropology.

Thick Description A thick description is a way to describe a scene, happening, or event in anthropology that draws on all of the senses, including taste, touch, smell, sound, and sight.

Transcribe To transcribe means to write out word-for-word what each person said in a conversation or interview.

Transcription A transcription is a written out word-for-word copy of what is said orally.

Translingualism Boundary crossing understandings of multilingualism where diverse languages in any one speaker's repertoire compose an integrated system. Translingualism is widely practiced in everyday communicative contexts but largely ignored or suppressed in institutional contexts.

Trans/script The term trans/script was first defined and used by Melisa Cahnmann-Taylor et al. to refer to compressed renderings of original transcripts that utilize techniques from poetry and the dramatic arts (scripts) to highlight emotional "hot points" and heightened language in the original discourse.

Trauma-Informed Trauma-integrated methods are ways of working that are responsive to the effects of trauma in participants and facilitators. This way of working seeks to avoid retraumatizing participants and increase learning effectiveness and self-sovereignty over one's own learning.

Turn A "turn" in theory references a cumulative shift away from one set of ideas and toward another within a community of scholarship.

Verbatim Coding Key word-for-word expressions, phrases, metaphors, similes, idioms, and words that stand out in a transcript as thought-provoking, compelling, resonant, or evocative and connected to macro and narrative coding.

Index

Note: Locators in *italics* refer to figures.

"A Blessing" (Wright) 121
"A Tibetan Picnic" (Banks) 127–128
abuse, experiences of 152–156
active voice 94
"adhan" (Tahat) 103
affective ethnography 48–51
after the field 159–160, 203–207
Agee, J. 91
agential realism 20
Albritton, M. 164, *167*
"Along The Ditchbank (Lang's Last Goodbye)" (Meredith Wilder) 45, 231
Alvarez, S. 116–117
American Anthropological Association (AAA) 6, 219, 238, 240, 242–246
androcentric bias 15
animacy 99
animal stories 96–100
Anishinaabe 48–50
annotated bibliographies 214
annotative lines 122
anthropology courses 10
anthropology, fields within 53
anthropomorphism 22
anti-miscegenation laws 45
antropoesía 160, 215–219
antropoetas 8, 215–219
Appadurai, A. 207
"Archives of Removal" (Murphy) 66
art: in creative ethnography 1–2; emotive and engrossing nature of 243–244; ethics and researcher responsibility 7; ethics of 231; ethnographers training in 4–5; identity as an artist and scholar 222–234, 238–246; museum displays 198–201; overlap with science 2, 241–242; risks of combining art with anthropology 226–228
art-adjacent spaces 11–12, 232
artful scholarship 130–135
artistic recovery 223
artmaking 2, 3, 11–12, 131, 134, 159, 223, 226, 231, 232, 241
arts-based education research (ABER) 10
arts-based research 10, 134, 178–186
Arumugam, I. 6
assonance 106
audience engagement 198–201
audio production 189–192
auto-ethnography 5, 86–89

Badkhen, A. 93
Banks, B. 127–128
Barad, K. 20
Bautista, O. 164, *167*
Becky (colloquialism) 198
Bednarek, R. 185
Behar, R. 209, 240, 241
Benedict, R. (pen name of Anne Singleton) 8, 219, 240
Bessire, L. 93–94
bildungsroman poetry 114–118
bilingualism: interviews regarding 130–131; non-human objects 22; as term 102; *see also* translingual poetry
Blumenfeld-Jones, D. 134
bordertowns 224
Brady, I. 239
Brake, E. R. 111–112
break out painting 91
Button Poetry 118

Cahnmann-Taylor, M. 7, 22–23, 58, 104–105, 242, 245–246
Cameron, J. 223–224, 225
Campt, T. 68
Cango, B. 98–99
Cantarella, L. 198
"Casa" (González) 21–22
Chatzipanagiotidou, E. 68–69
"Cherokee Mask Song" (Hopkins) 110
Chin, E. 198
cinema *see* filmmaking
classical materialism 25–26
Clifford, J. 2
close listening 71–75, 209–214
cluster writing 72
coding data 159, 169–176, *170*
Collins, K. 191
colloquial speech 116
colonialism: comics 32, 36; community and place 212–213; songwriting 223
comics 31–36, 178, 184
composite characters 159, 178–186
composition *see* music; songwriting
concentric circle model 229–231, *230*
consent forms 133
consonance 106
copyright issues 108–109
couplets, poetry 56–58
COVID-19 pandemic, masks in 184
Crapanzano, V. 66–67
creative ethnography: ethics and researcher responsibility 5–8; as field 1–4, 244; future of 244–245; toolkit approach 8–10
creative non-fiction: faction 76–79; after the field site 203–207; food and travel 125–129; someone else's life story 71–75; writing space and place 91–94
creative sensory ethnography 141–149
creative space 11–12
cultural differences, androcentric bias 15

Dawson, S. 88
"The Day of Shelly's Death" (Rosaldo) 156, 160, 216, 217–218
deep hanging out 232
deep listening 2, 189–192
Deger, J. 137–138
descriptive placemaking 91–94
Diamond, S. 239
digital audio workstation (DAW) 42
Diné country western bands 224
Diné music (jazz) 228
Dingwall, R. 5
direct translation 102–103
display creation 198–201
Dowell, K. 140
dramatic monologues 20, 23
drawing: comics 31–36, 184; mural sketches 162–165, *164–167*; writing about the unexplained 206
"Driving through North Philly" (Cahnmann-Taylor) 245–246
"Duplex" poetry 103

"The Economy of Progress" (Albritton) *167*
"Eighteen Ways of Looking at Property" (Cahnmann-Taylor) 131–132
Einzig-Roth, P. 163–164, *165*
embodied experience 121–124
emotional authenticity 74
end-stopped lines 122
endangered languages 108–112
enjambment 121
environmental futures 63
ethics: artmaking in ethnographic contexts 231; creative ethnography 5–8, 9
ethnographic artmaking *see* art
ethnographic fiction 3, 76–79
ethnographic gaze 215–219
ethnographic memoir *see* memoir
ethnographic poetry *see* poetry
ethnographic prose poems 80–84
ethnographic songwriting *see* songwriting
ethnographic soundscapes 189–192
ethnographic vignettes 39–42, 228
ethnography: as field 1, 3–4; training in the arts 4–5
ethnography about self *see* auto-ethnography
ethnopoetics 56–58, 238–246
Evans, W. 91
exact rhymes 106
exhibits 198–201

faction (creative writing) 76–79
Fairchild, B. H. 216
fairytale writing 73
Falcone, J. 78–79
after the field 159–160, 203–207
the field, meaning of 53
field recording 189–192
fieldnotes 203–207
fieldwork: ethical concerns 5–8; historical approaches 15–16; metaphors and similes 80–84; participant observation as a central research method 20; positionality 6; topics of study 53–54

fieldwork data *see* after the field
filmmaking: based on comics 36; observational videomaking 60–63; production values in practice 137–140
Finkelstein, M. 206, 207
First Nations 141–149
"Fisherman's Blues: A West African Community at Sea" (Badkhen) 93
"Five Minutes" (Peters) 89
"The Five Senses" (Brake and Hopkins) 111–112
flash ethnography 124
focal attention 190
food: cultivating appetite 125–129; sensorial anthropology 26–30
form-meaning relations 162–165
Foucault, M. 25
Franklin, B. 241
free associative writing 73
freewriting: photographic portrait 86–89; production values in practice 137–140; temporality and embodied experience 123; writing about the unexplained 203–207; writing into a poem's expanse 48–51
Friedrich, P. 239
funding for arts projects 231–232

Geertz, C. 76
genre 2
ghazal 56–58
Ghodesee, K. 2
Gilbert, E. 196
Gill, S. D. 184
"*Gimaazinibii'amoon* (A Message to You)" (Noodin) 48–50
global attention 190
"Going Native" comics 31–35, *33*, *34*
Goldberg, N. 196
González, R. 21–22
graduate courses 10
grammatical parallelism 109–110, 111–112
grantwriting 231–232
graphic novels 36, 164–165; *see also* comics
Griffith, N. 45

Hamdy, S. *164*, 165
Haraway, D. 26
Hegel, C. 198
Hendricks, J. W. 184
Herrera, J. F. 216–217
Hirshfield, J. 238
"Home" (Morrison) 213
homelessness exhibit 198
Hopkins, S. 110, 111–112
Horner, L. 88–89
Hugo, R. 245
humility 130–135
Hymes, D. 239, 240–241

"Iberian Chair" (Cahnmann-Taylor) 22–23
images *see* visuals
"Incident" (Trethewey) 103
Indigenous cultures: Anishinaabemowin poem 48–50; creative sensory ethnography 141–149; ethnopoetics 56–58; portrayal in comics 36
"Inez" (Jacobsen) 88–89
informed consent 169
installations 198–201, 242
institutional review boards 133
interviews: animal stories 96–100; artful scholarship 130–135; coding process 169–176, *170*
intimate experiences 65–66
"i.will.cross" (Jacobsen & Zia) 155, 231
"i.will.cross" (Zia) 152–154

Jacobsen, K. 16, 128, 233–234
Jarzabkowski, P. 185
Johnson, L. 118
journaling: paired journaling assignment 87; soundscape recording 191
journalism, distinction from songwriting 74
Justice, D. 56

"*Kabusha* Radio Remix" (Vidali and Phillips) 199
Karel, E. 191
Kashmiri conflict 152–154
Keats, J. 21
Klee, P. 91
knowledge production 198–201
Konopinski, N. 31
Kusserow, A. 81–84

"la jefa" (Alvarez) 116–117
language: interviews regarding second languages 130–131; non-Western literary and linguistic forms 56–58; songwriting in an endangered language 108–112; Spanglish 58; translingual poetry and scholarship 102–107
Latour, B. 26, 78
Lawrence-Lightfoot, S. 21
Le, J. K. 185

Levin, D. 121
LGBTQ families case study 170–176
life writing 71–75
listening *see* close listening
literature, non-Western forms 56–58
literature reviews 238–246; artful scholarship 130–135
"Long Way Down" (Reynolds) 114, 115–116
Longenbach, J. 122
Lovett, L. 128–129
"The Loving Kind" (Griffith) 45
lyrical storytelling 114–118

MacDougall, D. 63
Makaremi, C. 67
man-made objects 20
Marcus, G. E. 2
Marx, K. 26
mask-making 159, 178–186, *178–183*
materialism: classical 25–26; new 20, 21, 29
McCarthy Brown, K. 78
Mead, M. 137, 219
"The Medium is the Message" (Jacobsen and Parish) 233–234
melodic stress 108–109
memoir 3, 91–94, 193–196
metaphors, use in fieldwork 80–84
Miner, H. 15
"Minnie" (Einzig-Roth) 163–164, *165*
Miyarrka Media 137–138
Mol, A. 26
moral compass 5–8
Morrison, T. 213
"Motalava Come to Me" 149
movies *see* filmmaking
multilingualism 102; *see also* translingual poetry
multimodality 2–3, 8, 201
mural sketches 162–165, *164–167*
Murphy, E. 5
Murphy, F. 66, 68–69
museum displays 198–201, 242
music: coding process 169–176; creative sensory ethnography 141–149; food and travel 128–129; identity as an artist and scholar 222–234; scoring and composition 39–42; someone else's life story 71–75; songwriting from a photographic portrait 86–89; songwriting from newspaper articles 43–46; songwriting in an endangered language 108–112; writing silence 65–69
Mussa, J. *166*
Myerhoff, B. 138, 139

Narayan, K. 214
narrative poetry 114–118
narratives *see* storytelling
Navajo Nation/Diné Bikéyah 45–46, 125, 222, 224, 233
The Navajo Times 43, 45–46
Neruda, P. 22, 102
new materialism: analysis of food 29; non-human objects 20, 21
new phenomenology 26
"New Skies Above" (Xavier Albano, Djamiww, Naomi Sunderland, Vanessa Garrido, Fouad Ibrahim, Rosa Rantanen, Ahmed Zaidan, Nora Al Zubaidi, Raad Obaid Al Zubaidi, Kristina Jacobsen, Klisala Harrison) 145–147, 149
newspaper articles, writing a song from 43–46
Nixon, R. 62
"No Man's Land" (Jacobsen & Horner) 88–89
non-human objects, giving meaning and voice to 20–23
non-linear representations 162–165
non-Western literary and linguistic forms 56–58
Noodin, M. 48–50
note-taking from the field 203–207
"Notes on Spaces of Consciousness" (Karel) 191
"Nuestra Ciudad: Los Angeles" (Bautista) 163, *167*
"Number our Days" (Myerhoff) 139

observational skills, video 137–140
observational videomaking 60–63
"Odes to Common Things" (Neruda) 22
Olds, S. 216
Oliveros, P. 190
OpEds 43, 44, 232

paired journaling assignment 87
pantoum structure 56, 103, 107
parallelism 109–110, 111–112
Parish, J. 233–234
parsing lines 122
participant observation 20, 153, 224
Pattison, P. 175, 226
Pelosi, A. 198
performance, artful scholarship 130–135

persona poems 23
Peters, G. 89
phenomenology 121–124
Phillips, K. 199
"Phone & Spear: A Yuta Anthropology" (Miyarrka Media) 137–138, 140
photographic portrait 86–89
photovoice 63
Pirie, S. 243
pitch 97
place writing: descriptive placemaking 91–94; essentials of ethnographic writing 209–214; in song 43–46
play, as part of creating art 224–225
pluriverses 32–33
"The Poet X" (Acevedo) 114–116, 118
poetic prose 159, 203–206
poetry 3; animal stories 96–100; artful scholarship 130–135; ethnopoetics 56–58, 238–246; faction 76–79; metaphors and similes 80–84; non-human objects 20–23; non-Western forms 56–58; from a photographic portrait 86–89; temporality and embodied experience 121–124; terminology 8; translingual 102–107; turning around the ethnographic gaze 215–219; war and violence 152–156; writing into a poem's expanse 48–51
political issues, interviews regarding 131
Pollack, Deena 130
Pollock, Della 184, 185
portraiture 21
positionality 6, 7, 201, 231
poststructuralist turn 25
Prine, J. 89
production values in practice 137–140
proposal writing 213–214
prose poetry 203–207
public anthropology 198–201
public communication 162–165
public murals 162–165, *164–167*

"The Quadrant" (Stone) 123–124

race: Becky (colloquialism) 198; ethnographic displays and installations 198; interviews regarding 131
rapport-building 53
reflexivity: artful scholarship 130–135; after the field site 203–207; personal-professional dilemmas 6
Rego, M. 6
Reisler, P. 71
relationships 53
Rentzenbrink, C. 196
repetition 109–110, 111–112
researcher responsibility 5–8
restorying 184
rhymes: photographic portrait 87; rhyme schemes 44, 74–75; slant and exact 106; in songwriting 109, 228; translingual poetry 105–106
Rosaldo, M. Z. 215
Rosaldo, R. 4, 156, 160, 216, 217–218
Rosiek, J. 21
Rouch, J. 137

"Sam Stone" (Prine) 44
Sapir, E. 219
scholartistry 160, 238–246
science, overlap with art 2, 241–242
scoring (music) 39–42
senses: creative sensory ethnography 141–149; sensorial anthropology and food 25–30; "The Five Senses" (Brake and Hopkins) 111–112; writing through 121–124, 125–129
sestina 56
Shapiro, H. 216
shared anthropology 137
silence, in ethnographic representations 65–69
similes, use in fieldwork 80–84
Singleton, A. (pen name for R. Benedict) 8, 219, 240
Skinner, J. 130
slant rhymes 106
slow violence 62
Smith, A. D. 130, 131, 132–133
Snyder, G. 241
social structure 25
social theory as praxis 222–234
socially constructed interactions 25
Society for Humanistic Anthropology (SHA) 219, 238–240
"The Soldier Takes the Anthropologist to the Shooting Range" (Stone) 123–124
songwriting 3; coding process 169–176, *170*; creative sensory ethnography 141–149; in an endangered language 108–112; food and travel 128–129; identity as an artist and scholar 222–234; from newspaper articles 43–46; from a photographic portrait 86–89; someone else's life story 71–75
sonic ethnography 39–42

sonnet form 106–107
sounded anthropology 189–192
soundscape recording 189–192
soundscapes 39–42
soundtracks 39–40
space, writing space and place 91–94
Spanglish 58
"Spirit of Santo" (Banban Bamboo Band) 145, 148, 149
"Stale Refugee" (Kusserow) 81, 82–84
stanzas, poetry 56–58, 105–106
Stevens, W. 131
Stoller, P. *92*, 93
Stone, N. 123–124, 243
storytelling: animal stories 96–100; essentials of ethnographic writing 209–214; lyrical 114–118; restorying 184; and songwriting 71–75; writing from a picture 86–89
stream-of-consciousness writing 73
Syring, D. 98–100

Tahat, D. 103
Taussig, M. 206
temporality 121–124
thick descriptions: lyrical storytelling 114–118; observational videomaking 60–63; sensorial anthropology 25–29; turning around the ethnographic gaze 215–219
"This Old Porch" (Lovett) 128–129
trans/scripts 131
transcription 78, 98, 132–133
translingual poetry 102–107
trauma: trauma-informed group songwriting 142, 147–148, 149; turning around the ethnographic gaze 215–219; war experiences 152–156
travel writing 125–129
Trethewey, N. 103
True, M. 127
truth/Truth 73–74
"Two Men Die in Ditch Trying to Save Dog" 45

"Unadvisable" (Rego) 6
undergraduate courses 10
"Unheard Voices" (Mussa) *166*
Urban, G. 184

Vidali, D. 199
videography 137–140; *see also* filmmaking
villanelle poems 57, 105–106, 107
violence, experiences of 152–156
visual inquiry 163–164
visuals: comics 31–36; mask-making 159, 178–186; observational videomaking 60–63; photographic portrait 86–89; production values in practice 137–140
vulnerable observation 209–214

"Wakanda University" (Chin) 198
war experiences 152–156
Waterston, A. 65–66
"When You're a Retired American Studying Spanish" (Cahnmann-Taylor) 104–105
Williams, W. C. 134
Winn, L. 118
Wolf, M. 78
Wright, J. 121
writing: about the unexplained 203–207; descriptive placemaking 91–94; discovering what you truly want to say 193–196; essentials of ethnographic writing 209–214; from multiple perspectives 215–219; photographic portrait 86–89; into a poem's expanse 48–51; production values in practice 137–140; silence 65–69; temporality and embodied experience 123; through the senses 121–124

Zia, A. 152–154, 231

For Product Safety Concerns and Information please contact our EU representative GPSR@taylorandfrancis.com
Taylor & Francis Verlag GmbH, Kaufingerstraße 24, 80331 München, Germany

www.ingramcontent.com/pod-product-compliance
Lightning Source LLC
Chambersburg PA
CBHW070609270326
41926CB00013B/2470

* 9 7 8 1 0 3 2 4 2 9 9 1 5 *